TROPIC TENDENCIES

Pittsburgh Series in Composition, Literacy, and Culture

David Bartholomae and Jean Ferguson Carr, Editors

Tropic Tendencies

RHETORIC, POPULAR CULTURE, AND THE ANGLOPHONE CARIBBEAN

Kevin Adonis Browne

UNIVERSITY OF PITTSBURGH PRESS

Published by the University of Pittsburgh Press, Pittsburgh, Pa., 15260
Copyright © 2013, University of Pittsburgh Press
All rights reserved
Manufactured in the United States of America
Printed on acid-free paper
10 9 8 7 6 5 4 3 2 1

Library of Congress Cataloging-in-Publication Data

Browne, Kevin Adonis.
Tropic Tendencies: Rhetoric, Popular Culture, and the Anglophone Caribbean / Kevin Adonis Browne.
   pages cm. — (Pittsburgh Series in Composition, Literacy, and Culture)
ISBN 978-0-8229-6259-5 (pbk.)
1. English language—Caribbean Area. 2. English language—Caribbean Area—Rhetoric. 3. Popular culture—Caribbean Area. I. Title.
PE3302.B76 2013
427'.9729—dc23   2013023784

For my children, Layla and Kyle

Where there is no vision, the people perish.
—Proverbs 29:18

Be not afeard; the isle is full of noises,
Sounds, and sweet airs, that give delight and hurt not.
Sometimes a thousand twangling instruments
Will hum about mine ears; and sometime voices
That, if I then had waked after long sleep,
Will make me sleep again; and then in dreaming,
The clouds methought would open, and show riches
Ready to drop upon me, that when I waked
I cried to dream again.
—William Shakespeare, *The Tempest* III.ii

I've decided I don't want to be called Caliban any longer.
—Aimé Césaire, *A Tempest* I.ii

CONTENTS

List of Illustrations   xi
Acknowledgments   xiii

Introduction: A *Jour Ouvert*   1

Chapter 1. *Mas Rhetorica*: A Brief Discourse on the Caribbean Carnivalesque   10

Chapter 2. Structure, Strategy, and Rhetorical Parameters in Caribbean Expression   30

Chapter 3. From the Darker Side of a Schism: Performance and the Prophetic Masque   80

Chapter 4. "We Is People": Earl Lovelace, Ethos, and a Rhetoric of Vernacular Fiction   103

Chapter 5. Inhabiting the Digital Vernacular: The Old Talkers, the Caribloggers, and the Jamettes   128

Conclusion; or, Reprise for the Carnivalesque   155

Notes   167
Bibliography   187
Discography   197
Index   199

ILLUSTRATIONS

Figures

Figure 1. *3canal, Brooklyn, New York* 61
Figure 2. *Cocoa House, Roxborough* 65
Figure 3. *Unlocked on Coffee Street* 66
Figure 4. *Yard, San Fernando* 67
Figure 5. *Four Pirogues, Charlotteville* 68
Figure 6. *Corbeaux, Erin I* 69
Figure 7. *Pink House, Palo Seco* 70
Figure 8. *Brother Austin's House, San Fernando* 71
Figure 9. *Pink House Doorway, Palo Seco* 72
Figure 10. *Carib Street House, Western Side, San Fernando* 73
Figure 11. *Middle Class, Roxborough–Parlatuvier Road* 75
Figure 12. *Windward Road House I, Outside* 76
Figure 13. *Windward Road House II, Inside-Outside* 76
Figure 14. *Windward Road House III, Inside* 77

Tables

Table 1. Major strategic characteristics of the Caribbean carnivalesque 17
Table 2. Rhetorical modes (major characteristics) of Caribbean discourse 38
Table 3. Sample proverb forms 54
Table 4. Major strategic characteristics of the sermonic 56
Table 5. Orthographic features used in Internet chat 133

ACKNOWLEDGMENTS

First, Eva, my mother. Every single thing I do is an acknowledgment of you. Before anything else, I am your son. You are my primary source, my first experience of history. I am bound to look to you, and at you, and for you because you have unfailingly retained your greatest strength for my moments of weakness, as when I have grappled with the ironies of being a good son.

I grapple with other ironies, of course. Among which is the idea that I have been trained to believe that all acts—rhetorical ones, in particular—are acts of the will. As such, the idea of motive, as an indication of my awareness of that will, features prominently in the pages that follow. But I have not always been a rhetorician, and the capacity of my will has often been contingent on those who have brought me along, those who, at one step or another, have been exactly where I needed them to be. Opting for an overarching "everyone I know" seems lazy and perfunctory, so I would rather suffer the inadequacy that comes with only being able to name a few.

I could not have imagined a better graduate mentor than Keith Gilyard. I will never attempt to. The Barbershop—your office—is an institution, one where I have learned more than I could ever fully express outside of its walls.

Chuck Schuster, at the University of Wisconsin–Milwaukee, remains a champion. Liam Callanan and Valerie Laken, especially, understood. I remain grateful for Lane Hall's conversations about the magic of amateur photography even as I sought its rhetoric. Jennifer Johung. More than any other, your influence on some of the most sublime aspects of my thinking linger—so effective were you at reading its vulnerabilities and quelling my anxieties about them that, even in our long silences, I remember. Thank you.

My colleagues at Syracuse University have been magnificent, as has the entire staff. In particular, Eileen Schell and Lois Agnew, who have shared the responsibility of being research mentors and became acquainted with the project from its beginning. Your insight and curiosity about Caribbean rhetoric have sustained my energy, my willingness to refine my ideas. Steve Parks, your confidence and optimism are gifts. Thank you all.

I wish to thank the series editors, David Bartholomae and Jeanne Carr, at the

University of Pittsburgh Press, for their support. I am also indebted to Joshua Shanholtzer, whom I approached with this book, and Alex Wolfe, whose assurance in the later stages was invaluable. I must also thank my anonymous readers for their suggestions and encouragement.

I continue to benefit immeasurably from the wisdom of Elizabeth Nunez, whose importance as my teacher and great friend has never diminished, whose approval I seek without shame or hesitation. You have long been the compass by which I have oriented my course. And at other times, when my ideas have threatened to run aground, threatening to leave me as a castaway amid my self-made frustrations, more friends have kept me afloat. Perthrina Pegus, Gloria Ntegeye, Rene Farrow, Brian Adonis, Miguel Ayres, Michael Thompson, Michelle Bachelor-Robinson, and Joan Morgan: you have known (magically, I am certain) when I've been too busy to reach out and have instead reached out to me. You still know.

Joanna De Silva. Cousin and a far, far better photographer than I can hope to be. Having coursed both main and minor roads with me, know that I depended as much on your eyes as on my own. Keeva Blades and Kerry Callender have been tireless and reliable readers, your special mention earned because you took liberties with my reasoning, challenging me—literally, to the very end—to strive for clarity where only a hint of it was present. The frightening "So what?" dulled only through familiarity. We are more than obscure photographs of empty chairs in corners with flowery curtains, aren't we? Francette Hart-Ramsey and Lois Lewis, for your memory and for your research.

Lisa Kernahan, you are incomparable. You have contributed to this project. Not centrally, I am happy to say, but at the end, allowing me to see what I have imperfectly sought over the past few years. If there are words to express the gratitude I have for that, I have yet to find them.

Lesley Ann Capolino. You are one of my truths, constant and indisputable. Thoughts of you take me along Harris Promenade, past a train and a clock around whose still, nonworking hands a people struggles to make ends meet. Thoughts of you bring music and singing. You have seen me, soaking wet, and saved me. I am reminded, thus, of "Ulysses," San Fernando, 1988. I think of you and know that I am real—real, if only by association.

My relentlessly supportive family has kept me humble yet always remained willing to indulge my eccentricities. The Wrights and the Brownes are at the forefront of those who have kept me grounded throughout this entire process. I hope my choice not to name each individually is proof of my undying love for you all. Aunty Marjorie and Grampadaddy will bear the standard on my behalf. They continue to remind me that while exceptions were made for me, I am not exceptional. I am, and hope to remain, Kevin—just a little less clumsy or afraid. I love you all, if not equally.

Acknowledgments

It is impossible to please the dead, to make them proud. But honoring them now is a necessity. Throughout my life, I have been surrounded by spirits. "N. J." Muriel. Collins. Frank. Peter. Maureen. Lystra. Noel. But I reserve my most heartfelt thanks for my grandmother, Vena Browne. It was Vena who named me. It was Vena who didn't want me digging holes for a living. Granny. I should have danced at your funeral when Nicky and them was playing parang at the gravesite. I should have danced like I danced at your wake. And yet I am happy that, on those misguided days when the solitude of thinking and writing led me to believe I was alone, I was able to remember that there is still much more dancing left to do when the work is done. I may yet learn to dance while I work.

So there. I have not gone in search of mysteries. I have not made a study of jumbies, duppies, or deities. And yet I find myself so firmly situated in a pantheon of the vernacular that I am now forced to confess, to acknowledge the obvious: I have stood not on the shoulders of geniuses but on those of regular people, understanding that the accomplishment of carrying me as their burden far outweighs the ideas I find myself defending in the pages to come. Where I have faltered, the responsibility has been mine. Gaps and ambiguities, mine. Misunderstandings, mine yet again. Where I have raised questions without response, I will, in time, offer recompense. I have already paid a bigger price. Other burdens—of accuracy, of proof, of sustained inquiry and interest—are largely academic, idiosyncratic, and of my own design.

TROPIC TENDENCIES

INTRODUCTION
A Jour Ouvert

> Oho. Like it starting, oui? Don't be frightened, sweetness: is for the best. I go be with you the whole time. Trust me and let me distract you little bit with one anansi story.
>
> —Nalo Hopkinson, *Midnight Robber*

> Let's talk, then.
>
> —Plato, *Phaedrus*

LABOR DAY. CROWN HEIGHTS, BROOKLYN, 1999: there I was, standing half-naked in the middle of Eastern Parkway, covered from head to foot in blue paint. Head *bad*. My costume: horns, shorts, jungle boots, a rough tail, and a nearly empty leather rum pouch around my neck. *Watch me, nah!* A former Caliban, reclaiming myself in Brooklyn. A comfortably clichéd champion of my culture. A displaced Trini. A shameless measure of the condition that my physical appearance had defined, indulging in one of the few "pleasures of exile."[1] More Caribbean than I had ever had cause to be when I was in Trinidad.

The day had already begun to cool, and our band—the "Blue Devils"—had long since dispersed, its members moving back along the parade route to mix into the other bands, letting their drying, sweat-salted paint rub off onto bare skins and sequins that loosened with every gyration, trying to make the day last for as long as they could. Before long, I too would go back to join them. To have a time—wining, chipping, drinking, jumping, grabbing, pushing. But before I did, there I was, an overseasoned "bacchanalist" standing in blue, watching people twist and turn. And for a moment, I was that stripped man, driven back to the self-astonishing, elemental force that has driven me, at different times, to turmoil and to peace: the mind. For as Derek Walcott writes, the mind forms the basis of the Antillean experience: a shipwreck of fragments, echoes, a tribal vocabulary, and partially remembered customs that are not decayed but strong.[2] Stronger than ever. From a distance, those of us in the crowd—swelling, as we are often told, to the millions—seemed indistinguishable from one another, which is the case with crowds. More remarkable was the fact that up close, in the midst, when the differences were most apparent and seemed to matter less and less, all I was thinking about was home. Trinidad. And a familiar lamentation: home. Home: these faces, bodies writhing in the sun, too busy to acknowledge the cooling of the season, whose pleasure barricaded them as they waited for gunshots to cut (offbeat) through the soca, the stiffening bodies of police who resented them and barricaded their pleasure with disgust.

Home: the Caribbean. And I had never missed it more.

Strange it is that millions engaged in the contiguous struggle for pleasure could evoke a few islands and their citizens, citizens who, I am certain, would find it strange that I would choose to practice hyperawareness in the midst of a fête. But this is the case with crowds, as well as memories and histories: they help us reenact what Walcott calls "the gathering of broken pieces [that] is the care and pain of the Antilles."[3] Recuperative work. The kind of work that makes the perfect kind of sense (and that rum and revelry are unable to mask).

It occurred to me that a people should want to demonstrate, in no uncertain terms, that they consider themselves as worthy of recognition as any other people, not merely to get by from day to day, situation to situation, with neither a say nor a stake in the way those situations (and their very lives) unfold, but to have some role in shaping their destiny *as a people*. It should be as basic an imperative as the need to survive or to secure food and shelter for oneself and one's family. It is an imperative that is not so ambitious or impossible as attempting to undermine hegemony altogether; rather, it is one of having a reasonable stake in the status quo. Or at least it ought to mediate the conditions of our public interactions and some of our private ones. It occurred to me that our performances ought to be more than metaphors of our desires that dissipate when the situations change, when the euphoria of a sanctioned chance to explode in the public passes into memory. As I see it, then, one of the objectives of rhetoric seen from a cultural perspective is to preserve and solidify the prevailing aspects of identity among members of a particular social group. Another is to gain a deeper, more robust self-conscious understanding of effective discourse practices among members of that group and, in so doing, achieve the sort of praxis that can equip the members of that group for the life they imagine. And by designating such practices "effective," I refer to rhetorical activity's capacity to empower *rhetors*—practitioners of rhetoric—and members of the audience through active engagement, not simply to persuade them of this or that position. I am concerned with all these things.

People passed.

Half-naked kindred.

Stop.

Look. Look. Look again.

Stop. There is still more to come.

Wait, exactly how many Carnivals had I missed?

What if this Carnival, the opportunities we have to cohere, and the direction of our efforts were used to make something meaningful and lasting? But who was I trying to fool, really? Honestly, not even myself. I knew well enough what some of us did as individuals—those we count vicariously among our ranks—but what more could more of us do? Good questions, I thought.

Yes, but there would be a more appropriate time and place for that kind of thinking. More time to declare, on the grounds of fundamental subjectivity, that the vernacular rhetor, as much as the circumstances that bind him or her, is the occasion to which every situation that concerns this rhetor must be related. Instead, I acknowledged the profundity of the moment and went back to doing what I had come to do: wine, chip, drink, jump, grab, and push. But is this not the operation of nostalgia, that the methodological misstep of self-report can be so seductive, even at the expense of more validated evidence? Yes. Yes.

In the more than ten years since I stood on the Parkway, half-naked in blue, watching Carnival fade, I have had the time to consider my place. As I strive to establish a critical stance on the Caribbean, its people, and their rhetoric(s) in the less comfortable clothes of a researcher, the luxury of nostalgia has given way to restlessness. In the interstices, as I move from text to text, from topic to topic, I have been able to condense the flurry of earlier questions into two: What is the role of rhetoric in Caribbean popular culture? And if there is such a thing as Caribbean rhetoric—and there is—what is it? The initial exploration of these questions forms the focus of this book.

Having said that, I immediately find myself in a dilemma that will affect my course throughout the rest of this book: the attempt to *do* will often be overshadowed by the pressure to *outdo*. I find some comfort from the paradox, though, encouraged as I am by the fact that the possibility for rhetorical activity in the ecstatic rhythms of that evening could not be subdued by dollar vans and walkups any more than they could be subdued by slavery or colonialism. They must in some way be acknowledged. Caribbean rhetorical performances, as a practice of judgment and a critical redress to situations that necessitate forms of display, unfold as a vernacular response to situations that come about as the result of the greatest offense—*invisibility* and *silencing*. So, to put it plainly, the fundamental motive of the Caribbean practitioner is to be recognized—to be seen and heard—

in a way that capitalizes on the implied consensus of an audience familiar with his or her strategies. All rhetorical activity will therefore be oriented toward the attainment of that idea.

No rhetorical activity is possible without motive, which exists at the epistemic core of Caribbean expressive culture. For even though, as Burke writes, "the situations are real . . . [and] the strategies for handling them have public content,"[4] the successful deployment of those strategies—though in response to concrete situations—depends on the specific attitudes of the group for whom those strategies bear the most relevance and meaning. Therefore, while it would be acceptable to say that "in so far as situations overlap from individual to individual, or from one historical period to another, the strategies [can be thought to] possess universal relevance,"[5] such a concession becomes possible *only* in the most fundamental way: we are human beings; we recognize, make use of, and respond to symbols and situations as only human beings can.

This is, however, not the case when applied to specific contexts, their available inferences, and particular meanings, to which Farrell's discussion of the enthymeme's efficiency may be suitably applied: "While most cultures will profess to a conception of what is good or just, honorable or honest, the individuated meanings of any such conception are entirely dependent on the lifeworld or received traditions of the membership groups themselves."[6] The cascadoo resonates differently for some than for others whose navel strings are buried on rocky hilltops or mangroves. This is no mystery. In fact, a different sense of motive becomes clear when we consider (1) expressive strategies that help practitioners size up the situations of slavery, colonialism, neocolonialism, and nationalism; (2) the tools necessary for identifying sociolinguistic structure and outstanding elements; and (3) the prevailing attitudes toward language as an epistemic phenomenon that inhere at the fulcrum of experience and expression in specifically Caribbean contexts, making them specifically Caribbean. For some, the breakdown of the West Indies Federation in 1962 continues to show how nationalism in its narrowest forms can mimic staunch individualism and have fragmenting effects. Many still hold a grudge on behalf of their separate island nations, "overseas departments," and protectorates—not all independent, but sovereign in their own complicated rights. Yet these same people harbor a restless desire for a unity that has yet to reveal itself in meaningful ways, ways that lead to the materialization of those desires at all levels of society. As a prevalent rhetorical problematic, then, *how* we Caribbeans see ourselves becomes particularly relevant when we reflect on the larger democratic concerns we face and especially given the diverse composition of our Caribbean roots.[7] I believe an understanding of our rhetorical traditions helps address this, and it is from this corrective angle that I wish to embark on a discussion of what is expressed among Caribbean practitioners, as well as how and to what end.

That said, this project is constrained by the obvious factors: not only my specific expertise but also the impossibility of paying adequate attention to each tradition, all of them replete with their own complexities. The limitations are to be expected. Nonetheless, with regard to the full and equal participation of Caribbean people in all societies of which they are a part, this book is concerned with understanding and articulating the scope of the rhetorical tradition that enables participation among rhetors who consider themselves part of a Caribbean social formation and the network of desires it produces.[8] The book is also a response to the "Ellisonian-like invisibility" of Caribbean issues and concerns in the field of rhetoric.[9] Notable mention has been reserved for related fields—sociolinguistics, anthropology, education, composition studies—and from time to time the reader may catch glimpses and opportunities to discuss such issues more extensively. On the whole, however, the field of rhetoric in particular has been slow to pay close enough attention to this gradually increasing part of global society. Most important, although we members of the Caribbean community obviously all engage in and utilize rhetoric to our own ends, this book more specifically addresses how we identify similarities and engage differences, how we utilize traditional rhetorical methods to express and assert ourselves, and how we interact—successfully or unsuccessfully—in the wider public.

Implicit in my formulation of a Caribbean rhetorical tradition are two assumptions that recur and complicate any straightforward reading of the texts included here. First and foremost is the reference to "Caribbean" and what it means to the project—specifically, to whom does it refer? Most simply, I refer to those whose origins can be traced to the region, but the virtue of one's birthplace, though often a determining factor in one's allegiance, is matched in this project with the subscription to a characteristic way of framing the world and making meaning within it. I do not mean to invoke hegemony here (itself a privilege of an expressly *nonvernacular* power structure); rather, I am pointing to the spiritually possessing qualities of ideology and identification that result from the interplay of knowledge and interpretive practices that in turn emerge in recognizable forms within an array of texts produced by people who see themselves as Caribbean (though they may not have been born in the area). My second assumption is that the traditions—which are many and varied—are in fact deliberately rhetorical. This is a highly defensible claim based on the basic notion that extant traditions persist in response to rhetorical situations that prompt their emergence, and any response to a rhetorical situation is inherently rhetorical.[10] The more important question, then, is not whether Caribbean traditions are rhetorical but whether the adherence to them bespeaks a deep, abiding rhetorical knowledge. I believe it does.

My understanding of rhetoric also corresponds to Catherine John's suggestion that the range of expressions peculiar to Caribbean people is evidence of a highly complex system of mediated communication and an enduring collective identification with "an alternate register of consciousness, one that at its most profound seems to connect to ancestral knowledge in both conscious and unconscious ways."[11] Thus, while I do not claim that this is a singularly Caribbean rhetoric, I do claim that the examples I have selected typify a broad range of discourses reflecting the complex consciousness of the people connected to the Caribbean region. Each Caribbean rhetorical tradition, as a specific subset of that range of discourses, is a definitive symbolic action achieved by practitioners who deeply understand vernacular elements and strategically use them in changing contexts to interpret and articulate the world continuously. The identification with aspects of extant forms of knowing therefore becomes one of the fundamental imperatives of Caribbean discourse, giving shape to the more abstract and somewhat supernatural suggestions of the elements that constitute Caribbean identity on a rhetorical level. It enables us to put that knowing to use in the construction of identity and to have an impact on the societies of which we are a part.

Because rhetoric relies heavily on the intersection of myriad social and idiosyncratic factors and involves the mere probability of persuasion rather than the certainty of it, I must acknowledge the possibility that for any number of very practical reasons, a particular rhetorical appeal—whether collective or individual—simply may not take. While identification, agreement, and action are all possible, none necessarily manifests. The implicit persuasive aspect of rhetoric is therefore contingent on the general willingness of the social formations I identify to be referred to as such, a fact that will influence the degree to which rhetors either accept or reject the agenda of representation and assertion that, I believe, is explicit in this project. This can complicate the successful rhetorical enactment of what it means to be Caribbean in these times. In the perceived absence of an urgent need to identify as a supranational (regional) bloc, subnational differences among Caribbeans often rear up and cause narrow nationalistic nostalgia to prevail or persistent wounds to make their way into lore and calcify into culture, functioning as the localized embodiments of a rather abstract sense of emergent ethos: Jamaicans are overly aggressive; Trinidadians are very tricky; Bajans are just arrogant.

In fact, the choice to self-identify or differentiate is ongoing as those involved move between expressions of subnational and supranational identities with what seems the greatest of ease. And yet a sense of "being Caribbean" perseveres even as we flirt with the risks of greater dispersal and erasure in an inescapably globalized life, the unrelenting familiarity on which we rely for a greater sense of who we are and where we can successfully belong. This dynamic, like all rhetoric, is contingent on the situations we face and on a combination of personal, social, cultural, economic, and political leanings. I refer, for example, to the persisting sub- versus supranational tensions among natives of different Caribbean nations, contradicting the familiar (and false) notion that "all of we is one." This popular myth of ethnic and cultural unity has been used to characterize the Caribbean ethos as a desire for an implicit unity that has yet to be achieved. It relies on the presumption that "all of we agree." This is not necessarily always the case, however, as the conditions for "agreement" can frequently break down at various points of interaction and in times of peace or conflict.

Additionally, and as a result of the dilemmas caused by our variable affirmations, this discussion presumes that as a group, we Caribbeans remain in the dawn of our self-definition in global society. And we may stay there as long as the issue of a definable identity fails to be mediated on every level of our respective social interactions. This fact places us in a rather precarious position because of the vulnerability and susceptibility to competing social forces, not to mention the debilitating effects of hegemony. This position, however, provides an opportunity to construct an ethos that rests stably enough on a framework of traditional practices that persist and enable meaningful identification with others who share a stake in the effort to be seen and heard.

Using identification as one of the motives and consequences of an effective performance of shared meanings, Caribbean rhetoric builds on the sense of the familiar (doxa) in order to underscore shared interests and shared benefits that are probable in a given situation, meanings that have been acquired through experience and cataloged as a living archive of knowledge and expression that can then be activated, revised, and applied for particular consequences. All are based on a fundamental desire to be a part of the world and improve the quality of life while here. Highlighting this imperative as rhetoric requires leaving it open to critique. Nevertheless, with identification as an exemplary aim of symbolic action in general, Caribbean rhetorical performance allows its practitioners to effectively incorporate "products of . . . [the] highly energized interaction of history and memory [that] stand at the nexus of personal and collective memory" and put them to use in a range of social contexts.[12] Identification is, simply put, a fundamental carnivalesque process because it functions as an articulation of collective agency and cultural intention, existing in conflicting or oppressive situations as the expression of a realistic desire for successful participation in contemporary society and the benefits promised by it. Such participation enables (but again does not promise) productive change that is initiated by a representative social formation, in this case one consisting mainly of Caribbean people.

I approach this type of activity in terms of what I call the *Caribbean carnivalesque*, drawing on the most pervasive form of Caribbean public expression—Carnival—as a framing trope. Because this term involves the strategic interplay of numerous rhetorical modes and perspectives rather than a narrow reference to Carnival as a means of defining the Caribbean and its people, I use it here as a means by which Caribbean people can define the(ir) world and a lens through which they can see it. And while much scholarly work has examined aspects of the social, economic, political, and educational conditions that Caribbean people face, my project specifically addresses how they shape and are shaped by these conditions instead of merely reacting to them. Put another way, to pursue a Caribbean rhetoric is not only to ask *what* it is or whether there are dimensions we could identify as characteristically Caribbean but also to uncover the *practical use* to which it could ultimately be put given what we understand of the way rhetoric operates in local, regional, and transnational contexts. Raymie McKerrow's thought reinforces the exploration of these varied phenomena:

> To approach mediated communication as rhetorical is to see it in its fragmented, unconnected, even contradictory or momentarily oppositional mode of presentation. The task is to construct addresses out of the fabric of mediated experience prior to passing judgment on what those addresses might tell us about our social world. The process one employs is thus geared to uncovering the "dense web," not by means of a simple speaker-audience interaction, but also by means of a "pulling together" of disparate scraps of discourse which, when constructed as an argument, serve to illuminate otherwise hidden or taken for granted social practices.[13]

At stake is the struggle for a degree of agency that could facilitate meaningful participation among Caribbean people toward the critical attainment of a shared vision of prosperity, equality, and depth. Rather than rehearse the exoticism to which we (and our rhetorical traditions) are often subjected, I want to suggest a more practical view of Caribbean displays that rely on the vernacular tradition as a means of redress, of critical (re)invention. It can serve as an essential measure for effecting real change in a world full of nihilism and despair, fear and apathy, injustices and cruelties in our homes, streets, and schools.

The many iterations and enactments of the carnivalesque—whether in festivals, novels, videos, or the movement of bodies—are the contemporary expressions of that same legacy of display. They provide exemplary responses to rhetorical situations that allow us to explore the efficacy of an alternative approach (and analytical response) that can be considered "Caribbean" and demonstrative of what Wilson Harris called the "epic stratagems available to the Caribbean man in the dilemmas of history which surround him." According to Harris, the patent lack of "criteria for arts of originality springing out of an age of limbo" has forced audiences unfamiliar with these situations to compensate by imposing an inadequate notion of "Caribbeanness" to bridge the gaps in their own misconceptions.[14] Collectively, these texts can do some bridging work of their own because they constitute a nexus for the interplay and eventual negotiations of the Caribbean ethos, reflecting a vernacular awareness and the deliberate enactment of Caribbeanness toward material ends.[15] The interplay is such that if one were to consider *where* the rhetoric of Caribbean folk could be located, an answer would necessarily involve an alternative way of seeing that is, in fact, self-reflective, self-conscious, self-contained, and self-interested and that identifies prima facie with the vernacular subject. So what historically intransigent audiences missed—the fundamental intimacy of the relationship between an oppressive colonial social climate and the expression of public opinion—can be detected in the interstices, beyond the obscurities, where a sense of the Caribbean rhetorical tradition was actively and more effectively displayed.

The goal is not to explain the Caribbean to the reader. Rather, it is to initiate and (by way of description, analysis, and some speculation) sustain a conversation about the tasks we Caribbeans face. I must confess, though, that my Westernized conceit sometimes makes me wish I did not have to do this work, just as I wish that I had not been thinking of such half-deep and wholly unpoetic things on such a wonderful, dangerous day in Brooklyn. That is, I wish not that someone else had done it but that it would not have to be done at all. I wish that the entire corpus of Caribbean rhetorical activity were self-evident to whosoever cares enough to look at it and understand (without being told) that the people who embark on these activities have already understood themselves and continuously devise the reasons to address and transcend their respective situations. That yes, these activities are done *for their own sake*—that is, according to shifting agendas that manage both to elude and to demonstrate sophisticated thought that may be validated by this or that institution—but it is a sake with its own rationale. I wish more people—swelling, say, to a few million—understood that these reasons may or may not subscribe to particular methodologies; that they may or may not fit neatly into the host of terms available to us; that we could embrace these displays, become witnesses to their nature, their original otherness; and (whether we refer to them as rhetors, practitioners, speakers, actors, or dancers) that these are *people* who understand themselves better than we could hope to explain.

But here we are: at the tail end of a festival, I stumble upon a beginning.

Some things *must* be done.

CHAPTER 1

Mas Rhetorica
A BRIEF DISCOURSE ON THE CARIBBEAN CARNIVALESQUE

> Let no voice but your own speak to you from the depths.
> —Marcus Garvey, "African Fundamentalism"

> Methodologies passively assimilated, far from reinforcing a global consciousness or permitting the historical process to be established beyond the ruptures experienced, will simply contribute to worsening the problem.
> —Edouard Glissant, *Caribbean Discourses*

> Participating in carnival undermines the possibility of writing an objective account. This extraordinary experience, at once creative, transgressive, and intensely pleasurable, melts the cool detachment of the academic.
> —Geraldine Connor and Max Farrar, "Carnival in Leeds and London"

THE EMERGENCE OF AN ARTICULABLE Caribbean ethos occurred at a critical juncture in the history of the region. Referred to in the *Illustrated London News* as "parts of the world to which public attention [was] becoming much directed by impending changes in the main route of commerce,"[1] the region was of great social and economic interest in Great Britain for two major reasons. The peasant class in Britain's Caribbean colonies, which had risen steadily following full emancipation in 1838, had shown little interest in the global market until the last two decades of the nineteenth century, a fact that forced Great Britain to reinvigorate its efforts to manage the economic reconstitution of those colonies.[2] Additionally, as Roberto Cassá has observed, "the changes in schemes of production in the countries of the centre [brought on by the Second Industrial Revolution] led to a search for increased foreign markets for their manufactured goods."[3] As a result, greater emphasis was devoted to smoothing out the relationship between the peasantry and the plantations by modernizing export systems to accommodate new export crops, including cacao. These "domestic" activities coincided with the construction of the Panama Canal and the resulting emigration that drained local labor; by 1888, West Indian colonies had provided up to 90 percent of the labor force digging at Culebra, even though the British were never directly involved in the canal project.

In the shadow of imperial anxieties, traditional Carnival celebrations were endowed with the imprimatur (and de facto superiority) of European sensibilities, such that any derivative event would have been viewed in terms of the degree to which it assimilated the original or faithfully represented who these people—these black bodies—were thought to be. The intended audience was treated to the frivolity and apparent harmlessness of the scene, and these spectators were therefore discouraged from considering what the performance of Carnival meant to them, to their compatriots, and to the colonized black bodies engaged in it. This resulted in a complex misrepresentation of extant rhetorical tradition and a willful disregard for the performance of vernacular Caribbean identity and the expression of that identity in public spaces. Ironically, this same misrepresentation helps to emphasize the emergence of the Caribbean carnivalesque against a backdrop of colonial misunderstanding and as a result helps to underscore the festival's effectiveness as an exemplary and characteristically Caribbean response to complex situations. In short, it had the effect of masking the fact that there was a deliberate, dialectical engagement with official opinion. The crucial disconnection leaves a gap—an open space—between the attitudes of a colonial audience and the generative effects of carnivalesque performances.

Framed in the specific context of Carnival, rhetorical expression will always bear the risk of having its potential political awareness eschewed in favor of joy. But there is much to be gained from the risk routinely taken by practitioners, making it one worth taking. The *Caribbean carnivalesque*, as an exemplary practice, has the potential for activating consciousness among historically dispossessed people, thus enabling the desires of individuals to take form through collective practice. Beset by shifting contexts and mechanisms of power at home and abroad, vernacular Caribbean practitioners employ critical strategies of rhetorical display as a means of negotiation with other performers and with members of their respective audiences in order to foster, maintain, adapt, and (cor)respond to shifts as they occur. McKerrow suggests, for example, that "the initial task of a critical rhetoric is one of re-creation—constructing an argument that identifies the integration of power and knowledge and delineates the role of power/knowledge in structuring social practices."[4] In such a case, I am compelled to make a suggestion of my own: the Caribbean carnivalesque—the premier act of rhetorical (re)invention and the critical response to the shifting situationalities of everyday life—undoubtedly forms the basis of all dialogic performances related to the region and its descendants.[5] As we explore and reflect on the trajectory of Caribbean expression, from the initial attempts at utterance to the phenomenon of cybernetic disembodiment, the carnivalesque will stands out as a predominant feature and a necessary impulse.

As exhausted revelers will readily attest, the carnivalesque is more than a trope; it is also an embedded practice of culture and the definitive method for understanding and enacting the critical aspects of a Caribbean ethos. The carnivalesque has come to symbolize "freedom for the broad mass of the population and not merely a season for frivolous enjoyment," writes Errol Hill, who attributes to it "a ritualistic significance . . . rooted in the experience of slavery and in celebration of emancipation from slavery."[6] But the unadorned truth is that no other performances in the Caribbean repertoire are more public, and no other appeals to audience are more grand, graphic, visceral, contradictory, materially self-aware, and unapologetically desirous of democratic consequences, than those of the carnivalesque. This makes its importance considerable as a key topic in Caribbean rhetoric.

As it already was during my half-naked days in Brooklyn, the performance of the Caribbean ethos during Carnival is now under pressure from commercialization and a contemporary reshuffling of priorities that dictates its celebration and allowances as something of a gift, discouraging the circumstances that could lead to real resistance in public spaces: Carnival as a privilege rather than a right. I am therefore more inclined to consider the methods involved in addressing and negotiating this pressure. As far as Carnival celebrations are concerned, then, the festival is (and, I think, will remain) inadequate as a theoretical frame for the objects of study included in this book, for though the festival has been identified as a key signifier of "sociocultural complexity,"[7] its co-optation by corporate and middle-class cosmopolitan interests has done a great deal to undermine its rhetorical significance to a contemporary vernacular audience.

Understood conceptually, then, the carnivalesque does not merely encompass the traditional paradoxical tension highlighted by Antonio Benítez-Rojo, wherein "the groups in power channel the violence of the oppressed groups in order to maintain yesterday's order, while the latter channel the former's violence so that it will not recur tomorrow."[8] In addition, its complexities unfold (if they do not get resolved) in the course of everyday life, where Caribbean rhetorical activities—exemplified in the interplay of how Caribbean people *make meaning* and *what they make* of those meanings—are at their most common and most complex. Likewise, manifestations of the carnivalesque as I understand it exist in multiple genres, embodying, for example, the aural, oral, visual, and scribal aspects of popular cultural production and forming a repository of constitutive modes and motives. I will expand on this point later, but for now it suffices to say that the existence and deployment of these manifestations suggest the "celebration" of a formalized Carnival to be preceded by an ethos that determines the language, style, and worldview of Caribbean folk, providing a scope that is much broader and more far-reaching than the annually recurring sanctioned occasions for pageantry and light critique. When I use the term *carnivalesque*, I mean to evoke a deeply ingrained conceptual framework and not merely to deploy an adjectival function.

Caribbeanist scholars agree that the carnivalesque, originally conceived, represents vernacularized social action at an almost inarticulably complex level, incorporating African, European, and Asian languages, cultures, and consciousnesses to produce a characteristically Caribbean expression of "individual desires that interconnect . . . [to form] Caribbeanness' master network."[9] More specifically, there is no shortage of scholarship describing Carnival in the region as nothing less than a repositioning of an underclass that endured the oppression meted out by the plantocracy of the late eighteenth century, with the specific festival taking shape near the mid-nineteenth century. As a strategic response to the tragedy and conquest that constitute Caribbean history, emergent carnivalesque discourse was meant not to elide but to incorporate conflicting realities, subsuming the troubling history and making it contribute to the (re)invention and operation of major discursive forms that come into play to some degree in every text we produce. John Cowley augments this characterization in his initial description of the *diametre* (pronounced "jamette"), populated by the marginalized masses of the formerly enslaved postemancipation natives and immigrants who combined and conspired to be the real-life progenitors of the carnivalesque impulse:

> Unfortunates were seen as an incomprehensible *underworld*, and feared and loathed accordingly. Thus the *diametre* came to be made up of stickmen, singers, drummers, dancers, prostitutes (another meaning of *jamette*), *bad johns* (swashbucklers), *matadors* (madames), *dunois* (*jamette* rowdys), *makos* (panders), *obeahmen* (practitioners of magic) and corner boys. All were associated with a culture that revolved around the barrack-tenement yards of Port of Spain and similar locations elsewhere in the island. Migrant groups competed with one another, and more established settlers, for territory. At the same time, the *diametre* flaunted themselves (especially during the masquerade) to sustain their identity and draw attention to their plight in a society in which they were decried.[10]

Cowley describes an ethos of lived experience implicitly based on ways of seeing and constructively negotiating the world within the constraints of culture, class, and power. At bottom, therefore, is the notion that the carnivalesque functions as a discourse of counterdominance and negotiation that not only resisted the sanction of the ruling class but also publicly rejected it as fundamentally contrary to enacting an agenda in freedom. From this impulse, we can begin to extract the essence of a sophisticated rhetorical stance.

When considering the carnivalesque as an interpretive model for understanding public discourse, the theories of Mikhail Bakhtin are viewed as something of a default reference—that is, the notion of the carnivalesque as a form of discourse that coalesces among underclass factions and eventually wells up to threaten the official authority of the state. Taking Bakhtin broadly, for example, Selwyn Cudjoe reminds us that culture occurs as a system of signs that coalesce in response to a dialogic situation.[11] Cudjoe even goes on to approach the phenomenon of creolization through the Bakhtinian notion heteroglossia, from which he gleans the notion that meaning takes shape at the point of utterance, the idea that although appropriated words, symbols, and sounds can hardly be debated for their originality, they have all been infused over time with the intentions of the performers. Indeed, the carnivalesque has been used to signify the emergence of Caribbeanness itself. Cudjoe defines it, for instance, as

> a culture of laughter, picong, festivity, and ole talk [sic] that regenerated itself through the dynamic of a people's experience and defined itself paradigmatically through the first nascent outburst of the Carnival festivity in all of its polysemous and polysemantic richness. In this context, the creative transformative process that was taking place in the wilderness consisted of a situation in which the Creole inhabitants (the native population) took over. . . . Here, of course, one saw *the emergence of the subaltern, the emergence of the underground culture that was being submerged by officialdom and colonial rhetoric and practices.*[12]

Occupying the liminal space between revelry and revolt, the carnivalesque seems to bear the overtones of pragmatic self-definition and adaptability that make it particularly suited to engage and interpret a series of issues that emerge in shifting contexts. But Cudjoe's formulation here manages to position Caribbean people as a recipient audience that had either inherited or imitated the carnivalesque but in any case did not shape legitimate versions of knowledge, interpretation, or expression. The implication is troubling, particularly because it entrenches a popular myth of (mis)representation that trumped the development of authentic vernacular expression.

In contrast to Cudjoe, though, Benítez-Rojo sees the fundamentally binary structure of the Bakhtinian carnivalesque as anathema to the complexity of Caribbean culture, which is fully immersed in its own versions of the carnivalesque. In terms of culture, he suggests, the "complexity of the Caribbean carnival *cannot* be reduced to binary concepts . . . since it serves the purpose of unifying through performance that which cannot be unified (the impossible desire to reach social and cultural unity—sociocultural synthesis—that runs within the system). In this sense, and *only partially in the Bakhtinian sense*, we can say that Caribbeanness functions in a carnivalesque manner."[13] Whether Caribbean rhetorical activity emerges through imitation or originality, appropriation or abrogation, through the preoccupation with fragmentation and coalescence or the consequence of experiences that occur "in the wilderness," its complexity suggests a form of pragmatic expression peculiar to the region that remains to be adequately fleshed out. That said, there is more going on than just the bourgeoisie's general affinity for the grotesque or the poor imitation of that affinity by the underclass. It seems that, in order for the Caribbean carnivalesque to gain some foothold, we must relieve ourselves of the notion that Russian dialogism has any particular bearing on contemporary Caribbean discourse, except insofar as a useful vocabulary may be borrowed and judiciously applied. (And even then, we may, as Caribbeans, seek to stake an even greater claim on the term *Carnival*.) Bracketing, as Benítez-Rojo does, the notion of impossibility in favor of a more achievable probability, it becomes quite clear that the Bakhtinian carnivalesque will not suit Caribbean contexts, the neat application of familiar terms notwithstanding.

Other critics, too, overtly resist the tendency to frame aspects of the Caribbean in Bakhtin's terms, which they locate primarily in Russian dialogism, for even as the construct allows readers to problematize notions of the grotesque, mockery, laughter, and the mask that jibe with Cudjoe's definition, the limitations of Bakhtin's formulations are glaring when specifically applied to the Caribbean. Most notably, Gerard Aching has convincingly argued that, while useful in terms of a basic understanding of the carnivalesque as a strategy of oppressed people in general,

> Bakhtin's work on Rabelais's literature . . . elucidates homogeneous class formations that differ substantially from the multiethnic, transnational, and class-straddling populations that participate in carnivals and popular culture in the Caribbean today. . . .
>
> In this light, the examination of the uses of masks and masking as socially significant practices in the Caribbean must not only specify the contexts and styles of masking; such an inquiry should also go beyond simplistic binarisms by describing and interrogating the ways in which masks and masking devices are dynamically employed to (re)configure and (dis)place competing categories of (self) knowledge in extremely diverse settings.[14]

Aching's call to inquiry implicitly acknowledges not only the essential heterogeneity that would disqualify an application of Bakhtin but also the far more exigent rationale of framing Caribbean experience in *recognizably* Caribbean terms. In short, a Bakhtinian reading of Caribbean Carnival would constitute a misapplication of Bakhtin and, more crucially, aid in the continued marginalization of Caribbean folk who possess and seek to employ their own discursive methods. These methods evolved into a distinct tradition of rhetorical (re)invention in the context of a carnivalesque that—through the confluence of multiple sources—bears a nuance rooted firmly in the ethos of the islands, in the sensibilities of the people who live there and those who come from there. Read from this particular, critical perspective, the tenor of the carnivalesque changes significantly, with the term denoting less a symbolic exercise in joy than a calculated approach to a series of activities in material contexts. This complexity occurs prominently in contemporary theories of rhetoric. For example, regarding the interplay of materiality and symbolicity, Blair has claimed that while "symbols refer us consistently beyond themselves to their referential or meaning domains[,] . . . paradoxically, the symbol . . . teaches us to reach outside it for its meaning and to treat that meaning as if it were the real dimension of rhetoric, or at least the most important one. . . . [It] is problematic to treat rhetoric as if it were exclusively or essentially symbolic or meaning-ful. There are some things that rhetoric's symbolicity simply cannot account for. One is its consequence."[15]

Caribbean rhetoric operates similarly, along what can be considered a continuum of discursive substantiation; that is, it involves the metonymic synthesis of symbol and material through discursive (i.e., imaginative, linguistic, and physical) means, as illustrated in table 1. As a paradigm that can essentially make sense of the discursive activities of Caribbean people, it enables the contextualization of intent, action, reception, and reaction with a default *engagement with* dominating or oppressive forces; it synthesizes discursive processes with the strategic manipulation of language, material, and symbol; and it mediates adaptive practices and responses to dynamic consequences. In other words, it endows Caribbean practitioners with the flexibility to transcend myths of (mis)representation and move from mere performance to rhetorical assertion and then onward to actual praxis in the world. Exigency is heightened, furthermore, not only because of a general need to explore the intricacies of a Caribbean rhetorical framework but also because those intricacies can easily be overlooked or misconstrued—which forces us to realize that defining what Caribbean rhetoric *is* or *can be* is also a matter of determining what it *is not*.

RESISTING (MIS)REPRESENTATION

In rhetoric, the fine distinction between metonymy and metaphor is crucial to understanding not only the distinctions among contradicting depictions of the Caribbean people but also the Caribbean impulse to resist those depictions.[16] In essence—and I mean to be essentialist here—the differences that obscure the

TABLE 1. Major strategic characteristics of the Caribbean carnivalesque

Strategy	Carnivalesque characteristics (in relation to common corroborating rhetorical terms)
Syncretic	Vernacular articulations between *sacred* and *secular*; there is a combined reliance on *gnosis* (knowledge of the metaphysical) and *phronēsis* (practical knowledge, wisdom) that drives the resonance and effectiveness of this form. *Construction*: the establishment of the hero as a public figure of a group character (*ethos*) for secular demystification and confrontation of the status quo; some reliance on *ethos* (or even multiple/interchangeable ethoi), *bios*, and *parrhesiastic* delivery. The hero is constructed in syncretic contexts.
Divergent	*Diametre (heroic, dystopian, on display)* masquing: characterized by a tone that is demonstrably aggressive, acerbic, and negative. The agenda is constructed for the retention and articulation of revolutionary themes. *Trickster (heroic, disguised, on display)* masquing: characterized by throwing words, positive tone, passive expression, verbal focus, and revolutionary themes; the agenda is adaptive.
Convergent	*Prophetic Vision*: the tone is recuperative and positive with a major emphasis on sermonic. *Dystopian critique*: the tone here is apocalyptic and negative with a major emphasis on manifesto.
Conciliatory	Critical historiographic/revisionist remasquing and the application of the Caribbean carnivalesque in contemporary discourse as an overarching appeal for civic cooperation.

viability and complexity of the Caribbean ethos and identity have traditionally involved the application of one device (metaphor) where another (metonymy) would be more effective for articulating particular displays. And as I continue to make the case for a Caribbean rhetoric that coalesces as a series of carnivalesque displays in response to a historical situation, I want to illustrate its development as a deliberate response to misrepresentation, with the hope that we can move beyond viewing the activities discussed here as reflexive performance and instead consider their intentional application.

Western readings of the colonized body are fundamentally *metaphoric*, which is to say that the effectiveness of metaphor in representing the colonial subject hinges on that subject's *similarity* to European cultural representations (say, through the imitation of traditional European manners), with its use reflecting what may have been considered to be a "justified" transference of an opinion that was rooted solely in European imperialist ideology—an opinion held by the representative of a dominant power structure and directed toward the subject in question. Historically, the extant subjectivity of those being represented was irrelevant to prevailing notions of the carnivalesque, which was taken more or less as a Baudrillardian simulacrum manifested in accordance with the Romantic notion of the "picturesque."[17] Thus, by enabling the familiar to masquerade as fact, metaphoric imagery actually naturalizes the obscurity of the unfamiliar while giving the appearance of representing it as a crude approximation of an assimilated culture: colonialism is masked by an apparent metropolitanism, revolution reframed as mimicked sophistication that appears to eclipse primitivism.

Alternatively, a metonymic Caribbean gaze deliberately harnesses metonymy as a strategy to emphasize contiguity in two thematic areas: on the one hand, the masque and the people on whose behalf it is deployed, and on the other, the deployment of the masque and the larger system it is intended to critique. The Caribbean use of metonymy relies, therefore, on a sense of realistic representation based on the detection and perceived significance of recognizable, distinctive, and characteristic signs, arranged in a given text, that resonate with a vernacular Caribbean audience while simultaneously invoking the overarching system that is up for critique. As a consequence, it provides a discursive and performative bridge to a hitherto unexplored dimension of rhetoric that is rooted in the culture, identity, and ethos of the people from that region.

The classical tradition viewed vernacular rhetorical activity as a basic responsibility that was dutifully enacted in Athenian society as a right of civic belonging. But while this may be true of all rhetorical interactions in democratic societies (or societies that believe themselves to be democratic) from antiquity onward (and this includes nineteenth-century British vernacular society),[18] Caribbean vernacular practitioners were faced with a serious rhetorical problem, one that is underscored by Gerard Hauser's idea that "publics are emergences manifested through vernacular rhetoric."[19] The presumption is contingent not only on the fundamental *visibility* of that public but also on the willing reception of an audience. "If we were to listen," Hauser writes, "these are the ways by which they make their opinions felt"[20]—or to assimilate John Shotter's more poignant stipulation, "if we can let them *instruct* us in how to see them."[21] The dynamic Hauser describes is unfortunately not generalizable, tending as it does to reflect privilege rather than the likelihood of vernacular equity. Historically, black bodies of the colonial underclass did not have the privilege of taking citizenship for granted; rather, the status of citizenship was a thing to be granted (by favored birth primarily and secondarily by decree), not asserted through loud, insurgent, or violent means. Belonging was limited to the virtual invisibility of second-class citizenship.

That is, if a set of discursive practices does indeed provide the evidentiary base for studying and interpreting the constitution of social will among Caribbean practitioners, then we may reasonably conclude that the vernacular display was not so much the playing out of a carnival of inversion as a carefully constructed dynamic of rhetorical implication. By the same token, however, if no audience ever meaningfully participated, then the public enactment of citizenship by Caribbean practitioners would have been undermined by default, except among members of the internal audience, who would be speaking, as it were, to one another in a muted chorus. The expression of a vernacular ethos that emerges in response to such a situation *cannot* exist as a self-evident happening but occurs in conjunction with deliberate appeals to engage the participation of an audience that has determined the vernacular social status in the first place. These appeals in turn are provided so as to adequately instruct the audience, demonstrating how their recognition of the vernacular performance could allow vernacular desires to collectively materialize as a "public" in its own right.

In a historical Caribbean context, the *exigence* for being seen and heard, as well as the deployment of appropriate derivative performances that could have facilitated such recognition among the underclass, would have been inversely proportional to the receptivity of a nonvernacular audience. As a result of the nonvernacular audience's implicit resistance to being persuaded by that exigence, the potential risk to the practitioner would have been the forfeiture of a key desire: a practical public would be lost in favor of an idealized (i.e., perpetually marginalizing) status quo. So although there would have been a greater likelihood of persuasion among those practitioners who constituted an internal audience—the persuasive aspects existing, say, within a body of knowledge before the display and enduring after it occurred—they would have had to strive harder and continuously to achieve similar consequences with an external audience that would have been inclined to disregard the validity of public performances.

How then does Caribbean rhetoric issue a meaningful rebuttal to contradictory independence, the experience of colonialism, or the legacy of slavery from *within* a discourse that has historically constrained its development and curtailed the expression of will in public settings? To address these questions, given the a priori orientations of virtual invisibility, the desire for recognition, and the consideration of affect among the underclass, we must depart somewhat from Hauser's relatively holistic sense of the vernacular and turn to Robert Glenn Howard's notion of a "dialectical vernacular," which integrates disparate conceptions of "vernacular" that emerge from dual perspectives in a given social framework, a "subaltern vernacular" and a "common vernacular."[22] Taken together as a hybridized discursive system, a dialectical vernacular is described as "the agency derived from specifically being noninstitutional [while still being] able to introduce influence into the very system that rendered the enslavement."[23]

This kind of dialectical adaptability, or rhetorical flexibility, has characterized Caribbeanness from the outset and makes its formulations of performance and critique more suited for the metonymy of representation through the activation of masques than for the application of metaphor. Consequently, the same dialectical impulse saturates everyday Caribbean discourse and suggests that the "essence" of what is (mis)represented can be (re)claimed, (re)appropriated, and used as a "guiding agent" for understanding the material dynamics of an ethos that has hitherto been overlooked. The answers, in other words, can be achieved by looking at the carnivalesque activity through the strategic use of the masque. This analysis needs to be done both *materially*, through the interpretation of texts that reinstate subjectivity to the colonized body, the bodies of its descendants, and the texts they produce, and *symbolically*, with a consideration of the images and ideas that are manipulated by the underclass and have the potential to induce particular consequences for particular audiences. In short, it must involve an examination of the Caribbean carnivalesque as a rhetoric that is deployed *metonymically* as a response to situations within the imposed colonial reality, as well as the enactment of a vision, method, and (ultimately) movement forward in the context of that reality.

As with the spoken languages in the region—which developed gradually from separate languages to pidgins and then eventually to distinct creoles—the Caribbean carnivalesque had by the late nineteenth century endured major periods of fragmentation, imitation, and coalescence, becoming fully appropriated by the underclass as a public creolized expression. Following emancipation, the aristocracy-cum-plantocracy, already accustomed to a form of inversion in their own Carnival fêtes, turned to imitating the dress of slaves who had originally been imitating them.[24] More than a half-century later, the emphasis had shifted from the aristocracy to a system of rhetorical practice among the vernacular social class. A conduit to creolized rhetorical invention, the masque emerged both as a method of rhetorical (re)invention and as a means of illustrating the creolized expression of disparate ethics and the subsequent crystallization of those ethics in the everyday lives and identities of the people. As such, its use is both situational and deeply pervasive as an indicator of subjectivity that ties its adherents to the region and places them under significant pressure to give an account of themselves in response to the misrepresentations of official history.

A premier example of Caribbean rhetorical activity in public spaces, Trinidad's Carnival is replete with characters taken from European templates but intended to turn the gaze of the aristocracy back toward itself in parody, caricature, and grotesque critique; embedded in Carnival are representations of the supernatural and the mundane, the sacred and the profane, each for a specific rhetorical purpose. For example, evoking the supernatural increased the probability of equality among participants beyond anything that would have been achieved in otherwise inequitable material circumstances; reliance on the supernatural was subsequently fused to the mundane, a development that helped retain a connection to the known world and grounded the urgency for addressing social inequities in the material reality of the present. As a consequence, tropes of liberation and retribution—major themes among the underclass—were displayed as joint appeals for justice. Liberation would be sought through the act of public performance, while retribution would be achieved by actively implicating audiences in the performance and its consequences. This was a key tactic, for that audience included not just the sympathizing underclass but also members of the oppressive society who would have been obliged to witness and possibly participate. These characteristics highlight the complexity of rhetorical interplay that was evident in these festivals from the inception of their performance among emancipated slaves; they also underscore the contiguity of deep social motive and material experience.

As an official response to the insistence of vernacular practitioners, metaphor was transformed into myth and used much in the way Roland Barthes describes: as a system of communication determined by situations that enable objects to be *adapted to different types of consumption* by speakers and their audiences. A fundamentally ideological tool, myth is a potentially depoliticized form of speech that can remove "human meaning [from actors and events] so as to make them signify a human insignificance . . . , in short[,] a perceptible absence."[25] This removal of "human meaning" was achieved by superimposing comparatively depoliticized signifiers of European cultural memory—first Italian and then British—onto the vernacular carnivalesque event. The deliberate inclusion of familiar representations to mask differences that were still somehow recognizable to the intended audience had the effect of dehistoricizing the performance, excising the event from its context and its intended rhetoricity. The myth of the (mis)representative gaze therefore functions as a rhetorical display that threatens to counteract the relevance of the actual event; as such, it is able, through the invocation of a recognizable mythos of the European carnivalesque, to place extant British ideology on public display while simultaneously arguing for continued indifference to the rhetorical inclinations of the Caribbean body.

The rhetoric of British imperialist consciousness was designed to persuade the planter-class audience that colonialism was a necessity and a norm, with popular images contributing to the upkeep of social attitudes that would in turn reinforce a particular view of the colonies. The British historian James Anthony Froude, for instance, in an effort to undermine the growing call for reform in the colonies, makes the British position on colonialism so clear in *The English in the West Indies; or, The Bow of Ulysses* that it bears inclusion here.

> We made several similar small expeditions into the settled parts of the neighborhood, seeing always (whatever else we saw) the boundless happiness of the

black race. Under the rule of England in these islands the two million of these brothers-in-law of ours are the most perfectly contented specimens of the human race to be found upon the planet. . . . If happiness be the satisfaction of every conscious desire, theirs is a condition which admits of no improvement: were they independent, they might quarrel among themselves, and the weaker become the bondmen of the stronger; under the beneficent despotism of the English Government, which knows no difference of colour and permits no oppression, they can sleep, lounge, and laugh away their lives as they please, fearing no danger.[26]

This unfortunately popular rhetorical stance thrives virtually exclusively on the use of myth to emphasize the expression of a shared European consciousness while deemphasizing the public emergence and public expression of a Caribbean one. As I have noted, British audiences would have been inclined to take this particular act of mythic persuasion as an unremarkable fact of their default superiority. The official naturalization-neutralization of Carnival and the bodies engaged in it (re)configures the event as a performance of allowable liberation that occurs within definable (and framable) limits. An explicit claim is made about who controls, challenges, or understands whom, and an omnipresent imperialist agenda expresses a desire to promote a British interpretation of the Caribbean body to the exclusion of all others, a fact that allowed audiences to separate the event from its circumstance, thereby removing the overtones of violent reprisal. From a vernacular perspective, far less can be taken for granted.

The perpetration of metaphor as a mythmaking strategy goes further than simply suggesting that black Caribbean bodies ought to have been viewed and not necessarily seen, however. More problematically, metaphor was deployed to undo a major discursive activity by deliberately obscuring the public expression of the vernacular carnivalesque in favor of a more agreeable expression of mythic joy that seemed to recommend that a vernacular agenda be relegated to obscurity, where it would be allowed to exist outside the public view and thus be more tolerable to European sensibilities as a more or less "perceptible absence"—that is, the absence of real, material grievances from the public sphere. The subsequent impetus for addressing these grievances or correcting social inequalities would then be rendered moot. There is, of course, no gainsaying that subject positions and experiences are implicated in the act of seeing and of being seen, which in turn raises questions of the audience members' relevance and their roles in consequences. It suffices to say, however, that to possess a singularly Western approach to Caribbean rhetorical activity is effectively to possess a hard-wired ideologically driven method for *not seeing* others, which complicates how we are able to claim or be implicated in representative rhetorical acts.

IS *WE* WHO DOES WEAR THE MASQUE

We now stand to gain further insight into the rhetorical use of masquing, particularly how it differs from the use of masking as a form of concealment. Insofar as the production of texts by Caribbean people is meant to represent the region, its people, and their distinct sensibilities, the deployment of the masque as a form of vernacular epideictic extends its range of relevance to include a more robust interpretation of rhetorical activity. It serves multiple purposes in this regard: it is a nexus of subjectivities that are at once embedded and viscerally practiced as emergent display, it is a representation of the Caribbean subject in flux, and it exemplifies the contradictory role of the audience as a limiting and legitimizing agent implicated in the consequence of a rhetorical act. These factors can be combined to articulate the exigency and efficacy of the masque, regarding which Daniel Crowley makes a key distinction. Unlike the practice of covering one's face to achieve anonymity during Carnival, a masque indicates to the audience that the display is intended to draw on and amplify shared knowledge, whether from "history, current events, films, Carnival tradition, from the imagination, or from a combination of these."[27] Hence, the use of masques arises out of a necessity to resist absolute control through the deliberate presentation and possible resolution of social tensions, *not* simply as the release of tensions via sanctioned celebrations.

The tendency to focus on the mask as the apparatus for rhetorical activity among these marginalized people is at best a mistake on the part of an outsider. At worst, it is the reification of a presumed need among the marginalized: the notion that their rhetorical contingencies are fundamentally based on their need to hide what they do from their detractors, oppressors, masters, kings, prime ministers, or presidents. This leaves no room for the possibility that what is performed at the vernacular level may be what is intended. Masquing as a form of deliberate display is specifically tuned to the amplification of public social commentary for the purpose of agitation, dialogue, and possible change. The point, despite material limitations, is *not to hide* but to display and be displayed. It is the strategic practice of seeing and being seen that gives Caribbean practitioners a means of knowing the world through process and repetition, the construction of new knowledge, controversial meanings, and the insistence on alternative perspectives of reality. It therefore represents the recurrent taking and taking back of one's life through the collective ritualization and constant revision of liberatory practices that arise as a subprocess of rhetorical identification with members of an audience.

Likewise, the performances of people who play Carnival as dragons, demons, courtesans, and clowns are not to be read as essentially imitative. Viewed as masques, these performances instead stand to be interpreted as metonymic re-presentations that emphasize the contiguity of a Caribbean origin, ones on which a series of recognizable symbols is imaginatively deployed/displayed for an audience that is apt to understand and identify with what is being shown. Additionally, these performances function as material representations of vernacular critique that communicate particular intentions: members of the underclass, out of the necessity to re-emancipate themselves through assertion (rather than by edict), constructed the carnivalesque as an epistemological framework from the fragments of psychological shipwreck that persisted into the present, inflecting the tone of every Caribbean text.[28] Furthermore, it has already been established that Carnival allows the body to be defined as a vernacular text (and metonymically as one that is typically Caribbean) that can be located with relatively little difficulty because these bodies are numerous enough to constitute a majority in most former colonies. Not surprisingly, though, the body is not treated with much regard as a text that could most readily be located, put on display, observed, and read. The vernacular approach thus takes an even broader view of epideictic. In addition to offering the foregoing as strategies for revindication, it presumes the following three things: the vernacular body-as-text holds as much importance for the practitioner as the oral or written text; the black body, because of its ubiquity in colonial Caribbean society, is the most publicly accessible text; and the intended audience, as representative of the dominant/official institution, is not only the reader but also a *participant* in authoring the content displayed on the text.

Although the use of the masks as concealment surely fits within the scope of Caribbean rhetoric, this practice is neither contiguous nor coterminous with the motives that shape Caribbean intentionality and form the corpus of Caribbean rhetorical activity. This activity is not predicated on default avoidance or concealment, and the outflows that result in the establishment of rhetorical knowledge are not solely motivated by the need to avoid the very system that oppresses it. Instead, the masque thrives on the use of rhetorical display—*epideixis*—for the explicit purpose of achieving recognition and promoting a case for social change under oppressive or unjust circumstances. Considered by Aristotle as one of the three species (*eide*) of civic rhetoric, epideixis is defined as involving "either praise [*epainos*] or blame [*psogos*]."[29]

When viewed in its narrow Aristotelian context, epideixis appears (ironically) well suited to a Caribbean imperative that unfolds in contemporary public settings—that is, a conception of Caribbeanness as a *sensus communis*, making it an efficient, self-contained paradox that hinges on the articulation of an unflinching blame placed on a system for which there is, simultaneously, an affinity strong enough to elicit feelings of citizenship and belonging. The accompanying issue of temporality also makes the application of epideictic rhetoric somewhat apropos for Caribbean vernacular activities that seem to emphasize the urgency of a short-lived season of joy, specifically, the tendency of epideictic to appeal to "a kind of culturally grounded morality [that] collapses temporal distinctions so that past, present, and future needs and desires can be seen to merge" in a single event.[30] Comparisons notwithstanding, the need to emphasize the validity and viability of a rhetoric that exists on its own terms *supersedes* the convenience of an easy correlation between the classical idea and a Caribbean one. Carnival was not conceived as an encomium, nor does the perception and practice of everyday life essentially constitute the fictive, figurative limitations of lofty speech conventions for which epideixis was originally applied. Furthermore, in the case of classical epideixis, the immediacy of the performance does not necessarily require a corresponding immediacy of response on the part of the audience, even though there is the fundamental presumption of a receptive audience that is likely to get what it wants from the performance. This bears a certain degree of risk that the colonial vernacular practitioner cannot afford, particularly as these performances are designed to do more than reveal a community to itself alone.

Because epideictic performances "do not call for any immediate action by the audience,"[31] audience members have the default prerogative of *not* being moved once the occasion has passed; moreover, if they were to read the festival as a metaphor for Caribbeanness, they would also have the privilege of minimizing the performance of grievances to a temporary release of everyday social frustrations that, once expressed, would inevitably revert to the normal run of things. In response to such fundamental limitations, epideictic performance needs to be reconceptualized for colonial vernacular contexts and for a potentially unreceptive audience; like Carnival itself, to which it is being applied, it must endure a process of creolization not only in reference to a festival that can easily be constrained within a brief series of public events but also in reference to a vernacular ethos that extends into the everyday practice of public life.[32]

With the kind of epideictic performance that takes place in vernacular contexts, audience members occupy a hybridized role as both spectators (*theoroi*) and judges (*kritēs*). This makes the vernacular appeal to participation into a more direct act of implication because the audience, comprising representatives of an oppressive colonial system, would be under significant ethical pressure to act reflectively as witness *and* judge of its own complicity. In her reinterpretation of Aristotelian epideixis, Oravec makes a similar point, namely, that the epideictic practitioner "formulates principles derived from the common store of his audience, then applies these principles to well-known or typical objects or persons."[33] The key differences, however, may be illustrated this way: first, whereas epideictic was sometimes viewed in antiquity with great suspicion as a deeply self-indulgent, opportunistic, manipulative, and distancing practice, the epideictic practice in colonial vernacular settings was undertaken not by solitary individuals but by many individuals who constituted the underclass and who, as a consequence, produced a *collective* epideictic; second, the aristocratic and upper-middle-class audience to whom their major appeals and critiques were directed were not privy to the "common store" of principles, desires, or motives that shaped underclass life.

What emerges in the presence and performance of bodies, therefore, is the need for an explicitly pedagogical imperative that would satisfactorily implicate contrasting ethoi and direct the respective attentions of each toward a singular consequence. Consistent with the epideictic nature of the colonial vernacular, there is no presumption of an audience's acceptance (or even its awareness) of shared subjectivity with the performers; rather, the performance enables the ethos of the performers to cohere as an expression of desired citizenship that is amplified for public consumption, a fact that resists marginalization by suggesting an emergent, alternative ideology that enables new forms of expression, innovative forms of authorship, and deliberate visual reordering. The "lesson," as it were, would be implicit in the performance: the audience members' "learning" would be contingent on their presence, spectatorship, and self-reflection *in relation to* what they experience. As Perelman and Olbrechts-Tyteca show, "the argumentation in epideictic discourse sets out to increase the intensity of adherence to certain values, which may not be contested when considered on their own but may nevertheless *not prevail* against other values that might come into conflict with them."[34] The resulting cohesion of a collective vernacular ethos would thus not necessarily persuade the audience outright but instead would raise the probability of successful rhetorical expression, making persuasion *and* praxis attainable goals in the formulation and performance of Caribbean citizenship undertaken by members of the less-recognized collective.

The implicit suggestion that the mask be limited to its traditional connotation as a method of subterfuge and subversion results in a *decoupling* of intentions from vernacular performances and a reification of colonialist ideology intended to keep the marginalized where they were. Such a decoupling serves mainly to diminish the rhetorical power of the masquers for outsider audiences. But it also has the effect of heightening urgency and, through opposition, providing the imperative for resolution among Caribbeans. For whereas the maintenance of the status quo had its own uses for European audiences, vernacular practitioners actively sought to counteract the myth imposed by a normalizing European gaze. This reciprocal interplay underscores the nature of civil and public service that is essential to the concept of ethos in all rhetorical traditions—which, according to Hyde, allow people to create places where they can dwell with and for others.[35] In turn, such interplay feeds the epideictic impulse and "instructs the moral consciousness [to operate] for the good of the community" in which it is based and for which interest among practitioners may be the most intense.[36]

In viewing the rhetoric of Caribbean people, therefore, we encounter a significant difference between the ethos of the oppressor and that of the oppressed, one that distinguishes the Caribbean agenda, shaping both the nature and the consequences of performances. For Caribbean practitioners, ethos is not merely a matter of the goodness of citizens and their abilities to speak well enough to move an audience, thereby justifying their place in the community; rather, it is the conscious appropriation of the opportunity to perform an argument for the right to speak at all. It functions as a critical response, one based equally on the need to be differentiated from the colonial idea and the need to emphasize the breadth and complexity of Caribbean identity in conjunction with social and cultural manifestations that include creolized aspects of the very same idea: a performance of citizenship, an affirmative assertion of being of the world as much as in it.

Both the successful critique of embedded colonial practices and the subsequent embedding of emergent practices from a Caribbean point of view require establishing what it means to be specifically "Caribbean" rather than merely colonized and "postcolonized." The motives and effects of related practices must be viewed as going beyond the individual practitioner because of the imperative to have them apply to Caribbean people as the broad, cohesive character of a complex and fluid social formation. This is a problem that continues to plague the validity of discourses relating to the region and its descendants. In terms of the region's cultures, languages, and worldviews, Caribbean identity has been considered schizophrenic because it involves the tacit subscription to a series of existential predicaments: accepting the factors of oppression while rejecting its debilitating effects; resisting the persistent onset of ideologies that conflict with emergent or extant sensibilities; and claiming by right of inheritance those aspects of historical oppression that have been obscured while reclaiming that which has been obscured through deliberate misrepresentation. These factors help frame Caribbean identity as a paradox, a source of frustration that eludes proper distinction. Even the term *Caribbean* is at best fraught and provisional given the diversity of the region and the expressions of identity that sometimes divide along local, national, and international lines. Stuart Hall has suggested that it is impossible to locate an origin for Caribbeanness because "everybody there comes from somewhere else."[37] I see this fact principally as generative, for key aspects of this paradoxical identity can be activated to resolve the tension between, on the one hand, the false representation of Caribbean people that was placed at the center of mainstream discourse for public consumption, which induced a critical resistance to being so placed, and, on the other, the impulse to assert and enact an authenticated subjectivity that promotes insertion into the center to increase the probability of recognition, aspects that align with epideictic impulses. This outlook presumes, of course, that the responsibility for seeing Caribbean texts with new eyes, or in a new light, will persist among multiple audiences who must either recall or imagine (or both) a scenario or situation that is familiar and thus relative to what is being displayed: a public subculture that is, at all times, oriented toward the public disclosure of grievances as the complex synthesis of multiple influences that not only characterize Caribbean culture and identity in the course of Carnival but also come to bear in the carnivalesque criticism that may be employed as rhetorical method.[38]

Since all rhetorical performance is subject to slippage, this is not a failsafe theory. But we can make some fairly solid assumptions: however problematic the correspondence between shifting contexts may be, the freedom to express opinions in characteristically Caribbean terms suggests that there is a system of expression at work here that extends beyond a few days of splendor, reaching deeper and extending more broadly into the private and public lives of performers and spectators to influence those who attend or boycott the festival and affect those who have never known of it. This is because, *as rhetoric*, this system underscores the vernacular imperative to move beyond constricting limits. This engagement, then, implicates those who, through spectatorship or participation, either attend the performance or are informed of it. Carnivalesque practitioners understand, or are taught, that they are the actors and audiences, the authors and editors who, though constrained by social and economic realities, can still engage in forms of individual and collective activity that will allow them to navigate the currents of other discourses—power, for instance, or politics—if not change course altogether to their benefit. The practitioner understands also that being seen requires action, and being taken seriously depends as much on adaptability as it does on efforts of persuasion.

The carnivalesque, as I have indicated, represents more than can be observed in the streets, so to focus too narrowly on the event as celebration would be to elide a more fundamental imperative for equality and in so doing strip the display of its rhetorical qualities. One can, for instance, embody carnivalesque sentiments and, based solely on those sentiments, reject the festivities that take place without being outside the scope of the carnivalesque. If there is a problem with seeing the carnivalesque beyond festival boundaries, it is a problem of not seeing what is being displayed, of not understanding what is being said, and of not recognizing or acting on one's role in it.

In the quest to see, recognize, and understand what a Caribbean rhetoric can be (or is), we are also faced with a troubling chain of syllogisms: because Caribbean rhetoric functions in response to historical situations, and because Caribbean history includes a history of oppression, there is a great tendency to characterize Caribbean culture solely in terms of resistance, which leads to a comparison based in oversimplified contrasts. From that perspective, the extent to which

Caribbean culture is valid will hinge on the degree to which it emulates another culture. That "other" culture will usually be a mainstream culture that possesses the kind of credibility and stature to which the Caribbean (as a marginalized culture) could aspire. As a result of that implied tendency toward aspiration, the more meaningful tendency toward self-expression would be eclipsed in favor of a basic "we do that, too" approach. I suspect that this problem stems from the failure to mine and interrogate the sources of our respective cultures for a meaningful articulation of who we are. It may be that the problem is a failure to apply a workable hermeneutic rather than the lack of one altogether. The problem, in short, concerns not whether the contrast exists, or even whether we ought to approach Caribbean culture and rhetoric in oppositional terms, but whether we go far enough into *our own* systems to construct an approach that is sufficiently meaningful for us and useful for others. So when Caribbean practitioners "make *mas*" for the audience through the conscious manipulation of images and the variation of themes, they actually open a space for the interplay of conflicting discourses, the play of interpreted actions, and the prioritization of consequences that follow from the deliberate use of masques that audiences can witness or possibly engage with: they make a masque. The performance of Caribbean rhetoric, then, achieves its fullest expression when it confirms the individual's and his or her audience's roles in the carnivalesque context of masqued performance and the relationship these performances bear to the communities in which they are produced and performed.

CHAPTER 2

Structure, Strategy, and Rhetorical Parameters in Caribbean Expression

> The very cardinal sin is to depart from the language of everyday life, and the usage approved by the sense of the community.
>
> —Cicero, *De Oratore*

> Now imagery, in what we call expressions of popular wisdom, is deceptive, that is, it can be seen as first and foremost the indication of a conscious strategy. All languages that depend on images indicate that they have implicitly conceptualized the idea and quietly refused to explain it.
>
> —Edouard Glissant, *Caribbean Discourses*

> What is the source of my information? Pepper sauce!
>
> —Anonymous, personal conversation

FIRST, A CONVERSION: IN THE 1960s the anthropologist Roger Abrahams conducted fieldwork in Nevis, St. Kitts, St. Vincent, and Tobago. In a pioneering attempt to apply Kenneth Burke's rhetorical method to the analysis of the folklore and expressive culture that he observed in the region, he theorized that "the carrying out of rhetorical intent [or motive as symbolically enacted in specific genres] resides in the ability of the item and the performer to establish a sense of identity between a 'real' situation and its artificial embodiment."[1] Responding, as it were, to Burke's growing popularity in the social sciences, Abrahams rationalized his reliance on the dramatistic metaphor as a means to a single, recognizable end: having a voice in the conversation.[2] Framing rhetorical urgency as an "anxiety" brought on by an audience's need to respond to the immediacy of the message expressed in a folkloric performance, Abrahams argued that within a Burkeian paradigm, rhetorical exigence would be undermined by the very nature of the performance. In other words, a performance can succeed as symbolic action only if it *defuses* much of the urgency that it proposes through the strategic use of wit and the ability to foreground the *artificiality* of a situation instead of its *realness*. Symbolic action, as Abrahams understood it, would be activated for the specific purpose of distracting the audience members' attention from the substance of the performance. Both the speaker and the audience would have the power to control the effect of normative and antisocial performances, but only insofar as that control served to diminish the audience members' anxieties and their attendant need to act on what has been proposed in the performance.

From a vernacular Caribbean perspective, however, the stakes of a given rhetorical performance are perceived somewhat differently, such that any device that employs artifice solely to distract and entertain can be considered little more than a divertissement—a "pappyshow"—that not only is counterintuitive to the enactment of a meaningful agenda but also comes dangerously close to reifying hegemony. This is a problem of perception. The implicit suggestion here is that if these performances were to be considered successful, they would first have to be voided of their urgency and calls for action, designed instead to maintain dumb order among peasant communities and merely equipping members of these communities for a life of "getting by" instead of preparing them to "get through." In *The Man-of-Words in the West Indies*, Abrahams seemed to revise his Burkeian application. Abrahams found that a universalist—and decontextualized—approach to the "controlling power" of symbolic action could not satisfactorily be applied to Caribbean expressive features and situations because they appeared to operate within a completely different epistemic matrix. On the topic of the "competitive and highly contrastive superimposition of voices" observed in West Indian communities, for instance, he demonstrates a conscious turn from a strict application of pentadic analysis:

> It has become clearer to me that the dramatistic metaphor is ever in jeopardy of being overemployed and that, indeed, in describing all interactions with regard to "scenes," "scripts," "scenarios," "actors," and the vocabulary of mimesis, in general, we lose the particular virtues of such terms to describe actual performance occasions.... It becomes increasingly clearer to me that a ritual or festival, a game or a debate, is not a performance [for its own sake], and to describe them in performance terms is to break down certain ontological distinctions that we find useful to cling to.... The qualities of these enactments differ precisely because they are not theatrical but engage the audience in an entirely different way.[3]

Edouard Glissant notes that "the reductive force of imitation is deeply rooted,"[4] so I tread some dangerous ground even as I think of clearing a bit of it, for the burden of legitimacy is often carried at the expense of aspirations to originality. But Abrahams's move away from the generalizable opacity of traditional folkloric expressions and toward a greater specificity signaled an important awareness of the limitations of generalizability in the application of well-worn concepts in specifically Caribbean contexts, as well as a recognition of the risk we face in misreading them. We need not discard any particular aspects of a received method of rhetorical analysis, but their uncritical application will only further obscure our understanding of Caribbean expressive culture as a discreet system of rhetorical display that operates on its own terms among vernacular rhetors who explicitly express a desire to be understood primarily, if not essentially, in those terms.

According to Peter Roberts, Caribbean language exhibits many features common to all other dialects of English but possesses others that are unique to the region, ones that developed as a consequence of enslavement and subsequent circumstances.[5] Subtle features in Caribbean language range from intonations, such as a nasalization that stresses the affected vowel and changes the inflection of the word (e.g., *waa* instead of *want*), to more significant phonetic, morphemic, and semantic differences between standard Englishes and creoles.[6] As for the communication of more abstract Caribbean worldviews, the focus must shift to the relationship between intent and supralinguistic and paralinguistic qualities of affect, which have helped vernacular rhetors forge varying degrees of rhetorical (re)invention that, according to Paula Burnett, involve "the assertion of cultural self without the denial of that assertion to others, and the sharing of as much as can be shared."[7] This prompts us to consider the tactics and consequences that accompany syntactical features. I acknowledge the richness of these languages, but I am far more concerned with approaching their features as examples of deliberate performance. For Caribbean practitioners, the successful transformation of everyday experience into shared meaning results from the interplay of traditional discursive patterns and features, which I call *rhetorical modes*, that enable expression and support rhetorical invention.[8] They include code-switching, wordplay, circumlocution, call and response, boasting/shaming, proverbs, the sermonic, and nonverbal/visual semantics.[9]

These features suggest not only that a productive understanding of Caribbean language and expression relies on a consideration of *mutual intelligibility*—that is, the recognition of phonetic, syntactic, and semantic similarities that outweigh differences—but also that the resulting creolization reflects an actively practiced and vigorously defended strategic sensibility. Precipitated by the constellation of social, psychological, spiritual, and material consequences that have shaped the history of the region and continue to influence contemporary expression, these rhetorical features reflect the imaginative constructions of vernacular social reality; they also reflect and allow us to read the larger social realities of a creolized experience. Through them, Caribbean people are empowered to circumvent standard forms of communication in favor of more efficient delivery. As Caribbean people, we refer to and rely on them to filter the discourse of our myriad displays in ways both recognizable and relevant to us. Before I delve into illustrations of the specific forms, I think it would be helpful to contextualize the situation that helped give shape and exigence to the features in question.

ATTITUDES TOWARD LANGUAGE

With colonialism firmly entrenched in the West Indies, the purpose of English instruction was clear: "to diffuse a grammatical knowledge of the English language as the most important agent of civilization for the coloured population of the colonies."[10] But proponents of Caribbean creoles emerged early on. In 1869, for example, J. J. Thomas compiled *The Theory and Practice of Creole Grammar*. Thomas's text was unapologetically political, intended to facilitate instruction among French creole speakers and English speakers in Trinidad who knew enough about the creolization process to refer to their patois as "broken." Many had internalized the notion that "the lesson books of the colonial schools should . . . teach the mutual interests of the mother-country and her dependencies; the rational basis of their connection and the domestic and social duties of the colonized races."[11] In addition to providing a comprehensive study, however, Thomas sought (somewhat prophetically) to subvert the commonly held notion that the linguistic and intellectual abilities of creole speakers corresponded to their position at the bottom rung of the social ladder.[12] Thomas's efforts seemed to function as a deliberate attempt at social redress: to "dispel an error" that he said had "often been fatal to the interests of the poor."[13] Even on its own, his study illustrates the deep resonance and urgency of vernacular speakers' need to be understood in and on their own terms, with an accepted, acceptable, and codified system of linguistic agency that would reflect social competence among them. More recently, though, this project has given way to the need for a theory that could more effectively account for the development of native creoles in the Caribbean, specifically, one that would more seriously consider the dynamism of African linguistic elements in the formation of respective creoles, a factor the West African Pidgin Portuguese hypothesis, as a monogenetic theory, did not seem to satisfactorily accommodate. The creole hypothesis also appeared to provide the needed balance, or at least explain the linguistic dynamics, between European superstrate speakers and African substrate speakers, offering a continuum along which language acquisition and communicative competence occur. Embedded in this theory is an approach to rhetoric that seemed also to articulate cultural awareness and intentionality with regard to a particular language situation.

The "creole continuum," as John Rickford puts it (citing David DeCamp), "refers to a situation where a continuum of intermediate varieties develops between creole and standard poles as creole speakers experience increased motivation and opportunity to modify their speech in the direction of the standard language."[14] As a supporter of this theory, I suggest that the consequences of history and the greater exposure and opportunity to participate in mainstream culture resulted in heightened pressure to assimilate and gain higher communicative competence with the standard forms. These negotiations with language mirrored developments in larger social perceptions of what it meant to be Caribbean, coming at a steep price that often included ridicule, exile, fear, reprisal, and shame at both ends of the continuum. And as Mervyn Alleyne has observed, "between these two points of view, the truth seems to be that these societies are contradictory, conflict-prone and insecure, ambivalent in outlook and attitudes, ambiguous in their formation and in their functioning."[15] Alleyne seems to imply not only that language, as a definitive method of expression in creole societies, is methodologically sound but also that it functions as one of the most effective demonstrations of existential awareness. Having contributed to the development of an oral self-expression, we are obliged not only to speak ourselves into being but also to continuously display and describe the shifting dimensions of a Caribbean existence. Kamau Brathwaite provides examples of "nation language" that serve to illustrate this layered impulse, reshaping but not undoing what he called "the contours of an English heritage."[16] Brathwaite's observations highlight the paradox of vernacular being, as do Thomas's, and illuminate how we might approach Caribbeanness through language in order to link historical sociolinguistic contexts to the development of rhetorical practices and affect. Rickford concurs, noting that "pidgins and creoles are often centrally involved in problems of social, economic, and political development in the communities where they are spoken: in attempts to reform and upgrade the educational systems, and in efforts to establish a new cultural identity or forge a new means of artistic expression."[17]

Another more recent example of the explicit resistance to decreolization is the 2010 publication of the Gospel of Luke—*Jiizas: Di Buk wi Luuk rait bout Im*—in Jamaican patwa. As part of the Creole Bible Translation Project,[18] undertaken by the Bible Society of the West Indies (whose earliest work dates back to 1985), *Jiizas* has revived the issue of linguistic complexity and social negotiation in mainstream considerations of the legitimacy of Caribbean languages and language users (not to mention the apparent "underevangelization" of Jamaica).[19] Pastors and congregants have come down on opposing sides, arguing about whether Jamaican creole translations can adequately express the complexity of their Hebrew, Greek, or English counterparts.[20]

Overall, though, scholars have convincingly demonstrated that in their diversity and complexity, Caribbean languages—*what* Caribbean people say and the specific forms characteristic of the languages they use—are systematic and productive and must be approached as languages *in their own right*. They are not corruptions of the standard due to the speakers' cognitive deficits or inabilities to assimilate; rather, much like the speakers themselves, these languages exist in deliberate relation to and in contention with privileged forms. A significant aspect of this theory and its practical application, as far as rhetoric is concerned, is the correlation between the oral displays of language and their inherent affective qualities: the notion that the speakers played a deliberate role in the development of the creole and that they opted to use it in a range of purposes and contexts, both because of and in spite of pressures to adhere to the standard language.

Rather than frame Caribbean language as a sociolinguistic *reaction* to a set of social circumstances, then, I will examine the degree to which the process of creolization emphasizes some of the foundational aspects of rhetorical (re)invention as a negotiation (among other things) of linguistic ambivalence. Frantz Fanon warns that "to speak means to be in a position to use a certain syntax, to grasp the morphology of this or that language, but it means above all to *assume a culture, to support the weight of a civilization*."[21] The rhetorical situation that Fanon describes here emphasizes the fact that strategic choices lie behind the decision to speak a particular language in a given situation and with a given audience and that those choices are fraught with social tension (not just the problematic inculcation of the binary distinction between the "proper" and "improper"). In terms of language use, potential difficulties in ethos must be negotiated once one has chosen to identify (or differentiate) oneself within a linguistic gauntlet. This tension is at the heart of the rhetorical ambivalence that Caribbean speakers experience, even in their interactions with other Caribbeans. As I intimated previously, and as Fanon affirms, language ambivalence is a point that Caribbeanist thinkers understand implicitly and seize as a theme for discussing the broader dimensions of identity in the Caribbean; their critical stances on language bridge important gaps between what people say, their intentions or motives, the effects of their language on certain audiences, and the responsibility associated with these performances. Louise Bennett's narrative poem "Dry-Foot Bwoy" illustrates how such ambivalence is negotiated, as well as the potential failures of that negotiation, viewed from the perspective of a native Caribbean.[22] In the poem, the spectrum of ambivalent sentiments ranges from sarcastic concern to ridicule, from explicit sympathy for the victim of ridicule to implicit frustration with a sociolinguistuc system that necessitates such performances. In expressing this diversity, the poem helps to illustrate the negotiation of linguistic ambivalence as part of a moral imperative to which the speaker seems to adhere—and that stands at the heart of the ambivalence toward the "dry-foot bwoy." Indeed, this ambivalence fuels the critique and justifies the speaker's scorn, as well as her pity.

For the speaker, the critique addresses not the standard in and of itself but the attitude toward language that the "bwoy" presumes is his. His performance is a pretense, the assumption of a linguistic mask that fails to impress his audience. The "foreign twang" is at first (mis)taken as some sort of illness, a symbolic cold from which many a weary traveler has suffered. He is seen, on a basic level, as an oddity: a somebody in search of a language and a virtual nobody without one. But further, the speaker's sentiment and the subject of the poem—Mary's son, whose travels have left him linguistically conflicted and socially awkward—emphasize the deep ambivalence that endures among users of contentious language varieties and the audiences who witness their use in all genres of expression and cultural production.

Aggravated by a protracted banga season, or what Patrick Bryan calls "the Scylla of low wages and the Charybdis of unemployment," creole speakers learn to negotiate hard times and the seemingly irreconcilable tension between survival and ambition that has characterized the marginal classes of Caribbean society from emancipation to the present day.[23] They do this in part through the performance of tradition, where language negotiation represents not just the process of creolization as a metaphor of sociolinguistic evolution but also the very condition of being creolized, an awareness that leads to the oral expression of Caribbeanness that endures in contemporary times. This in turn supports the effort to understand the rhetorical use of language in relation to its symbolic and material yields. For instance, in Jan Carew's *Black Midas*, Shark, the protagonist, reflects on his own sociolinguistic ambivalence: "Books had made me divided in myself and I knew I would remain that way as long as I lived. On the one hand, the language of books had chalked itself on the slate of my mind and, on the other, the sun was in my blood, the swamp and river, my grandmother, the amber sea, the savannahs, the memory of surf and wind closer to me than the smell of my own sweat."[24] Shark's dilemma provides a more nuanced dimension to Prospero's boast concerning textually based knowledge and Caliban's subsequent complaint in *The Tempest*.[25] But whereas Shakespeare's protagonists could articulate only the author's apparent empathy, Carew's Shark is far better equipped to make an explicit appeal for equality and critique its absence. The metonym is clear: the "books" are not books, no more than the division Shark describes is his alone. Carew, through Shark, provides the reader with a critique of a larger, more perverse issue of self-determination that is forced to take shape under oppressive educational and social conditions. Because no person or set of people is simply predisposed to oppression, in an asymmetrical power relationship of the type Shark experiences, Carew suggests, there is always an inordinate pressure to "acquire" the standard in the way Rickford describes, often begrudgingly so. Similarly, with G., the protagonist in George Lamming's novel *In the Castle of My Skin*, the theme figures prominently in his musings:

> Perhaps we would do better if we had good big words like the educated people. But we didn't. We had to say something was like something else, and whatever we said didn't convey all we felt. We wouldn't dare tell anybody what we had talked about. People who were sure of what they were saying and who had the right words to use could do that. They could talk to others. And if they didn't feel what they were saying, it didn't matter. They had the right words. Language was a kind of passport. You could go where you like if you had a clean record. You could say what you like if you know how to say it. It didn't matter whether you felt everything you said. You had language, good, big words to make up for what you didn't feel.[26]

Rhetorically, Lamming does more than construct a basic we/they binary to highlight the linguistic gulf that language users must traverse to achieve communicative competence (whether through the legitimacies of appropriation or mimicry). This is certainly evident, but the author also superimposes a theory of his own sociolinguistic experience as part of a more extensive cultural memory. And he accomplishes this while simultaneously forcefully speculating on the nature of language among the "educated" speakers to whom he and his peers stand in contrast. The passage indicates that the vernacular speakers are endowed with a deep abstract "feeling" hampered by the perceived inability to express those abstractions. They are thereby relegated to the penumbric margin as a matter of linguistic inadequacy and embarrassment. Speakers who reside exclusively on the other end of the continuum have a different problem. They possess the vocabulary and skills of effective communication—the "right words"—as well as the flexibility to "talk to others." What they seem to lack, Lamming implies, is an awareness of the "feeling" they would need to express. Here, Lamming concedes to the overarching social reality that their communicative prowess would let "people who were sure of what they were saying" compensate for any deficit of underlying "feeling."

Like Shark, G. recognizes the effects that divergent, ambivalent language attitudes have on one another. In the passage quoted, Lamming describes the problem as an interlectal articulation of life experience, not simply a situation in which language users who are familiar with being either obliged or forced to negotiate with certain social standards merely *choose* one or the other. Lamming's narrator and his friends go beyond choice to figure out a course of rhetorical intentionality with regard to language, a result that can come about only because they are acutely aware of the ideological strain that accompanies language choice. Shark and G. both represent the Caribbean vernacular rhetor's ongoing turmoil with the imposition of language and ideology that threatens to eclipse *all they know* with *all they know they must learn*. The weighted contexts of identity formation and assertion in the Caribbean, which resulted from the combination of vernacular traditions and European inculcation, underscore

TABLE 2. Rhetorical modes (major characteristics) of Caribbean discourse

Mode	Primary genre(s)	Characteristic(s)	Rhetorical motive(s)
Code-switching	all oral, textual, or scribal genres	deployment of multiple linguistic registers	resistance, assertion
Wordplay	all oral, textual, or scribal genres	pun, innuendo, slang, improvisation, exclamatory idiophones	prowess, power display, sexuality, profanity, vulgarity
Circumlocution	dialogue, music	indirection, misdirection	avoidance, aggression
Call and response	sermon, speech, musical performance	call by the rhetor and response by audience	bonding, authorization, acceptance
Boasting/shaming	picong, calenda, music, sermon	intimidation, profanity, mockery, exaggeration	criticism, prowess, hierarchical display
Proverb	proverb (aphorism, apothegm, axiom, maxim, saying)	symmetry, chiasmus, repetition, succinctness, metaphor, formulaic format	causality, threat, natural or universal order
The sermonic	all oral, textual, or scribal genres	sermonic (messianic and jeremiadic)	instructional, cautionary, liberatory
Nonverbal semantics; visual semantics	steups, kuya mouth, twist-mouth, cut-eye, gesticulations, dance, flight, travel reportage, narratives of exile, photography, film, graphic design	oral and physical embellishments in tone, intonation, or action; moving/stationary bodies in physical space, acting, acted upon	critique, physical performance, negotiation, power, resistance

speakers' sensitivities to the oral displays of cultures that took shape in the crucible of Caribbean reality.

RHETORICAL MODES

Negative views of Caribbean orality persist, maintained by many creole speakers who, in their encounter with empire and its derivative institutions, feel compelled to valorize the status of standardized English and the corresponding marginalization of their respective creoles; worse, they too often succumb to these tensions at the expense of their representative cultural expressions. However, if the imperative of rhetoric is to promote the judgment of its participants, then we must establish categories of vernacular creole expression as legitimate forms of argumentation despite the way Caribbean language may be maligned by some and misunderstood by others. For clarity, I highlight these modes and their representative genres in table 2, briefly explaining how they are activated.

The rhetorical modes serve as the traditional foundations on which contemporary epideictic performances are based. Speakers who are consistently exposed to and consciously use these embedded forms are particularly attuned to their preponderance at all levels of interaction. Now, while no doubt everybody can appreciate a little shit talk, the general tendency is to take these features for granted as part of the everyday operation of culture. Take, for example, Ezra Griffith's description of "shit-talk" as "a Bajan form of discourse . . . conducted in fluent patois and centered on just about any conceivable subject as long as it [does] not personally concern any of the participants." Griffith provides several specific characteristics:

> The conversation was fuelled by rum and the pork chop, a centrepiece of Bajan cooking. The expression "bare shit-talk" refers to shit-talk in its most concentrated form.
> Not everybody could participate in bare shit-talk up in our gap. Participants had to have outgoing personalities and had to be willing to make argumentative assertions with unbridled confidence and, generally speaking, in a loud voice that was accompanied [by] hand gestures signifying premeditated arrogance. . . .
> Such arguments rarely relied on any objective element to make the case. A preference for one of these two world-class cricketers [Don Bradman or Frank Worrell] was best established with a loud voice, artful cricketing motions, and the capacity to hold forth extemporaneously, employing assertions unambivalently.[27]

Griffith accurately depicts features that must work interdependently for shit talk to *be* shit talk and, further, to be *bare* shit talk. These kinds of social situations are recognizable to others from the region because they often mirror similar contexts found from island to island: the ritualistic elements of food and drink, the confident style, the motion of hands to complement verbal delivery, the arrangement of facts, and the reliance on particular appeals. The richness of the features Griffith identifies, however, is subsequently undermined when the modality is juxtaposed with arguments that rely on evidence, the "objective elements [needed] to make a case."[28] Put another way, although this portrayal may have been intended to highlight a particularity of Caribbeanness, it seems to elide the greater complexities of vernacular expression. A more nuanced examination is necessary. In many brief conversations about the subject, I have often repeated the definition of rhetoric a mentor gave me: "Rhetoric is the practice of using language to influence the choices other people make." More than anything else, this account cuts to the quick of my interests in words and their effects. A practitioner influences choices. A rhetorician considers those choices and their influences. Then again, when the choice itself is which language to use, things can get a bit complicated.

Code-Switching

The tensions of appropriation and abrogation are inherent in the practice of code-switching and can form the horns of a rhetorical dilemma that multilingual practitioners routinely face:[29] the performance of difference, no matter how strategic, involves explicitly acknowledging the inequalities that underscore the very differences being performed. In the context of asymmetrical power dynamics, therefore, it becomes crucially important to determine how to say what needs to be said, what language should be used to say it, and when it should be said.[30]

Similarly, the lines of distinction are not always as clearly drawn for the speaker, even with the deliberate interplay of basilectal, mesolectal, and acrolectal features that determine intent and affect.[31] That is to say, some of we does do it for fun. Some of we does do it for spite. And some of we does do it for so, but it don't ever really be just for so. Even so, it still have a whole set of Caribbean people digging a real horrors with the way how they does talk and interact with this one or that one on a day-to-day basis, not just in the literature and thing, but in real life.[32] And is like they don't get tired of jumbieing their own children for talking the same way, for doing the same thing.[33] And like is forget they forget that what they theyself learn about language (and that the attitudes and them that develop as a consequence) was often learned by the hook or the crook. I can still hear them.

> Not "some of we does do" but "some of us do."
> Not "I done eat" but "I'm finished."
> Not "ova dey" but "over there."
> Not "reverse back" or "go *down* downstairs" or "go *up* upstairs."

On top of that, they steady taking basket from the uninitiated as to whether the talk they talking is not only "correct" or "proper" but also meaningful,[34] all despite the rich, complex linguistic and intellectual traditions on which their talk is derived and the overarching sociopolitical significance that accompanies it. And dat eh no shit talk neither.

In other words, to talk like me eh know nothing about proper, and (especially) if I know, I eh care is to throw nonstandard sand in standard rice. To talk (and write) like this involves a rhetorical choice; it is done on purpose and for a purpose, not spitefully but for spite. I doing this to show you a form, that is, to make a point, to demonstrate a particular ethos that is grounded in specific language use.

Put another way, even though many Caribbean people hold that their language varieties—varieties some of them speak exclusively—are broken, improper, and inferior, their code-switching performances are steeped in rhetorical intent that can be traced to their collective cultural identification.[35] The choice either to creolize the standard or to standardize the creole signifies attempts to use language as a tool to broach critical conversation in recognized and recognizable terms in order to facilitate discourse. According to Ashcroft, Griffiths, and Tiffin, these measures "mark a separation from the site of colonial privilege" and underscore a strategy of polydialectal communication.[36] Our worldviews unfold, therefore, as a complex culture of vernacular expression, recognizable on the linguistic level not only in terms of tone or syllable stress but also in terms of semantic inventions and the strategic arrangement and application of rhetorical forms. To reiterate, then, we use the language *for so* (that is, easily, without any great difficulty), but *never really just for so* (that is, not just for display but in response to a range of specific motives).

Such motives are more subtly evident in Merle Collins's "Shadowboxing," for example, as the narrator describes the attendees at a birthday party that will later form the backdrop for a lengthy discussion of the political environment in Grenada. Notice how, before any political conversation per se becomes apparent, Collins switches seamlessly between the standard and creole forms to appeal to an audience that understands and expresses its Caribbean sensitivities through such language:

> Desiree looks around the table. There will be seven of them—Danton, the biggest boy, born the year of the invasion, said he was doing something in the piece of ground behind the house and he would come soon. Trust Danton to find something to do right at this time! Anyway, seven of them including Danton: her mother, Miss Ty, sitting there with her grey afro and cream pant suit and looking well nice—figure slim and trim, not like she, Desiree, getting bigger every day; Tantie Velma, who take her in after she get pregnant with Danton and run away before Miss Ty find out—Tantie Velma looking like young girl in tight jeans and pink sleeve-less top in spite of her size; Dawn, hair pulled back with that green and red band round the roll at the back—the child look good with that style, she have the face for it, the high forehead and the father big eyes—Dawn with her eyes on the television though it not on.[37]

The shifts neither impede the accuracy of the description nor detract from Collins's other depictions. Even more subtly, the initial utterance in Walcott's "Pocomania" also evokes the ethos of creolized speakers and performers in their symbolic, cosmological, and spiritual encounters. Operating almost in contrast to the more extensive "Jamiekan Baibl" project, language is used here to foreground the apparent paradox of godly perfection and material fallibility: *"De* shepherd shrieves in Egyptian light."[38] At another point in the continuum, the poet Michael Smith launches a scathing linguistic performance in "Mi Cyaan Believe It," juxtaposing basilectal language with the deliberate, scornful acknowledgment of persistent aspects of colonial domination.[39] The speaker's thinly veiled references to two nursery rhymes—"Humpty Dumpty" and "Little Boy Blue"—effectively evoke aspects of empire in the metropolis and in the colony with a performance that criticizes the education system that was intended to eradicate such speech, as well as the social milieu that contradicted what colonial subjects ought to have learned about the beneficence of their rulers. Again, language is the masque the speaker uses to amplify the oral display that the audience is bound to notice: "Mi seh mi cyaan believe it."[40] The speaker implies that while he has neither the privilege nor the inclination of the elite, he realizes that the fragility they both share is most likely to be expressed in the arena of partisan politics (used here as a synonym for "class") that maintains the separations that he and his children ("picni") have little choice but to endure. If there are implicit questions in "Mi Cyaan Believe It," a line that Smith repeats throughout the poem, they may be articulated thus: "*How* can I believe? Why should I?" Conversely, though, there is little doubt that Smith was ever really puzzled over how—or how effectively—he would engage with overwhelming disbelief in the face of glaring social injustices. Similarly, there is, along with his outrage, the parallel desire to believe and to effectively articulate the paradox, interspersing incredulity with resistant hope.

Wordplay

In the context of Caribbean expressive culture, wordplay can be described as the manipulation of discursive devices, such as metaphors, puns, and repetition, to cast a veil of ambiguity, complexity, misdirection, humor, or critique in a given performance. These performances require cleverness and spontaneity if the speaker is to "trope" effectively—that is, to "turn" the meaning of the word, image, or sound to suit the context of the exchange. When such devices are deployed for specifically rhetorical means, however, they suggest that concealment is not really the objective.

A play on words will usually do more to disclose than to conceal, making the act of concealment (and not the thing being "concealed") into the joke. That is, the practitioner exhibits just enough savoir-faire to avoid censorship with an overtly offensive delivery but does not attempt to avoid offense altogether. The attempt at wordplay amplifies the topic at hand, such that the audience understands *precisely* what the speaker intends. We see this, for example, with Anthony "Gabby" Carter's use of puns in his song "Dr. Cassandra." With this application of the masque, Gabby shows that sufficient guile is not synonymous with covert intentions. On the contrary, the key here is *not* to hide the intended meaning of a given word or phrase or to maintain an air of play that would unduly euphemize the delivery and thus take the edge off a potential offense. This tactic can free the practitioner to take certain liberties with the audience and potentially free the audience to take liberties with the performance itself.[41] For example, the pun on penetration—injections expressed with the onomatopoeic *jook*—is put in play to euphemize rather than avoid a direct sexual proposition.

Gabby is not attempting to mask the fact that his request is sexual: the pun on "coming" is obvious; the sexual act is metaphorically represented as "medicine" that only Cassandra can administer; and there is the additional reference to the sexual act as "pressure" that, at least in Gabby's view, only Cassandra can "cool down." To avoid provoking the ire of his audience, he attempts to validate the relationship, suggesting that the arrangement between himself and Cassandra (for which he "did not have to pay") is legitimate, even as the numerous repetitions of the act itself interspersed with Cassandra's declaration serve to demonstrate the sexual stamina they both share. According to Gabby, "[She] jook, jook, jook, jook, jook, jook, jook, jook, jook, jook, jook."[42]

The pun is also a feature in Gregory Isaacs's rockers hit "Night Nurse," which had many an unsuspecting child singing along to the "emergency" of plaintive sexuality, a "pain" that kept "getting worse." The effectiveness of rhetorical wordplay is further seen in its use as a mode for critiquing issues that are made palatable through the lens of sexual innuendo. Slinger "the Mighty Sparrow" Francisco is the master of this move. His oeuvre of calypso tales, which includes such classics as "Saltfish," "When It Bald It Better," "Jook for Jook," "Leggo Meh Stick," and "Bendwood Dick," makes ample use of punning as the preferred device. Notably, "Congo Man," which was released in 1965 and banned in 1969,[43] progresses through themes of invasion, capture, sexual consumption, subjectivity, and disgust. Using the most taboo of indulgences for the black man—contact with a white woman—Sparrow discusses the problems that follow from an encounter between the "civilized" and the "savage" when the curiosity of the former comes into contact with the bravado of the latter. The cannibal Congo man resolves his immediate situation by "eating" the women and all they represent. The debilitating effects of the Congo man's consumption of the white female body, which he "eat until he stomach upset," include a voracious obsession with what whiteness offers and an experience that Sparrow has, to his great envy, never had.

The admission, however, raises a question: does Sparrow really envy the Congo man? No. He neither envies him nor wishes he were in the same position, for he has suffered from the same effects and knows them all too well. His suggestion—that had he been in the same position as the Congo man, he would have returned the women safely to their husbands—highlights the false comparison between himself and his "big brother." In reality, neither of them has a particular allegiance to the white man or woman. The trick of his comparison, of course, is that even though Sparrow gives the impression of civility, chivalry, and generosity, noting that he has never eaten the meat of a white woman, his sympathy remains with the Congo man, the black precolonial ancestor. Consumption has corrupted him, a fate common, if not essential, to the colonized mind. It is also a point of fundamental resistance for Sparrow or, less likely, the benefit of circumstantial fortune. The concern here is not that white women are particularly delectable or desirable for Sparrow or the Congo man (he is already a headhunter when they meet him) or that Africans are essentially savage (after all, he did "cook" one woman before eating her). Rather, it is the irony of influence that each society has had on the other, the preconceived notions each possesses, and the potential dangers such ignorant encounters could yield (and have yielded). Sparrow manages, with a masque of sexually ambiguous reference, to turn the offense on the offending subject and to ask which is the more reprehensible act and why. Rather than absolve the audience—whether as perpetrator, critic, or both—from the failings being critiqued, Sparrow's wordplay suggests that they are more intimately involved in the display.

The calypsonian David Rudder also uses metaphor (albeit in a less ribald manner) to emphasize audience members' collective and individual reactions to economic hardship, with the fête functioning as a symbol within a commentary on the failings of national politics, specifically, the People's National Movement (PNM). In "Madness," Rudder describes the social madness that ensues, offering details that contextualize the issue for the audience:

> I jump the wall about twelve o'clock and
> I gone inside
> Stand up there in the people's fête
> My eyes open wide
> Everybody inside there like they are feting hard
> But when I look at their faces mamayo
> Like they are going mad
> It must be the budget that the man
> From Whitehall did read
> 'Cause all of them inside of there like
> They suck a crazy seed
> That kind of head couldn't come from weed

Rudder uses this as an entry into political commentary: he symbolically storms a "political party." The metaphor thus functions as a vehicle to describe an occasion in which the dual notions of control and chaos contribute to vernacular social behavior, attitudes, and expectations that manifest as a masqued display within a worldview that Rudder analyzes and shares with his audience.

In something of a contrast, 3canal's "Mud Madness" argues for a primal—that is, antirationalist—approach to life during Jour Ouvert (Jouvay), the early morning opening of the Shrovetide Carnival. The group's stated rationale ("Everything is mud. From mud then back to mud again") is based on ritual and an understanding of the cyclical nature of life.[44] It is in effect a claim that life does not end but continues, echoing Genesis 3:19 ("Dust thou art, and unto dust shalt thou return"), which is a staple in Christian and syncretic funeral rites. This, however, is a material, earth-based reading of experience that eschews lofty notions of the otherworldly in favor of more visceral celebrations of life and death, unity, freedom, and letting go. As Carnival begins, 3canal's "Mud Madness" is a call to action, an assertion for those "children running" to have a chance to belong or to take that chance. The ritualistic "letting go," then, is necessary in order to enable one to "hold on" as part of an organic whole.

In the Caribbean rhetorical tradition, wordplay, including the use of similar-sounding words that differ in meaning and context, is often utilized as a prelude or segue to commentary undergirded by a sustained critical sensibility. This aspect relies on a contiguity of the referent object to the punned object. Take the following example overheard in a kitchen: "I just kicksing in the house, man. Them kicksing in Parliament. I does kicks in the house."[45] Derived from Winston "Explainer" Henry's "In Parliament They Kicksing," the pun on *house* directly refers to the houses of Parliament (Trinidad's Parliament was modeled after the British system of government, though its two chambers are the House of Representatives and the Senate). The pun shows the speaker's implicit and acute understanding of the political structure of the country, not to mention an underlying dissatisfaction with the goings-on there. Furthermore, the speaker uses an additional semantic marker, that of "kicksing" (joking), setting a benign "kicksing" engaged in at home against a potentially damaging "kicksing" performed in Parliament, where the stakes are apparently higher and the consequences for regular citizens more telling. The sentiment expressed here is related to the notion that "joke is joke, but damned joke ain't no joke." Further, the speaker makes a value distinction between private and public behavior, showing an acute awareness of place and audience. Because public behavior, especially that of politicians charged with maintaining the nation's equilibrium, carries with it significant responsibility, the speaker implies that Parliament is no place to "kicks." Explainer emphasizes the irony of a government that shirks its duties by kicksing, while the overheard reference to "just kicksing" implicates specific members of the audience by drawing on a pun that they presumably recognize. The speaker is thus able to direct the course and quality of the exchange.

In Jean Binta Breeze's short story "Sunday Cricket," wordplay is also used as an improvisational tool, effectively redirecting audience members' attention from distraction to persuasion. The story's narrator expresses grave disappointment at having to attend church instead of a cricket match she had planned to see with her friend Bredda B. Resolved to endure the service by the most expedient means, Bredda B opts for sleep. As the service goes on, the intensity of a guest pastor reaches high pitch, and the congregation bursts into applause:

> De whole church give a firm an loud clap han. Is dis rise Bredda B, im jump up quick, like im late fi heaven, clappin im han an hollerin out "Im mek a double century or im out?"
>
> As soon as dis come out im mout, de laughin bus out fresh from de back an de vex face dem turn roun from de front. Sista B put dung her hymn-book an staat head out troo de side door so can come een troo de back door fi im. My madda face tight like no joke cyaan mek fi at leas a year.
>
> Is Bredda Jerry save de day, ah have to give it to dat man. Im answer Bredda B right back. "Out? Out? Nooooo.... Not out, never out. We have a openin bat dat never out. None like Him been aroun for centuries. An church, if you have Him on you side you cyaan lose, no, you cyaan lose. My openin bat, your openin bat. Mek im lead dis team today. Jesus! What is His name? ... Jesus! Call on His name ..."
>
> De whole congregation bawl out, "Jesus." All de backbencher dem come een, "Jesus."[46]

Circumlocution

The art of circumlocution operates predominantly in the service of verbal strategies, which include avoidance (indirection), challenge (direction), and trickery (misdirection). As such, it deals broadly with the technique of "saying without saying," whether out of fear, passive aggression, or the need to strategize within debilitating constraints. In its first form, avoidance, the intent is to minimize the probability of confrontation by taking steps to ease tension, as Aldrick attempts to do in Earl Lovelace's novel *The Dragon Can't Dance*:

> What could he really tell Fisheye? Fisheye had charge of the boy, and if he wanted to beat him, what could he [Aldrick] do?
>
> "Shoulda go and lift some weights before I come to talk to him," Aldrick thought. "And learn some jujitsu." And it was in this spirit that he approached Fisheye.
>
> "What the hell you doing there alone on this culvert, man?"
>
> Fisheye didn't answer, and Aldrick might have suspected that all was not right; for this manner of approach, this aggressive and anticipatory and conciliatory humour[,] was the means by which men said to each other what they had to say, while avoiding conflict. "I just bring home your son. I hear you does beat him for nothing."
>
> "So what?"
>
> "So," he plunged on, for he was aware of the boy standing tensely beside him.

"So, I come to warn you. If you beat him again I going straight in the gym and lift some weights and learn some jujitsu and come back for you."

"I ain't making joke tonight," Fisheye said coldly. . . .

"I still have to talk to you about the boy," Aldrick said, turning to leave.

"You better don't talk that talk tonight."

"When I lift the weights I will talk," Aldrick said.

"Lift plenty," Fisheye said.

Aldrick walked home very slowly. He was not happy with himself.[47]

Whereas Aldrick uses indirection, playing at aggression to deflect Fisheye's rage, circumlocution can take an understated though more antagonistic form, as with Cleothilda's half-hearted admonition of Sylvia in the same novel:[48] "Sylvia seemed unconcerned; and as she bent in that jubilant curtsy to take up her bucket, and Guy started to ease away, Miss Cleothilda, *intent on blunting Sylvia's triumph and asserting her own power,* calls out sweetly, 'Sylvia, wait! I think I have a dress here that could fit you—*if your mother would let you take it.*'"[49]

Call and Response

Described by Geneva Smitherman as "spontaneous verbal and non-verbal interaction between speaker and listener in which . . . the speaker's statements are punctuated by expressions by the listener,"[50] the practice of call and response has a number of purposes, including (but not limited to) politeness, incitement, and acknowledgment, the intensities of which differ according to different speaking situations. Call-and-response interactions may even involve a temporary reversal of primary speaking roles—that is, the caller becomes respondent and vice versa. Typically, call and response involves an interaction between performer and audience that is meant to encourage the performer, to urge that he or she continue speaking, that what is being said is not only appreciated but also appropriate to the context. For example, when members of a group meet, the particular language they use determines certain codes of behavior that can either renew bonds of common identity or signal a difference. I might greet another Caribbean person by asking, "Wh'am now?" (What's happening now?) or "What's the scene?" Or when entering a room for the first time, I may repeat my greeting, "Morning, morning" or "Night, night," to which I will likely receive a response that may also be repeated. Similarly, to certain Caribbeans I will say, "Respect," which has a number of different meanings ("hello," "thank you," "I agree," "calm down," or "respect") depending on the context of the conversation or rhetorical situation in which it is said. Each of these statements, used effectively, provides the necessary comfort and access to further conversation, letting the speakers proceed with the knowledge that we are *authentic* Caribbean people with common experiences and frames of reference. No need to perform the learned Americanness, for example. *Not around we. We* understand. In contrast, some speakers choose not to offer such sentiments in the same form to non-Caribbeans, choosing rather to greet in the standardized form: hello, good morning, and so on.

The response thus functions as an authorization that lets the speaker know that the listener is sympathetic and receptive and that it is no imposition to go on. The performer in turn acknowledges the participatory role of the audience, soliciting responses by asking questions or even pausing strategically during the course of a performance so the audience has the opportunity to respond. Performances such as these are designed to implicate the audience in the performance, with the call and response marking the perimeters of a particular performance so those in the audience are always aware of their roles and responsibilities.

Chief among these responsibilities is the necessary suspension of disbelief to receive the full intended effects of the performance, which can range from indoctrination and the reinforcement of a worldview to elaborate explanations of the way things are in the world. According to Smitherman, call and response "enables traditional black folk to achieve the unified state of balance or harmony which is fundamental to the traditional worldview."[51] Though it is observed very often in a sacred context—that is, at a church service or other religious gathering—call and response is performed in secular social contexts as well. This form of dynamic interaction can, for example, take the form of openings and endings that occur with tales:

Storyteller: Crick?
Audience: Crack!

Storyteller: Crick, crack!
Audience: Monkey break he back for a piece of pommerac!

Storyteller: Mout open?
Audience: Tory jump out!

Storyteller: Wire Bend?
Audience: Story end.[52]

Conteur: Tim-Tim.
Audience: Bois Chaise.
Conteur: Qui sa Bon Dieur mete assu Laterre? [What things has God put on Earth?]
Audience: Toute chose. [Everything.][53]

Conteur: E di queek [or Mesieur]
Audience: Quack.[54]

Caribbean practitioners in contemporary settings outside the region also use call and response to establish, develop, and maintain connections between themselves and their audiences. This bond can be described as the combined psychic and physical attachments that exist in varying degrees of intensity between the performer and the audience. It is achieved and maintained by establishing identification, with the response confirming the subject's acceptance of a particular identity and the interaction thus creating a bond that supersedes the limitations of the current location, connecting the audience instead to its cultural roots. This occurs through directional identification—that is, the means by which the ethos of the performer and that of the audience are aligned as a singular entity through conscious acts of *distribution* or *convergence*—designed to reinforce the performer's intent as being in line with the welfare of the audience. The performer can be either the distributor of identifying aspects that members of the audience actively accept on a subnational level or the locus for collective identification on a supranational level.

Distribution can be achieved in a number of ways. Many performances, for example, begin with the *salutation*, a strategic acknowledgment in the form of an unapologetically unadorned roll call between the rhetor and the audience. The following example illustrates a standard practice at Caribbean parties:

> Anybody from Antigua?
> Anybody from Barbados?
> Anybody from St. Lucia?
> Jamaica?
> Trinidad?
> Tobago?
> Guyana?

To each successive inquiry, members of the audience respond in the affirmative (often most energetically for their own native country), taking umbrage should their country be neglected from the roll; some performers have been known to include almost every island and as many cities as they can recall just to avoid breaking the bond.

Other performers do the opposite, inverting subject-referent positions and displaying themselves to the audience as inclusive examples to be emulated. This strategy is as common as the previous form, implemented through identifying aspects that the performer represents and on which the audience can converge for a common experience of the performance. Nadia Batson's "Caribbean Girl" accomplishes just that. Batson negotiates with the audience, attempting to supplant presumed penchants for subnational attitudes with a collective—that is, supranational—sensibility. Rather than solicit her audience based on disparate nations, she notes that the audience collectively defines her Caribbeanness: the composition of her audience "brings out" the Trini, the Bajan, the Vincy, the

St. Lucian, the Antiguan, and the Jamaican in her. In turn, she presents herself to the audience as "your Caribbean girl." By tapping into the similarities that inhere in the various musical traditions and persist in individual Caribbean societies, the astute performer works for coalescence, thereby making nativity something of a moot point even while alluding to birth and to being brought into existence. The performer is their connection to the mutual tradition, using familiar aspects to convene and maintain the contemporary enactment of a Caribbean ethos. Depending on the strength of the bond that the performer has established over time, salutations may often go unspoken, the acknowledgment of the audience articulated in cheers. For some performers, appearing on stage is salutation enough, though the savvy performer will rarely begin without refreshing the bond previously established with the audience. And what can begin as straightforward interpellation can often develop into full-fledged collaborative choral performances and evoke the foundational dialogic bonds at the heart of vernacular interaction.

Of course, the possibility of breakdown occurs when, whether live or recorded, the performance fails to deliver, breaking the psychic bonds or altering them in a significant way. Provided that such a disconnection does not occur and the delicate relationship remains intact, the practitioner's prophetic, critical, or liberatory agenda may well be enacted and positively received. This involves, among other things, a call to action that can motivate dynamic social activity and counteract cultural amnesia by generating a response.

Boasting/Shaming

Disputatious verbal exchanges set the backdrop for the boast, which allows practitioners to display their virility, strength, and verbal prowess. In "Stepping Razor," Peter Tosh opts for directness instead of wordplay, using simile to warn his enemies with a boastful tone that he is not to be trifled with, that even though he might seem unimposing, he is "dangerous, dangerous." Another example of this, "picong," is known by various names—old talk, blagging, and shit talk, for instance—but the essence of this rhetorical exchange is singular in focus and precise in its effect. A key figure in the picong tradition is the Midnight Robber. Speeches were traditionally delivered extemporaneously with a single objective: to show that no other robber was better. Vasco De Freitas offers a sample:

> Rollo the Ganja is here, so don't be surprised because you have never yet seen me here before! But I was in this trade for many many long years, roaming for my father. I passed through Bulgaria, Sweden, Copenhagen, Denmark, Australia, Hungary, Russia, Crussia, and also [incomprehensible] and I have never yet get destroyed....
>
> The day I was born the world greatest tribulation was ever known. Deafening

thunder rolled for more than forty-eight hours consecutively. Over six hundred villages, cities, and streets were washed away by floods and hurricane. And here comes a vision! So hand me the mysterious weapon, similar to the weapon that Samson defeated the Philistines with. And if you want to die a criminal death, I shall send you to the lonely wilderness where the birds of the air and wild and ferocious beasts of the dark jungle were [incomprehensible]. . . .

Down from the eyeless regions of the lost century came I invincible, undauntable, and impregnable criminal master. More actual sound efforts are incorporated into the delivery of speech. When I speaks he cry and sobbed and rubbed his eyes like a child. Men, women, children wail. . . .

Wheresoever I lay my battling arms, green grass may never grow, sun may never shine, lightning may never flash, thunder may never roar, volcanoes refuse to explode, and even mankind refuse to grow! . . .

Or in a picong in a calypso war when your paltry verses are done with your dunce head, I will have some fun. I will give you rocks to eat for bread and you will be numbered among the dead. Your body will be going down the road, but your spirit will remain under my control. For whenever the death bell toll my flag unfurl for rebellion.[55]

The rhetorical complement to the boast is the shame it is intended to cause in the opponent (though it differs fundamentally from the kind of shame Aldrick feels when his pretended boast fails to work with Fisheye), and even performers in different genres during the Carnival season are subject to De Freitas's scorn. In De Freitas's Robber speech the boasting focuses on the performance itself, with a great deal of rehearsal having been invested in achieving the most effective delivery. But such boasts are also deployed as an overture, a prelude to more decisive action. In *Solibo Magnificent*, Diab-Anba-Feuilles offers a boast before beating Doudou-Ménar to death:

You . . . you . . . you don't know who I am? . . . [If] you don't know who I am, just ask around. Devil is what they call me, and I am the worst thing that ever happened to you, you got that, and if I start fighting with you it's to the death, until I drop over your body, for I am ready to die, oh Jesus give me the last rites, I am going to die over her dead body! *sé mô man lé mô!* it's a real-real death I want!

. . . Christ! No one saw the billyclub fly up and crash down on her head. . . .

. . . There isn't a thing that can get you out of the grip of the Devil who's going to break your bones one by one! I've got superpowers, and I'll poison your soul, your body, your sex![56]

As a counterpoint to the secular boast in *Solibo Magnificent*, a prelude to murder, religious occasions too allow for shaming, either through sermonic confession or the calling out of members of the audience. This calling out is somewhat circumlocutory in form, since it does not directly identify the subject; rather, the subject is implied. Enhanced by the successful conversion of a woman who "suddenly ... burst into tears and threw herself forward in a confused outpouring of confession,"[57] the calling out is achieved in this example with the repetition of a universal "You":

> "You who stand outside the palings of grace scoffing and jeering, you who feel too proud to humble yourself before what is Great and Good, remember it will be noted against you in that Book of books that on this night you heard the call and rejected Christ. You said to him, away with you, I have chosen the enemy. You who hide because you're ashamed, you'll be found out, and you who run because you're afraid, you'll be caught."[58]

In spite of their apparent circumlocution, such strategies often hit their mark.

Proverbs

When we falter, and many times before we do, the oft-repeated lessons of caution, promises of doom, or even the possibilities of brilliance in strategic folly are frequently delivered to us in the form of proverbs. The proverb is fundamentally an appeal to the authority of established modes of knowing, to perceived and accepted truths. They take the form of gnomic markers that are deployed to help define either the ethos of the performer or the general tone of a certain rhetorical performance. Key features of this are succinctness and subtlety. That succinctness is evident in the linguistic structure—the grammatical and syntactical features—but also in the layers of meaning, context, space, and time in which the statement is delivered. A mother, for example, uses a familiar proverb to caution her son: "Friend does carry you, but dey doh bring you back." The proverb stresses not so much a distrust of friends as a sense of personal responsibility. When presented following a particular event or instance, the same statement can also serve as commentary and a form of confirmation of the proverb's effectiveness, simultaneously reinscribing the tradition's authority. Proverbs signify a psychic equivalent of that place we can go to when, with nowhere else to go at a given moment, something must still be reached for, must still be said or done, simply because the moment calls for it. When my uncle Peter drowned, for example, people who attended the wake uttered the same words (now a truism confirmed by his death): "Friend does *really* carry you. They don't bring you back."

In addition to providing instruction, proverbs testify to the resilience of the communities from which they emerge, for they record not arbitrarily recalled sentiments but rather ideas that, having worked effectively, are worth remembering and repeating. Some proverbs embody aspects of the sacred ("t'ief f'om t'ief make God smile"); others, the secular ("good sense beat obeah"); while still others bridge the sacred and secular to achieve their maximum significance ("when you come a church, bring you own hymn book [and try no read from mine]").[59] Many contemporary proverbs—or those using the proverb form in context—refer to sports, drawing on metaphorical commentary (e.g., "stay in your crease," a cricket reference) that Caribbean people recognize. Structurally, as indicated in table 3, they employ familiar devices, including metaphor, symmetry, chiasmus, and irony.

Roberts argues that in form, meaning, and context, Caribbean proverbs are saturated with the negative because the historical domination of Caribbean people forms the core of their vernacular experience.[60] These degrees of negativity stand out in the previously provided examples. They include, for instance, negative wording (e.g., *no* or *don't*), negative moods or themes (e.g., death, defeat, and loss), and negative context-determined purposes (e.g., deterrence and correction). Yet these proverbs exhibit more than just negativity, even though many begin there. In the slavery-colonialism dynamic, Europeans obviously had much more cause to be positive than did the Africans, who were on the receiving end, but Roberts seems to be hinting at a deeply ingrained and critical *response* to situations. "The strategy of the proverb is to direct by appearing to clarify," writes Abrahams, "by simplifying the problem and resorting to traditional solutions"; he goes on to say that a "proverb works primarily by *cloaking* a recommended course of action in the garb of artful expression."[61] Giving this a more positive account, we might describe proverbs as securing a practical wisdom, or phronesis, that reflects the normative phase of a vernacular worldview that has developed through sustained practice in response to traditionally negative experiences. Derivative sentiments make this clearer.

In "Bajan Litany," for example, Bruce St. John uses proverbs to foreground his suspicion and the potential folly of regional imitation in the areas of politics, industry, and economics: "Follow pattern kill Cadogan (Yes, Lord)."[62] Notice the parenthetical's call-and-response dynamic and its role in underscoring the overall critique of an audience that goes uncritically along in the pattern of the mainstream. Louise Bennett makes a similar move in "Independance," using the comparative ignorance of "dumb animals" (the hungry puss and marga dog) to comment on the skewed sense of actual independence in Jamaica during the 1960s.[63]

When applied for rhetorical effect, as they typically are, proverbs can amplify the effectiveness of arguments by endowing practitioners with abstractions of symbolic reference that provide audiences with the *option* of ignoring the obvious lesson—or its repeated delivery—in favor of a symbolic and comparatively less problematic mask. Thus, by giving "the impression that much thought has at some time been given to the problem to which the proverb is presently addressed," the speaker can take shared knowledge for granted and be more succinct with the delivery. This enthymematic activity does not mean that the prov-

TABLE 3. Sample proverb forms

Metaphor	Symmetry/asymmetry	Chiasmus	Irony
Chop don't leave mark in water.[a]	Before face an' behind back no a one.[b]	Go buckra cow-pen fe count cow, no drink him milk; but when you drink him milk, no count him cow.[c]	Servant does ease you foot but hurt you heart.[d]
Cockroach ent have no right in fowl party.[e]	One day for watchman; one day for t'ief.[f]	Good thing not cheap; cheap thing not good.	Many a mauger cow you see a common a bull mumma.[g]
You have to play dead to catch corbeaux alive.[h]	Dog don't eat dog.[i]	Money is no problem. The problem is no money.	Good nature make nanny goat tail short.[j]
A old stick of fire don't take long to catch.[k]	Dog don't make cat.[l]		Friend does carry you, but they don't bring you back.[m]

[a] As in matters of faith and suspicion, some offenses, though impossible to prove, are equally impossible to refute

[b] What you do in secret is not the same as that which you would do in plain view.

[c] If you transgress, don't wait around to get caught (*buckra* is a metonym denoting a white man or the plantocracy). The translation is mine; the proverb comes from Lawton, "Grammar of the English-Based Jamaican Proverb" (127).

[d] Luxury often comes at too high a price, often one's own peace of mind. Do for yourself what you can instead of depending inordinately on others.

[e] Know your place, where you are welcome and where you are not. Know yourself and where you belong.

[f] Have patience. No system is perfect, particularly systems of exclusion. Everybody will have an opportunity, or make one, in due time.

[g] We all come from the same place, despite the power differentials that get constructed later on. The translation is mine; the proverb comes from Lawton, "Grammar of the English-Based Jamaican Proverb" (127).

[h] When all else fails, subterfuge (trickery) is sometimes the most effective strategy (corbeaux are vultures).

[i] Beware of nepotism. Only a fool would expect, in this case, that you would eschew favoritism and turn on your own. Of course, in the most dire times, a dog is likely to eat anything.

[j] Kindness is too often taken advantage of. The translation is mine; the proverb comes from Parsons, "Proverbs from Barbados" (324).

[k] A comment on nostalgia and the activation of memory, this means that dormant passions—love, especially—are easily aroused. The translation is mine; the proverb comes from Parsons, "Proverbs from Barbados" (324).

[l] Certain results are to be expected in certain situations, particularly in reference to the operation of fundamental systems. One should be aware of the difficulties that inhere in situations of fundamental difference.

[m] This self-explanatory adage is widely applied as a caution in a variety of situations.

erbs themselves are intended to mask meaning per se or absolve the audience of understanding that meaning; it suggests only that the members of the audience will already be either sufficiently familiar with the proverbs' general(izable) sentiment to need no extensive explanation or sufficiently familiar with their logic to understand how it may be applied in different situations. Thus, if we assume that audience members opt to respond to the obvious—that is, the intent behind a proverb's deployment, its respective situation, and its desired consequence—using proverbs increases the opportunity for generative interaction.

Enabled by the symbolic references that offer alternative interpretations of what may be obvious, traditional proverbs help form the bases of dialogic proofs that adherents use to formulate their understandings of the world. The activity suggests attempts to abide by the normativity expressed in these notions; however, although these proverbs retain much of their structure and may provide the essence of successful oral transmissions, they are subject to improvisation, modification, and applicability. That is, they evolve in terms not only of structure (linguistic and syntactic) and use (context and place) but also of meaning. For example, combining the two proverbs "you can lead a horse to water, but you can't make it drink" and "where horse does reach, jackass does reach" might result in a more layered commentary: "Where horse does reach, jackass does reach. But if they both get led to water, only a jackass wouldn't drink." This can be interpreted as meaning, more or less, that despite the presence of overarching inequalities (say, with the stark absence of Caribbean scholars in certain fields of study) and disadvantages, only jackasses will fail to take advantage of the opportunity provided to them.

The effectiveness of proverbs and their derivative hybrids lies in their ability to weather repetition without devolving wholly into cliché, a quality that is ensured by the timeliness of their applications and their overall flexibility. As a catalog of human interaction and the unfolding of events in the natural and supernatural world, proverbs enable practitioners and audiences to articulate and respond to principles of behavior based on logical, aphoristic models and to simultaneously shape the potentials and probabilities of future interactions and consequences.

The Sermonic

The sermonic tradition in Caribbean rhetorical tradition typically uses one or more of four major components that rely on the arrangement of broad rhetorical appeals to achieve the desired effect: a *confession*, the expression of a *jeremiadic thesis*, a series of *appeals*, and a concluding *meditation*. These features are laid out in more detail in table 4.

In Earl Lovelace's novel *The Wine of Astonishment*, when the community can no longer accept the religious persecution it has had to endure for gener-

TABLE 4. Major strategic characteristics of the sermonic

Feature	Main characteristics
Prostration/confession	Self-referential and self-deprecating gesture; designed to identify with the audience and to minimize separation between practitioner and audience, who must be united in struggle to achieve success or meaningful change
Jeremiadic thesis	Direct or indirect articulation of exigence, usually a crisis or problem currently afflicting society as a whole, with repercussions on a local, regional, or global scale
Appeal	i. *Pathetic*: appeal to emotion, primarily with allusions to tragic circumstances (slavery, colonialism, etc.), the effects thereof (trauma and nihilism), and the capacity for transcendence; emphasis on pathos as the predominant means of implication
	ii. *Dialogic*: appeal for interaction that grows out of the urgency expressed (mainly, but not exclusively) in the pathetic appeal; emphasis on aspects of Socratic dialogue and logos
	iii. *Dogmatic*: a more rigid appeal, designed as a formative set of concepts for constructive social operation that corresponds to a shared vision; emphasis on aspects of parrhesia, bios, and ethos
Meditation	Appears at the beginning and/or end of a performance; operates as a practical demarcation of discursive boundaries (akin to the formulaic beginnings and endings that appear in some folktales)

ations, Bee, the group's religious leader, launches into a sermon that exhibits all these features. I reproduce the entire discourse, highlighting each sermonic component:

> And Bee raise his head from his reading and look at the few of us packed close together in one corner where the building wasn't leaking, and his voice was low and the rain was soft, beating on the roofing, and we was quiet and listening.
>
> "Brethren, tonight I come to bow my head and to lift up my head," Bee say and right away his words touch me and I answer, "Blessed!"
>
> [Confession]
>
> "I come tonight," Bee say, "to make a confession and to give a direction."
>
> And Sister Ruth cry out, "Sweet Jesus!" and raise the hair on my head.
>
> "I come tonight," Bee say, "as a man who stumble in the wilderness for nights, and my eyes open now. I see the light! I see the light!" Bee cry out, "I see the light!"

Structure, Strategy, and Rhetorical Parameters in Caribbean Expression

"Amen," the congregation say.

"Brethren," Bee say, his voice soft now and sorrowful and brave and pleading, "I is the shepherd that cause the sheep to go astray."

"... astray ..." And we was answering him, leading him on, drawing out his words with our own as in the old way.

"... that have you moving from mountain to hill, so we don't know ..."

"Jesus, we don't know," the congregation say.

"I mean," Bee say, "we don't know if we is fowl ..."

"Say it, Leader."

"... or feather. If ..."

"Merciful Father."

"... we black ..."

"Jeesus!"

"... or white. If ..."

"Oh Lord!"

"... we going ..."

"Going, Saviour, going."

"... or coming. If we up ..."

"Jehovah!"

[Thesis]

"... or down. We don't know who we is."

"Tell us, Leader. Tell us who is we."

[Pathetic, Dialogic Appeal]

"We," Bee say, "... we is Shadrack, Meshack and Abednigo that burn in the fiery furnace and ain't come out yet ..."

"Tell it!"

"We is the day that don't have no rest ..."

"Saviour!"

"We is the grass that they cut and trample and dig out and sprout roots again ..."

"Beloved!"

"We is sticks that bend and don't break. We is Egypt ..."

"Oh Jesus!"

"Ethiopia ..."

"Lord!"

"We is Judah ..."

"Oh Israel!"

"... Solomon, the Queen of Sheba. We is love that rise up, the earth that don't fall down. We is corn and water."

"Amen! Amen!"

"I is the shepherd of the sheep and the servant of the Lord,"
[Dialogic, Dogmatic Appeal]
Bee say. "And if we must worship . . ."
"Beautiful Lord!"
" . . . If we must worship, we must worship in Spirit . . ."
"And in truth, Jeesus!"
"If we must worship we must worship with a ringing of the bell and bringing of our souls with a joyful noise unto the Lord . . ."
"Ooh Lord!"
"Who is greater than the Lord?"
"Yeeah!"
" . . . for he will carry out . . ."
"Yees!"
" . . . and he will bring you. He will search you and he will turn you . . ."
"Jeesus!"
" . . . He will touch you with his right hand."
"Oh God!"
"Lift up your voices, oh ye hills!" Bee cry out.
"Yeees, Leader!"
"Lift up your voices, oh Jerusalem! Lift up your voices, oh Judah! Lift up your voices, Israel! Lift up your voices, oh Ethiopia! Lift up your voices . . ."
"Yeees!"
[Meditation]
And now with the congregation answering him, Bee voice was getting stronger, and all the sadness and anger in his soul poured down in his words.[64]

More than a mouthpiece, the speaker is charged with the task of "taking us there" and bringing us back, trying all the while not to lose the audience or get lost in the liminal space he must cover in the move from point to point, between history and future, reality and possibility. In Lamming's *In the Castle of My Skin*, the narrator describes the rhetorical awareness inherent to the success of a sermonic scene: "The voices had stopped singing and the preacher stood again. He made the plea for the others' salvation while the worshippers like a supporting cast reinforced it. They understood perfectly when they should intone the amen, or break into singing. And they knew what hymn suited the particular incident."[65] In the following example, the evangelical preacher strikes a more solemn though no less familiar tone in his sermon. The jeremiadic thesis is used implicitly to underscore the certainty of death and the well-known refrain that "many are called, but few are chosen," though the emphasis in this sermonic moment lies on the dogmatic appeal: "You must make your choice now, for I say that for such of you, and there are many here, I put it to you that there will be no tomorrow. For you there will be no tomorrow."[66] Embodying the psychic, physical, and emotional aspects of interaction, the sermonic is one of the foremost vehicles for expressing syncretic forms, as well as the separate aspects of the sacred and secular that play out in the public and private spheres of everyday life.

In addition, we can see how the sermonic opens up onto other possibilities for rhetorical action and social change. Consider, for instance, Eva's observation at the end of Bee's sermon in *The Wine of Astonishment*: "And now with the congregation answering him, Bee voice was getting stronger, and all the sadness and anger in his soul poured down in his words."[67] Here the application of the sermonic, in terms of the carnivalesque, yields opportunities for the analysis of action and interaction, motive and motion, and (I think especially) call and response that are deployed to help draw up the soul, emerging from Bee as a voice getting stronger—strong enough, in fact, to allow the words themselves to be a symbolic container for the expressions of anger and sadness caused by material circumstances. The congregation's pains are poured as well into their own words, thus enabling the worshipers to rise and negotiate the constraints of the occasion. Lovelace shows that the performance and effect of the sermonic are not just about celebration as escapism; nor are they just about the "Amen" and the clap and then the return home hoarse, voiceless, and empty-handed. It can't, in other words, be *just for so*. To be rhetorical, in my view, the performance must not only aid in the encounter with and understanding of the world but also increase probabilities for improved circumstances. The sermonic paves a way out of struggle. But how to make the implicit explicit? The carnivalesque, as an altered state of vernacular consciousness, confirms the speaker's Virgilian role, as Bee's performance illustrates, through (or between) symbolic action and deliberate activity. The sermon calls not only on a supernatural power to render aid but also on the practitioners to act in response to what they see and hear.

Predictably, the sermonic sometimes appropriates the biblical to demonstrate the scope of performers' collective resolve, their sentiments regarding both the nature of material reward for work done and evidence of an abstract desire for justice, as illustrated in "Rivers of Babylon," a song written by the Melodians' Brent Dowe and Trevor McNaughton:

> By the rivers of Babylon,
> Where we sat down
> And there we wept
> When we remembered Zion.[68]

Rather than the basic subscription to masking and misdirection, the selective thesis, seen in the song's only partial use of Psalm 137, seems to emphasize negotiation as the means of dealing more directly with seemingly insurmountable struggle. Typically associated with the plaintive songs of Rastafarian Nyabinghi rituals, the more overtly revolutionary content of the song actually lay in the parts of the hymn that remain unsung. The pathetic sermonic appeal to grief as a prelude to action makes sense in the light of the remaining text, which portrays liberation and the fall of Babylon as an inevitable consequence. It is also reasonable to presume that relevant audiences would be familiar with the different sentiments of the entire psalm, for biblical selectivity, a sermonic subcategory, was a strategy already in use by members of the clergy who, under the direction of the plantocracy and elites disaffected with emancipation, used the Bible to justify the continued oppression of peoples in the new Caribbean. Following promises to God that his people will not forget him in the midst of their sorrow, the message turns when the speaker adopts a tone of vengeance that is unmasked and unmistakable:

> Remember, O Lord, against the sons of Edom
> The day of Jerusalem,
> Who said, "Raze *it*, raze *it*, to its very foundation!"
> O daughter of Babylon, who are to be destroyed,
> Happy the one who repays you as you have served us!
> Happy the one who takes and dashes your little ones against the rock![69]

Nonverbal/Visual Semantics

Not all that can be said should be said; conversely, not all that should be said can be. These gaps arise primarily from the inadequacy of words. Thus, whenever words seem to fail in the course of verbal interactions, Caribbean practitioners resort to nonverbal semantics to express themselves or to augment their verbal expression. By referring to them as *nonverbal*, I do not mean to limit the matter solely to oral performances that seem to defy enunciation or to the embodiment of passive gestures. Verbal performances are usually accompanied by elements of physical movement or inarticulable sound. Rather, nonverbal semantics can be described as the somewhat more abstract realm of what Rickford refers to as "'ordinary' rituals involved in everyday behavior: how people walk and stand; how they greet and take leave of each other; what they do with their faces and hands when conversing, narrating, or arguing, and so on."[70] In "Turn Thanks to Miss Mirry," for example, Lorna Goodison describes a series of nonverbal semantics as an alternative to standardized forms of language expression:

> She could not read or write a word in English
> but took every vowel and consonant of it

FIGURE 1. *3canal, Brooklyn, New York* (2009)

> and rung it around, like the articulated neck
> of our Sunday dinner sacrificial fowl.
> In her anger she stabbed at English, walked it out,
> abandoned it in favor of a long kiss teeth,
>
> a furious fanning of her shift tail, a series of hawks
> at the back of her throat, a long extended elastic sigh,
> a severing cut eye, or a melancholy wordless moaning[71]

The *steups* (also *cheups, stchoops, chups,* or "kiss teeth," as in Goodison's poem) is the noise produced by sucking air through pursed lips and along the side teeth; in cases where the actual sucking sound is not used, the gesture is euphemized somewhat either by uttering or writing the word ("Chu," "Chuh," "Steups," etc.) or by pursing the lips *as if* to steups but stopping short of making the sound— saying without saying. The duration of the steups relates directly to the degree of these sentiments; the longer the steups, the more egregious the issue on which it is meant to comment. There are also derivatives of the steups that manifest in certain contexts where the full steups will not work as well. These include the "twist-mouth," the motion of twitching the lips to the side to express or emphasize a noteworthy or ironic point, and the "kuya mouth," which resembles the twist-mouth except that it is usually deployed as a substitute to pointing with the hand. The lips, then, are used to bring attention to either a person or situation on which the practitioner chooses to comment in secret, that is, without the knowledge of the subject on whom the practitioner is commenting. The steups, represented textually as an onomatopoeic word, is used to express disgust, disrespect, insubordination, impatience, anger, and frustration. Conversely, it is also used to effectively show empathy, regret, and relief.

Nonverbals also communicate that the practitioner *intends* to be seen and heard by the subject. Thus, in response to the extended speech of the Midnight Robber, replete as it is with insults and threats, an offended (or defeated) practitioner is likely to steups. Moreover, if a particular performance, such as a lecture or sermon, fails to stir or to produce any satisfactory effect, an unconvinced audience member may steups to show disapproval. For instance, during the composition process (or a lecture preceding it), many of my Caribbean students felt compelled to steups in frustration when they felt unable to craft what they hoped would be a "proper" response to their essay prompts. Others repeated the action when they received their papers and the results were not what they expected. Instead of conveying a sense of powerlessness or surrender that would effectively bring an end to any perceived assault, their steups constituted a form of argumentative engagement that influenced the tone of their interactions with me.

The "cut-eye," when deployed for a direct effect, functions as an insult that invokes the subject's silent (though not invisible) argument with a perceived opponent. According to Rickford, "the argument is waged as much with words as with eyes, each protagonist 'cutting up the eyes' on the other in a threatening and belligerent fashion. But there may be no verbal argument at all. In any situation where one wishes to censure or challenge someone else, or convey to him that he is not admired or respected, a *cut-eye* may be conveniently employed."[72]

The cut-eye involves moving one's eyes horizontally, vertically, or diagonally, as if surveying another subject, for the purpose of communicating dislike or disapproval. When faced with it, the attentive practitioner who wishes to be effective will either adjust his or her delivery to avoid more of these negative responses, avert the eyes to maintain the integrity of the interaction, or simply terminate the interaction altogether. The storyteller, calypsonian, pastor, poet, and politician all gesticulate for rhetorical effect and enhance the effect of their verbal delivery with motion. As far as gesticulations go, the cut-eye is among the most subtle and most effective. Sometimes, of course, physical performances can be taken to form the total expression. Figure 1 shows the members of 3canal engaged in three examples of nonverbal semantics during their performance of "Good Morning Neighbor" in 2009.

From the left, Roger Roberts looks and points up to the sky; Wendell Manwarren grasps the mic with both hands and looks directly at the camera; and Stanton Kewley looks out onto the general audience, his right hand in what can be called an emphatically instructive gesture, as if saying, "Dis is de point allyuh should be listenin to!" Individually, each member's action is significant and can be viewed discretely for its own meaning, but together they achieve a multiple dimensionality to the group's delivery, a synergy that is consistent with its overall rhetorical project: liberation through consciousness. There is, presumably, the appeal to a higher power, the personalized appeal to an audience of one, and the broad appeal to the congregated audience that relies on the teaching motion to do the "talking." Together, these make for a holistic delivery of a very basic message: "Good Morning, Neighbor." "Good morning, neighbor" is a greeting, obviously, but it is also a trope for unity that must be worked on continuously as part of a dialogically structured interaction.[73]

This performance by 3canal suggests that a rhetorical attempt at unity succeeds to the extent that it brings the audience both psychically and physically closest to achieving unity, though it does not and cannot ensure it. The band nonetheless shows how it can be achieved; the audience members must be present to immerse themselves, physically and psychically participating in the performance by engaging with the performers in the process of creating a "real presence."[74] Relying on Shotter's analysis of epideictic display, we might say that the success of such engagements "occurs *only* when we enter into mutually responsive, dialogically structured, living, embodied relations, . . . when we cease to set ourselves, unresponsively, at a distance" from the performance.[75] The entire performance includes not only delivery and reception but also the response that the audience is in a sense charged to deliver. Thus 3canal appeals for unity as an activity, which depends on *presence*, the literal act of *being there*, of showing up.

Dance provides another comprehensive example illustrating the scope of textuality that can emerge from the utilization of nonverbal semantics. Suzanna Sloat has pointed out that the dances of the various islands, each with its own language, "evolved in somewhat different ways, but with a noticeable common dance language or vocabulary" that evokes the mutual intelligibility sociolinguists have noticed in the different creoles of these islands.[76] As a mode that privileges embodiment, dance allows the dancer to enact an agenda through physical performance; at the very least, it signifies the dancer's psychic awareness of the situation that demands this kind of engagement: not just a dance *for nothing* but a physical display of rhetorical intention. This can seem to resemble escapism from the pressures poor people face, as it does in Cogill and Barrett's poem "Dem Belly Full."[77] Rather than succumb to a litany of social injustices, people are entreated to forget their sorrows, troubles, sickness, or weariness "and dance."[78] When Bob Marley set the poem to music, he presumably understood quite well that dance can hold a liberatory force based not on escaping from these issues but on reprioritizing them; that is, dance supersedes troubles, sorrows, sickness, and weariness and allows the dancer to provide a physical response. It bears, in other words, a rhetorical force that can be activated to deal with these problems. And if it can be activated at will, then only a small step remains between the dance and its rhetorical utility.

For example, in Paule Marshall's *Praisesong for the Widow*, Avey Johnson goes through a spiritual reconnection with her grandmother through a series of visions. These visions concern herself and her grandmother on the Sea Islands off the coast of South Carolina, but they occur and intensify while Avey is on a cruise in the Caribbean. When Avey ends up in Carriacou, at the invitation of an elder who is returning to the smaller island off Grenada for the Big Drum festival, Marshall exposes the reader, through dance, to the spirituality shared among African Americans and Caribbean people. Avey's grandmother was a Shouter, engaging in practices similar to those of the Shouter Baptist, Kumina, and Shango Baptist sects of the Caribbean. The elders congregate to perform a sacred dance, the Juba, and for Avey their movements are surprising and frightening in their familiarity. She reluctantly begins to dance, to feel, to become one again with the features of spirit that bind rather than succumb to those that separate. Having gone through the rituals of expurgation and purification, her will reactivated, she is able to dance: "arms bent, she began working her shoulders in the way the Shouters long ago used to do, thrusting them forward and then back in a strong casting-off motion. Her weaving head was arched high. All of her moving suddenly with a vigor and passion she hadn't felt in years, and with something of the stylishness and sass she had once been known for."[79] Avey's inclusion in the practice of the vernacular tradition stresses not only the resonance of persistent cultural elements in the African Diaspora, further evidence of their obvious intersections, but also the fact that some of these elements get expressed through the body in motion rather than with words, depending on one's willingness to show up to and participate in the rhetorical event.

In the event that showing up is not entirely possible, or the dance cannot be performed, or bodies are not actually present or represented but implied, audience members still ought to have options—of implicating themselves, for example, in certain displays to the degree that they may be able to convincingly identify (with) a particular performance or display where actual attendance would not be possible. Thus, beyond what we may be willing to presume about the performative intentions demonstrated on a stage by the members of 3canal or in a circle of dancers in the Beg Pardon of Marshall's Carriacou, audiences should be able to glean compelling examples of symbolic action from other "visual events," a relationship Mirzoeff describes as "the interaction between viewer and viewed."[80] The following few pages reproduce photographs I took during visits to Trinidad and Tobago between 2003 and 2011. I offer them merely to serve a broad definitional purpose, to help illustrate how images can ultimately serve vernacular rhetorical agendas, specifically with regard to masquing as strategy.

Common to all vernacular images is the necessity to be viewed as an authen-

FIGURE 2. *Cocoa House, Roxborough* (2006)

tic demonstration of a vernacular existence. Even if the ultimate contents of their propositions go beyond the strictly vernacular, the symbolic representations of such images ought to be taken broadly in the context of their own terms (including those of the photographer). Such an idea may not seem obvious when looking at *Cocoa House, Roxborough* (fig. 2).

Bricks. Mortar. Beams. Light. Cocoa. Tobago.

By contrast, when we look at *Unlocked on Coffee Street* (fig. 3), where graffiti from "Ayana the . . ." to "CRITICS CREW" appear to tell viewers most of what they need to know about this particular surface—a door to an abandoned business on Coffee Street, San Fernando—we may conclude that the surface was intended to function more like a traditional text and less abstractly than the Cocoa House. Even the hinges, locks, and latches seem to hold the text together—amplifying its relative cohesiveness as a "written" text.

Both images demonstrate aspects of a rhetorical agenda that may or may not be obvious to a viewer, especially a passive one. But should we be so cavalier about the vernacular as to presume that no such agenda exists, that these images were produced for their own sake? No. Without launching into a full-scale analysis of these images, I argue that we who have had to (and, in many instances, continue to) wrestle with the issue of being seen and heard simply do not have the luxury of presenting ourselves or our ideas as a series of inexplicable and indecipherable obscurities, not even in situations where those obscurities could be used in the

Figure 3. *Unlocked on Coffee Street* (2011)

service of complexities.[81] This activity jibes with what Sonja Foss argues is the "pictorial turn" in rhetoric,[82] an even further departure from Platonic idealism, though a highly logical representational strategy for those who seek not idealism but recognition, even if that recognition is of an equally mundane nature: everyday life, its comings and goings, events that are as likely to cause a knowing smile as to foment rebellion, to cause a cut-eye or a steups, the recognition of time as it passes and the things that pass with it—our lives and livelihoods, for example, or our houses. So as we consider the idea of visual semantics within the scope of nonverbal expression, I think it is vital to extend some attention (however briefly) to visual images—photographs, specifically.[83] In such cases, not only do the symbols (when used with rhetorical intent) resonate with viewers who recognize them, but they have the affective capacity to engage a relatively unfamiliar audience. The images therefore bring with them the probability that what appears unfamiliar could evoke familiar meaning.

Basically, I want to highlight the need to complicate assumptions that can arise from the cursory examination of vernacular images, assumptions about anything from heartfelt nostalgia to exotica, the errant pleasures of imagined exile, or the paradoxical relationships between tourism and industry, the challenging practice of everyday life among idle consumers and those who are idly consumed. One of the greatest vernacular imperatives is the adequacy of the display in terms of what the audience can actually be allowed to see. This holds true even in the virtual absence of specific human rhetors and subjects, whether that rhetor is behind the lens or purposely left out of sight. Consider *Yard, San*

FIGURE 4. *Yard, San Fernando* (2011)

Fernando (fig. 4), for instance; any impulse toward the consideration of spatial and material opportunities provided by this (or any) image should come as no surprise, especially since in making the case for a legitimate vernacular rhetoric, having a space in which to practice it is an essential concern. This includes the symbolic spaces available to us, as well as those we are willing and able to create and represent in response to a perceived exigence. Let *Yard, San Fernando* serve preliminarily as an example of what I mean.

So what do glass louvers have to do with rhetoric? Perhaps many things. Perhaps very little. But they certainly have the capacity to indicate both that the photographer intends to "say" something to viewers about what he or she sees and wants them to see and that the viewers are invited to respond, in various ways, to the images themselves (devoid of any consideration of the photographer's intention) and to determine, on their own, what the image is "saying" to them. So whereas John Szarkowski argues that the essence of the photographer's craft is "to quote out of context,"[84] I prefer to approach his point of view from

FIGURE 5. *Four Pirogues, Charlotteville* (2008)

that of a rhetorician who must simultaneously consider the deliberate insertion of motive and rhetorical choice in the composition and creation of the image, for, as Szarkowski continues, the central problem facing the photographer involves determining both what to include and what to reject.[85] The choices, of course, can be infinite. Regardless, whether the scene is immediately familiar or not, the basic composition in *Four Pirogues, Charlotteville* (fig. 5) suggests a degree, however slight, of deliberate contrivance.

The pirogues, while randomly anchored, result in a comparatively ordered latticework of fishing poles laid out against the backdrop of the sea and just beneath the horizon provided by the high coastline.[86] It is possible that the apparent contrivance of the image, read aesthetically, underscores not only the interplay of order and disorder but also the inextricable relationship between the two, the idea that we can have no idea of order without one of chaos. Easy binaries aside, the photograph is capable of communicating notions that go beyond the false primitivism of the region and its people, notions that may reflect a desire to be included in a broader humanism rather than be subject to narrow appeals. There is not much drama in the image. The fishermen whose boats lay anchored were comfortably ashore. No one sees "Axehead," whose eyes were blue, ringed and half-blinded in gray. But what else need be said about the scene? In a word: more. For me, the meaning of the image is not solely about *what* it includes but also about *how* it enables the photographer to presume on the viewer's reception of symbols for material effect:[87] given that the photograph also attempts an argument from a material perspective, viewers are invited to consider the significance

FIGURE 6. *Corbeaux, Erin I* (2011)

of each aspect of the photograph *in relation to* the people they are intended to represent. As such, the audience is then authorized to make further presumptions about the relationships among images—in terms of symbol, material, and space—what they mean, and to whom. Juxtaposing images permits interactions among them. How, for instance, might an audience read *Four Pirogues* in relation to *Corbeaux, Erin I* (fig. 6), which also features pirogues and the sea, as well as two of the more ubiquitous images of Caribbean beach and fishing culture, the palm tree and the three "corbeaux" (American black vultures)? What might one conclude about lifestyles, about the vitality of one over the hopefulness of the other, a sense of routine that waits to be renewed or one that seems to long, more desperately, for revival? An embarrassment of riches or of poverty? And what if such viewers were inclined to draw their conclusions exclusively with regard to the rhetoric of the images rather than their apparent aesthetics?

A similar set of questions may be asked of the rhetorical relationship between *Pink House, Palo Seco* and *Brother Austin's House, San Fernando* (figs. 7 and 8).

FIGURE 7. *Pink House, Palo Seco* (2011)

Whereas viewers are limited to speculation with the previous series, a different sense of the rhetorical situation emerges with additional context in this case. The wooden jalousies on both structures are typical of early Caribbean architecture, which was designed with ventilation and "beating the heat" as top priorities. The order implied in such a construction style is not difficult to miss, as the rough parallelism offers more than enough for an aesthetic reading—about, say, the ironies of postindependence, or the obstinate ghosts of colonialism past.

The close-up shot in *Pink House Doorway, Palo Seco* (fig. 9) helps illustrate further how one might recast an image in terms of its rhetorical significance. The images of jalousies and their easily observable parallelism suggest that the only distinctions between an aesthetic reading and a rhetorical one are the extent to which the photographer's imposition of a specific context supports the viewable details of the image and the extent to which the viewer's consideration of context and details invokes meaning and provokes a conscious response. The fact, for instance, that *Pink House Doorway* shows a doorway to a house that, like the one depicted in *Brother Austin's House*, is currently occupied helps reinscribe the materiality of the image (or rather, the lack of materials, which subtracts from the structure's apparent consistencies), which goes well beyond the image itself. The structure shown in *Pink House* is so weatherworn that one of its doors has lost half its jalousies as well as its baseboard, a sheet of aluminum roofing covers a window, jalousies above and around are missing, and a window is entirely open. The modifications made to the structure shown in *Brother Austin's House* are even more pronounced, though ironically the consistency of lines may tempt

FIGURE 8. *Brother Austin's House, San Fernando* (2003)

the viewer to overlook the scale. The house's role as dwelling and artifact is made more difficult to ignore by the satellite dish, which the house, despite its imposing façade, can only partially obscure. More context leads to more meaning, further increasing the image's rhetorical potential to disclose its apparent obscurities. Thus, the structural inequalities become even more pronounced as more layers of relevance are added: *people have lived there and have died there.* Some live there still.

This is part of the rhetorical work that images can accomplish. Rather than "speak" only for itself, and on its own behalf, the vernacular image can help clarify whatever it displays, serving as a visual amplification of what it records. Let me explain what I mean with a more specific example. The building shown in *Brother Austin's House* belonged to my grandfather's brother, Austin. When I made the photograph, in 2003, I was standing less than six feet from the place where, in 1988, I had seen my grandfather take his final breaths. The dish across the street belonged to one of the four most prominent families of morticians in the area.[88] Their prosperity was derived from the lives and deaths of their neighbors; by itself, that prosperity forms a rudimentary contrast to the state of the house in the foreground, but taken with its source, it points to the longevity of structures, the interdependency of communities, and the intricacies that one can encounter in a matrix of morality, mortality, and immortality.

This is but one of the ways images come to *mean*; that is, even as temporal

Figure 9. *Pink House Doorway, Palo Seco* (2011)

relationships are spatially and visually condensed and (re)framed in this situation, they provide meaningful options to the audience based as much on what is added as on what the viewer may be willing to consider. This is a conclusion corroborated by Foss,[89] but one need not dig that deep to realize that the material factors in these images add up to many things, which may include the inhabitants' desire for better conditions, their critique of the direct effects of the status quo on them, or their submission to the status quo despite its effects. For the audience, the key is to understand these vernacular visual events as providing rhetorical commentary that can be supplemented with a story. Because such an image ought to be taken, at least in part, on its own terms, and those terms are not immediately apparent to uninformed audiences, each image is an *invitation* to the viewer to figure out—or ask, or at least acknowledge—how vernacular

FIGURE 10. *Carib Street House, Western Side, San Fernando* (2011)

rhetors construct and come to terms with the range of situations in which they find themselves. For example, I may further contextualize the location of Brother Austin's house with respect to that of the structure shown in *Carib Street House, Western Side, San Fernando* (fig. 10); this is my grandfather's house, which is adjacent to his brother's, a placement that allows for a literal juxtaposition as well as a symbolic one. This contextualization increases the probability that an even broader conversation may more amply unfold with regard to my motives as photographer, memoirist, and rhetor. Of course, there is little guarantee that a viewer would ask. Inquiry is never guaranteed. But that should not deter the rhetor from having a response. So, as we return to *Yard, San Fernando*, we see that the space defines a path that leads, clear enough, through objects imposed and created; it leads, inevitably, to wrought-iron fences, spacious verandahs, an ominous white concrete house, and roofs comparatively more intact. The yard commemorates.

Aside from all that, it is particularly noteworthy that while the space itself cannot illustrate the full scale of the histories and influences that form its border and background, the interplay of its multiple features *combine* to define its vernacularity, baring it to the audience. *Yard, San Fernando* offers viewers options for negotiating with what they encounter, thereby providing choices for them to implicate themselves in what the image of the space, and the space itself, may have to offer: come in, pass through, look around, stay, leave. At the very least, it is intended to *display* a set of meanings, not hide them. Granted, no image can tell of all the things that have occurred in the scene it represents, all the lives that have been lived. No image needs to. None of these images *needs* to tell it all. The salient parts will do. For, despite the life expressed in *Yard, San Fernando*, an overarching context exists from which they cannot escape, and that context will (eventually) define the wider characteristics of the vernacular image as a rhetorical text, in addition to determining how localized and personal the context may be for the rhetor and certain members of his or her audience. Michel de Certeau intimates, for example, that certain strategies simply lack the means to be kept to themselves because they exist within the limits of hegemony.[90] As such, these pictorial arguments suggest a form of assertion, critique, and strategy that occurs in plain sight—albeit emerging from the interstices and margins, they remain in conversation with and exist *despite* the hegemonic constraints that shape daily life. And, lest we go too far from masquing as I conceive it, note that the overgrowth and decay depicted in *Middle Class, Roxborough-Parlatuvier Road* (fig. 11) only amplify the illusion of well-known vernacular subjectivities—which include the desire for upward mobility, symbolic mockery based on a material reality that can only *appear* to have been achieved, or abandoned aspirations to the trappings of relative success—while leaving other aspects sufficiently obscured (either for history's safekeeping or for the audience's imagination and inquiry). If there is no need for everything to be shared, then sharing everything would be unnecessary.

It is important to note, additionally, that in taking these photos I made no attempt to conceal what may be perceived as typical vernacular details, even though the images may sometimes appear to transcend them.[91] Rather, I sought to creatively use the apparent schizophrenia not only of the old and the new but also of what has come, of what was brought, and of what has stayed, as well as what I meant to communicate to or even argue about with an imagined viewer. The series *Windward Road House I, Outside*, *Windward Road House II, Inside-Outside*, and *Windward Road House III, Inside* (figs. 12, 13, and 14) together clinch the point.

As I have alluded to earlier, these images complicate the role of the viewer. Above all, though, they reinforce the subjectivity—the material "realness"—of the vernacular gaze. This is important for many reasons, particularly in situations where the images not only say something effectively but manage to say what words simply cannot. If pressed, I would note that this final series takes the

FIGURE 11. *Middle Class, Roxborough–Parlatuvier Road* (2006)

viewer inside, progressively deeper into the inner parts of a house that, at first glance, gives the impression of standing on its own. And so the metaphor begins to coalesce. In addition, this structure bears the characteristics of a traditional Caribbean "case" house, erected on posts a few feet above the ground to enable transportability and provide a relative measure of safety in the event of a surge inland from the Atlantic, which lies only a few hundred yards away.[92] Though it stands uninhabited, as is made evident by the encroaching bush around the house and at its steps, and with its missing panels showing the obvious signs of having seen better days, the house itself refutes Froude's argument that "there are no people [in the West Indies] in the true sense of the word, with a character and purpose of their own."[93] Aside from Froude's unfortunate error, and consistent with the masque, note that the entire series argues through amplification for what I believe the viewer ought to have seen from the very first frame: the themes of balance and integration, colonial imposition and eventual decay down to the very root of imperial structure, the literal uprooting of new growth to underscore the old growth of roots spread across a wall, imposing their own order of natural latticework on the parallelism of partitions and handmade jalousies. It is what it should be: a both symbolic and material representation of the Caribbean, a metonym of its own larger material condition, limited in its scope, as (ultimately) any other argument about these topics could be.

FIGURE 12. *Windward Road House I, Outside* (2006)

FIGURE 13. *Windward Road House II, Inside-Outside* (2006)

FIGURE 14. *Windward Road House III, Inside* (2006)

Let me be clear: I consider this kind of work, as well as further inquiry into it, potentially revolutionary in motive if not also in outcome. In *What the Twilight Says*, Walcott argues that "all revolutions begin amateurishly, with forged and stolen weapons, . . . and just as a comfortable, self-hugging pathos hid in the most polemical of West Indian novels, so there was in the sullen ambition of the West Indian actor a fear that he lacked proper weapons, that his voice, colour, and body were no match for the civilized concepts of theatre."[94] As I near the end of this chapter, I am forced to admit that the specter of "amateurish revolution" has been the cause of an enduring anxiety, one that I have harbored as a scholar and on which I will continue to rely. At no other time has this anxiety been more pronounced than when I claim a text—any text—as rhetorical. "Cockroach don't have no right in fowl party," some would say. Nonetheless, with respect to realizing and responding to the exigence of practicing conscious selfhood on a theatrical stage, what is true of the art practiced by vernacular rhetors is true of all the arts, of which rhetoric is a key example. And as I consider my people (vernacular in our ways), I am now obliged to make a case to an audience about things we have taken for granted so well that they meld to form the everyday. I consider, also, that we are apt to declare our subjectivity in plain sight, as plainly as does the graffiti montage in Perry Henzell's 1973 classic *The Harder They Come*: "I WAS HERE BUT I DISAPEAR [*sic*]" appears first on a rusted sheet of galvanized roofing only to reappear on another rusted fence: "I WAS HERE";

"HERE," emblazoned on a wall in red letters; "SEE ME HERE," a sign on a motorcyclist's back; and, on a wall across from a police station, "Iam EVERYWHErE."

We are everywhere, even if we seem not to be visible.[95] This is one of the ironies of the obvious, isn't it? We are often likely to miss things right before our eyes. And so, when words seem to fail or prove inadequate for the purpose at hand, the spaces and things we represent in our images have a part to play, not the least of which includes the ways they support the notion that rhetorical effectivity relies on symbol and material as much as do our ideas of how visual arguments may be constructed, how their material features may be arranged, and how their attendant symbols may be deployed.

As the examples in this chapter show, these modes do not operate discretely. Rather, they overlap, mixing with other modes for optimum effectiveness, with each of them acting as a supplement to the others. In their most basic roles, the rhetorical features help ground the abstractions of Caribbean meaning in the form of identifiable expressions. Their functions within the larger discussion of the Caribbean rhetorical tradition cannot be overstated, for Caribbean rhetorical performance is not simply a matter of linguistic diversity or similarity. Beyond demonstrating mere language variety, traditional rhetorical devices are used to shape, modify, reinforce, or even ensure certain consequences. The features resound at some of the most visceral levels of our identity, marking us "Caribbean" wherever we are and helping to sanction performance as struggle and art—indeed, as a form of revolution that is rhetorical in every way. The critical self-awareness achieved in dialogic contexts enables the dynamic transference of ethos from performer to audience, with the hope that an audience will aspire to a level of accountability that carries over into everyday life and beyond the circumstances of the performance. These performances—or those imagined in the absence of a physical performer—are transformative acts that help Caribbean people grapple with challenges, social and political injustices, atrocities they have endured, their histories, and their futures. Their effect, therefore, should be considered (and not only in the degree to which performers are able to align intention with reception).

Obviously, the entire corpus of Caribbean expression cannot be relegated to the examples I have considered. The important point, however, is that even just scratching the surface of any genre of Caribbean expression will uncover what we mean to say, evoking distinct vernacular characteristics that continue to be practiced. No conversion is necessary. In the end, however, Glissant's epigraph is not as simple for me as it may be for those I represent. Caribbean people may by and large take their activities for granted. Not so for me. So I close on this note: the Caribbean rhetor's obvious and predominant focus on narratives of vernacular identity and the histories inherent in their displays suggests a dual approach that is both an ethically based aesthetic undertaking, for it is sustained by a responsibility to present and represent, as faithfully as possible, the intricacies of that identity for our aesthetic consideration, and a rhetorical enterprise, also ethically based, that gestures more directly toward the development of a discursive model and allows a distinctly Caribbean identity not only to flourish but also to do "work" on our behalf. Islands that repeat themselves should produce islanders that reinvent themselves, whether faced with changing circumstances or filled with a desire to address circumstances that appear oppressive, static, or merely inadequate.

CHAPTER 3

From the Darker Side of a Schism
PERFORMANCE AND THE PROPHETIC MASQUE

> Don't even try, stranger, to understand it.
> —David Rudder, "Tales from a Strange Land II: Crossing The Bridge"

> Me speak to all the children. Me speak to everything that moveth and liveth pon the earth. . . . And me say what me see ina dem heye [what I see in their eyes]. Me see [what] type of intention ina dem heye—a where music is. Me no know if me ha dem look dey, you know. But me know which musician me can look pon and know if im is a real musician.
> —Bob Marley, "Talkin" (track 3), *Talkin' Blues*

> We never thought of the lyric. The lyric was there, it was cute, but we didn't think of what it meant; but at that time, nobody else would think of it either, because we weren't as morally open as we are today and so, a lot of stuff—really—no excuses—just went over our heads.
> —Andrews Sisters, in John Sforza, *Swing It*

THE CARIBBEAN RHETOR'S EXPRESSIONS OF language, culture, and identity articulate an ethos that grows out of the internalization and subsequent externalization of rhetorical strategies, practices, and tradition as public performance; each performance embodies the idea that *who feels it, knows it,* and *who knows it, tells it.* Consistent with the operation of the carnivalesque in the conception of cultural identity and rhetoric, the music of Caribbean people is a collaboratively composed record of Caribbeanness, of the ways in which knowledge is created, distributed, appropriated, manipulated, and then redistributed as tradition on public display in the shifting and constraining contexts of local and transnational life. As both the bearer and distributor of that knowledge, the most effective performer will be one who embodies and can combine the various sensibilities of his or her audience to address issues that unfold beyond the immediate discourse community. For while we vernacular rhetors may well face a shared supranational imperative to which we perhaps can all aspire collectively, we simultaneously feel the sway of myriad subnational characteristics supplying the terministic screens that filter such an imperative for us. As members of an audience in need either of guidance or affirmation, we depend on the performer to negotiate those poles of differing sensibilities for us—and *with* us—because the critical consciousness we ultimately seek relies on the synthesis of things felt (perceived) and things understood (conceived).

Rhetorical maneuvers of this sort are as prevalent in their contemporary forms as they were historically, albeit significantly less popularized than are other, more commercially buoyant but vacuous counterparts in music (and cultural production more generally). Performers have nonetheless managed to retain a pattern of rhetorical motive and performance that comes out of attempts to reconcile tradition with innovation or to tailor each to the other in ways that matter. And what does this require of the performer? Above all, it requires a more than passing familiarity with the features being deployed, something like a shared understanding of the many degrees of rhetorical effectiveness that the tradition's various modes provide. This shared understanding is significantly determined by the creativity of masqued displays in the areas of confrontation, disputation, and direct instruction. This fact would be lost on performers such as the Andrews Sisters and Robert Mitchum, people who, enamored with calypso music, failed to grasp the significance of songs such as "Rum and Coca-Cola" (a criticism of the U.S. occupation of Trinidad during World War II and the consequent erosion of social order) in the way they were intended.

So to the initial sayings, I add another dimension: *who don't hear will feel*. At least, that is the saying as I remember it (and use it). In common usage, the saying is an ominous component in the catalog of cautionary phrases. It is usually deployed as an unmasked threat of reprisal, censure, or some other form of punishment issued by one powerful entity—say, a stern mother or a repressive government—over an entity that, either unaware of its lack of power or unhappy with it, proves itself a resistant upstart, a "hardened" child, perhaps, or more important in the Caribbean experience, an urban underclass. I want to introduce an alternative reading of the phrase, however, one that more effectively frames audience reception in the specific context of vernacular epideictic activity, which I discussed in chapter 1. Even if an audience opts to ignore a message (that is, not to *hear*), its capacity to *feel* the message makes a transmission highly probable. As such, effective rhetorical implication (wherein the audience is made to share in the outcome of the performance, whether through guilt or complicity) is achieved. That is, successful rhetorical performances in this vein are not simple exchanges of intent for persuasion among audience members but the result of a number of potentially persuasive interactions that operate verbally as well as viscerally. Who don't hear will feel.

The popularity of Caribbean music is a literal testament to the resilience and versatility of vernacular discourse, having endured because the contemporary listening audience is actively called on to identify with (and thus collectively respond to) the topics and strategies these performances embody. In general, this music's versatility is undergirded by a problematic conception that so closely aligns the development of music with fragmentation and coalescence—situations it was no doubt partly intended to address—that it inordinately serves the myth of Caribbean intellectual and sociocultural simplicity. For example, the ethnomusicologist Peter Manuel opts for the crucible metaphor, describing the region as marked by a "particular combination of white political power and black demographic power, and of insular isolation and maritime cross-fertilization, . . . [in which] these musical elements simmered, effervesced, and eventually bubbled over."[1] While there is the presumption of a well-earned reflexivity in the formation of Caribbean music, the consequences of that reflexivity can too easily be construed as stemming *solely* from a basic or even instinctual reaction to a rhetorical situation in which the people who produced them seemed to bear no significant agency. In other words, the metaphor of the crucible suggests that the *situation* allowed a certain degree of craftiness or, at best, the mastery of mother wit to cohere. This depiction, however, too easily implies that these subjects were only *acted upon*, the music "bubbling over" without the presumption of an equally important stirring up of constitutive intention.

Syncretic features, the result of social pressures, obviously lie at the heart of Caribbean music, but the purposeful appeal to a broad audience involves the deliberate secularized integration of sacred, folkloric, and revolutionary references. That is, Caribbean popular music distinguishes itself as rhetoric in ways that demonstrate more sophisticated and systematic motive and invention. Just as West African slaves, limited by their physical environments and the inaccessibility of viable escape routes, had to fashion means of active and passive resistance retained from native traditions, contemporary performers continue to engage in these traditions to facilitate the transference of messages through the manipulation of sound, silence, symbol, and conscious embodiment. Their social responsibility is infused with what the tradition provides in terms of both individual perception and a shared worldview.

PLAIN TALK, BAD MANNERS

Calypso, despite having gone through more than two centuries of evolution, still bears many structural and ideological features retained from the vast repertoire of sacred and secular songs that were brought to the region. These features are not merely embedded in the tradition as relics of a forgotten past but endure as syntheses of phronetic and gnostic interpretations, resulting in performances that reflect a cognizant accumulation of common wisdom fused with knowledge of the divine (as well as the varied forms of expressing them both). Among the underclass, the desires for agency and praxis were predominantly voiced by the chantwell,[2] whose power was language. "The word was magic," writes Rohlehr, "its form, incantation, its purpose inspiration and celebration."[3] Emerging in the late nineteenth century, chantwells were the vocal leaders of this oppressed social class, emboldened by their constituents to exhibit an ethos that complemented and contradicted their disfranchised status as virtual nonmembers of "respectable" society.

The predominant mode of delivery, the calenda, was sung first in Yoruba, then in French creole,[4] and (much later) in English; having made its way to Trinidad from Martinique, Dominica, Guadeloupe, St. Lucia, Barbados, Jamaica, and the Grenadines, the calenda provided the structural form on which calypso music was originally based. These early prophetic articulations of agency were developed to disrupt normative sensibilities with appeals and complex allusions, remaining in practice despite the gaze and pressure of authorities.[5] The chantwell was the proto-calypsonian—singer, griot, and chronicler, the embodiment of vernacular epideictic sensibilities—who was entrusted with the transmission of urgencies, injuries, problems, praises, and other mundane matters of rhetorical import. Take the following example:

> When I dead bury my clothes.
> I don't want nobody to cry for me.
> When I dead bury my clothes.
> Put everything in the cemetery.[6]

A few things are happening in this example. First, the political subtext of this particular calenda is not far beneath the surface, not too heavily masked, maintaining an air of tension that the ruling class would rather have ignored. It presumes a warrior's ethos, relying on a direct, logical appeal for justice that had its intention/attention directed toward the apathy of the ruling class. Additionally, there is an explicit acceptance of death's inevitability, even preempting its occurrence. Not "if" but "*when* I dead." It suggests a series of questions regarding possessions, inheritances, and legacies that are amplified in the context of socioeconomic and material pressures. What valuable possessions were there to leave behind given that land ownership for former slaves and their descendants was highly unlikely in the postemancipation era? What will or inheritance would be left? Aside from the obvious preoccupation with material objects, what stands out most is that the song petitions strongly for the speaker (and, to some extent, the performer and audience, as well) to be remembered: while burying the clothes would take care of the physical traces, the song's repetition ensures that the request (and the person making the request) will not fade altogether. It is, in short, a desire for immortality, which can be achieved only through collaborative practice. This is an admittedly secularized reading, but songs such as this one are clearly not plaintive appeals to the sympathy of the ruling class for undue special treatment—"I don't want *nobody* to cry for me." Furthermore, the appeals are inspired by an impulse to make oneself clear rather than by a need to be concealed. These strategies of collaborative confrontation, critique, and memory issue from the perspective of a marginalized vernacular sensibility that subsequently shapes the ethos of the traditional calypsonian, as well as the role traditional rhetorical concepts play in the prophetic discourse of contemporary Caribbean musical performance.

As descendants of the chantwell, calypsonians command the rhetorical modes sufficiently well to make a lengthy discussion of them here more than a little redundant. It bears saying, though, that their vernacular strategies work as deliberate forms of identification and rhetorical implication, a practice performers use to achieve a sense of authenticity and discursive utility among members of the audience. This strategy was also demonstrated in original songs that actively co-opted familiar Christian symbolism, ones that the historian Louis Regis suggests were delivered "in anticipation of a bloody triumph over the Europeans who had tried to impress upon them the sacrosanctity of such symbols."[7] The resulting practice not only relied on a prophesied deliverance out of the hell of oppression for some soon-to-come otherworldly reward but also fused the representative aspects of protest and resilience in the physical realm to aspects of spiritual reward in the ethereal one. On a more physical plane, the threat expressed by the speaker in one such song, to "eat . . . the white man's flesh [and] . . . drink . . . the white man's blood," could hardly be confused.[8]

Steeped as they were in confrontation, disputation, and display, these songs underscored the early desire for self-assertion and self-determination at the turn of the twentieth century within the diametre, where traditional codes of conduct superseded the significance of official rule and often the adherence to it. The pressures of censorship by the ruling class and law enforcement that culminated in the Canboulay Riot of 1881 had been fairly successful in pushing the stick-fighting bands back to their "incomprehensible underworlds" (and with them the majority of chantwells who were the voices for "societies" of batonniers such as the Damas and the Wartloos, who were often engaged in battle).[9] The calenda was subsequently banned in 1884 as part of the Peace Preservation Ordinance (formerly the Torch Ordinance of 1884, ratified January 25), but the tradition was actively maintained despite efforts to suppress it.[10] In the wake of the Water Riot of 1903, however, calypso reemerged in the public sphere, but now without the bands of stickfighters it had been the calypsonians' exclusive role to lead. This era of the "oratorical calypso" renewed anxieties among the elite, which took measures not to provoke further insurgence. Above and beyond the resistance to oppressive social pressures, however, the early calypsonians were also directly engaged in demystifying the extant circumstances at the core of most of their suffering.

Chief among these performers was Raymond "Atilla the Hun" Quevedo, whose prowess as a masquer could hardly be doubted, as his later songs and continued advocacy on stage, abroad, and in government forums have amply shown. In 1935 Atilla recorded "History of Carnival" with Gerald Clark's Serenaders in New York, an event that seemed to anticipate calypso's ascendency "from a scandal and hideous Bacchanal" to a comparatively "glorious carnival." Atilla boasts that calypso, as an art form, had indeed come a long way from the traditional melodies sung in relative obscurity by equally obscure chantuelles;[11] they had been promoted, as it were, to being played on American radio stations. America: never really the outside world and seemingly always in need of new articulations, its people searching for ever-broadening perspectives. When used as a standard, the United States served less as a promised land than as a foil against which calypsonians were able to place the common hardships of the local underclass in greater relief.[12] The familiar pressure, compounded by the irony of calypso's reception abroad, was not lost on Atilla, who commented in less than covert terms on the traditional scorn calypsonians were made to endure at home. In "History of Carnival," he lamented that "a prophet has no honour in his own land," drawing the remark from John 4:44, for though calypsonians and their songs were derided in Trinidad, foreign studios—such as those known for recording the work of Rudy Vallee—had embraced the form. Vallee himself embraced them. Whether the calypsonians were treated as novelties or peers, the overall contrast with their treatment at home was telling. But Atilla's critique did not end there.

Later, addressing the Trinidad Legislative Council on matters of amendment to the exceedingly restrictive Theatre and Dance Halls Act of 1934, Atilla exclaimed, "[Calypsonians were] . . . showing up the behavior of these people whom we have above us and whose lives we thought should be an example to their less fortunate—well, I cannot say brethren, sire, as that would be a contradiction in terms—but whose lives are not what they ought to be: an example of less fortunate people."[13] Here Atilla casts a disappointed eye toward history even as the market seemed open to him and his contemporaries. The gesture was not simply one of complaint; following World War II, calypsonians had endeared themselves to American G.I.s and were doing quite well, as "History of Carnival" suggests. At the same time, it was an effort to identify with the ethos of the traditional calypsonians, many of whom were deliberately censored and sidelined. Of course, such imperatives were not limited to the immediate discourse community; they would carry over onto the international stage with seemingly relative ease. Years earlier, during the war, Atilla's 1937 calypso commemorating Franklin D. Roosevelt's visit to Trinidad had borne this out. To those for whom "Roosevelt in Trinidad" appeared complimentary, Atilla could not have been more so. Beginning with a general observation that the president's visit was a great privilege for the people, Atilla then turned to a series of compliments, touting Roosevelt's personal charm, his control of urbane sensibilities, and his modesty as the chief diplomat of "the Great Republic."[14] Atilla's display must have been as flattering as intended, even though he had vehemently argued that "no one without a West Indian background" would "ever be able to appreciate or understand" the genre.[15] Yet to audiences whom experience had shown a less friendly face and tone, and who were very familiar with the good intentions that often precede subjugation, Atilla's epideictic was of critique, not of praise. The singer was not masking his critique but instead very plainly describing and dismantling the features of Roosevelt's mask. That is, the ostensible compliment was in fact a commentary on U.S. foreign policy and military strategy, particularly as it related to the Destroyers for Bases Agreement, a treaty between the United States and the United Kingdom. This agreement, enacted in 1940, allowed the United States to use various British military bases for a period of ninety-nine years; not surprisingly, Trinidad and the region's other British colonies—the Bahamas, St. Lucia, Jamaica, Antigua, and British Guiana—had been pawns in the early negotiations for the treaty.[16] Audiences likewise understood the saying "all skin teeth ain't joke." Roosevelt had come, Janus-like, to intrigue his audience with diplomacy and to protect U.S. interests. Atilla's "compliment" was in fact a warning, for those who had ears to hear, that the colonies were still subject to the might of the United States, as well as its whims, vices, and perversions.

What becomes apparent in all this activity, then, is the evolution of masquing beyond the "initiatic purpose" of concealment and the "verbal delirium" of creolized oral practice.[17] It is a fact that encourages us to consider not just the symbolism that serves as "verbal parallels to a pattern of experience" but also the materiality of particular rhetorical performances and the experiences they create.[18] Whereas the mask elicits a tendency toward wordplay and punning so as to conceal the intended message, the practice of masquing in prophetic calypso involves the willingness to speak out when no one else has—to break the silence or maintain the noise, embodying something of a parrhesiastic display—and to do so, by whatever means seem most effective, to generate an organic collaborative text. *Who vex, loss*. Partial though it may be, the performance exemplifies how the experience of one's Caribbeanness is expressed and interpreted through music. It remains consistent with the carnivalesque tradition, in particular with the prophetically inflected themes of commentary, entertainment, education, and uplift. In an interview with Cornel West, Harry Belafonte discussed rhetorical intention as a masquing strategy that confirms the persistence of an impulse demonstrated in his own music during the "calypso craze" of the 1950s:

> When I sing the "Banana Boat Song," most people see it as some whimsical, fanciful little tale that brings charm and delight to the listener. But to me, it's about a human condition that was very real to me as a child in Jamaica and very painful and extremely oppressive. . . . I always thought that if people came to embrace my art and began to sing my song, they would want to know who I am. And if I could get them to the next level of that curiosity, I would politicize them to death.[19]

Comparing Atilla's apparently complimentary performances to Belafonte's unadorned political motive reveals not only the consistency with which calypsonians were able to make themselves "understood through the subtle associations of sound" but also their capacity for making their deeper intentions clear.[20] Following the uneasy socialization process that involved both a conservative retention of ethnic separateness and a movement toward integration with a society that continued to malign vernacular expression as satanic, these performances equalized public discourse through amplified displays of motive.[21] Whether by invoking the materiality of the drum in response to local ordinances or the indictment of a U.S. president in the shadow of colonialism,[22] the calypsonians clearly viewed their audiences—supporters and detractors alike—as rhetorical equals. They were thus able to strike an important Manichaean distinction between the just and the unjust, the one(s) making the appeal and the one(s) responsible for the conditions that make the appeal necessary. Negotiations of everyday struggle reconstituted as the consequences of motive appear less like the interminable oppression of inferior victims and more like a people's attempt at dialogic interaction, for they were based on circumstances that could be openly addressed and possibly changed on a platform of moral, if not economic, parity.[23] This understanding of motive can be applied with relative ease to the majority of traditional songs, extending across the entire range of Caribbean cultural production.

Many calypsonians—and their audiences—certainly suffered as a consequence of the socioeconomic paralysis they were made to experience. For most, their portion was not prosperity but widespread disfranchisement. But as authorities went to greater lengths to censor calypsonians, the latter opted to display the very things for which they should have been punished, invoking the miscreant spirit of the Canboulay in full view of the public and its policymakers.[24] Traditional vernacular impulses continued to thrive—despite the corporate and political efforts to silence them—because circumstances demanded voices that could persuade a people to pull together, rise, and possibly take action.[25] For those in the calypsonian's immediate audience, most of this action would have to be performed in a protracted season of political malaise, forcing them to respond in equal measure to metropolitan interference and the localized conceit of state-mandated nationalism.

THE PEOPLE CALYPSO

The British West Indies Federation experiment had failed by 1962, less than five years after its inception, in 1958. Though the resulting fragmentation seemed to exacerbate the issue of independence for the member nations—beginning with Jamaica and Trinidad in 1962 and ending in 1983 with St. Kitts and Nevis—the desire for self-rule resulted, not surprisingly, in the exposure of bourgeois pretensions.[26] Dissatisfaction, unrest, and rebellion among the underclass were difficult to ignore; they proved even more difficult to overcome. No nation emerged unscathed. In Jamaica the escalation in violent conflicts between supporters of the People's National Party and the Jamaica Labour Party led to the Suppression of Crime Act and the Gun Court Act, moves intended both to disarm the public and repress the likelihood of proletarian radicalism. The accused were held indefinitely, and trials held in accordance with the acts were (not surprisingly) conducted in camera, out of public view, ostensibly to eliminate the threat of witness intimidation. In Grenada, following an armed coup that deposed Eric Gairy as prime minister, the hard-line socialist rule of Maurice Bishop came to a bloody end when he was executed along with other cabinet ministers. The subsequent U.S. invasion sought to quell the emergence of Marxism in Grenada (having failed to do so in Cuba) and that island's eventual incorporation into the Soviet bloc. In Trinidad, the liberal authoritarianism espoused by Eric Williams had successfully overcome the Black Power Revolution and the consolidation of unions; further repressive developments included the Public Order Act, which was delivered piecemeal as the Firearms Act, the Sedition Act, and the sabotage bill. Other upstarts, such as the National Union of Freedom Fighters, were also summarily dispatched by the notorious "Flying Squad." Crackdowns. Order. Williams, nicknamed the "Pussonal Nonarch,"[27] was poised to serve as patriarch to a nation in apparent need of a benevolent and fearsome father in the wake of the revolution. A contemporary stage had been set.

Having been sanctioned to perform a protective role on behalf of their audiences, prophetic calypsonians rely on impulses that are supported primarily by their selective interpretations of symbolic and material references, drawing from a range of ubiquitous wonders and signs gleaned from experience.[28] These are then activated publicly, as part of a methodology for achieving praxis while counteracting nihilistic tendencies coming to bear on a social scale. There remains, among this group, a dual emphasis: a dystopian critique characterized by the practitioner's directly addressing *the establishment*, speaking as an intermediary for the masses, and a prophetic vision characterized by appeals directed to *the audience* from the perspective of an observer who identifies with the marginalized masses. As a result, the calypsonians' discursive performances attempt to balance sermonic discourse with a desire for critical consciousness. In other words, their songs traverse the distance between psychic and social poles, between implicit ways of knowing and explicit ways of living, between crippling nostalgia and the progressive action of cultural memory, and between psychic trauma and the manifestations of a hope that must be constantly reinforced.

For some calypsonians, these late twentieth-century developments were only reminders, the continuation of a familiar misery for which hellfire and brimstone was the only logical prescription. Regis argues that "the calypsonian exposed to numerous religions and even more magicoreligious practices would cultivate a mind-set which tends to explain the otherwise unaccountable in these terms, and as the political kingdom offers countless examples of what *to the Trinidadian mind* seems inexplicable, it is only natural that the calypsonian should use religious metaphors to account for such phenomena."[29] In 1987, for instance, Leroy "Black Stalin" Calliste set a familiar theme of Judgment Day retribution in "Burn Them," in which he entreats God and then St. Peter for an opportunity to judge and punish leaders whom he holds guilty of crimes against humanity. Having felt "the full weight" of injustices in local and transnational contexts, Stalin has had enough and is ready to loose his retribution on them. None would escape his wrath: Karl Hudson Phillips, a former judge of the International Criminal Court and attorney general of Trinidad and Tobago; P. W. Botha, a former prime minister and then president of South Africa and staunch proponent of apartheid; Margaret Thatcher, a former British prime minister who had refused to place sanctions on South Africa and was thus complicit in its brutal success. In Stalin's vision, they all burn. Even "Reagan going in de fire too!"[30]

The most effective rhetorical strategy is one that prefigures the response to particular situations, while the versatility of such strategies increases the probability of affect. So Regis's point regarding the calypsonian's articulation of the sacred to negotiate the secular is well taken. Unfortunately, it also substantially absolves audience members of any complicity in the fulfillment of a rhetorical act, effectively contradicting the prophetic agenda and undermining their shared responsibility in the achievement of outcomes. From the standpoint of rhetoric—more specifically, in consideration of the carnivalesque notion of implication that occurs from the outset of any given performance—the calypsonian's audience cannot simply be presumed ignorant. In fact, the opposite is true: the audience is very much aware. Audiences do not simply take a reprieve from drudgery or wait, like empty vessels, to be filled solely with a calypsonian's take on a particular topic; rather, they are always already able to engage *dialogically* with the performer. When listeners nod, they do so intently. Describing some examples of "alternate patterns of persuasion and social influence" in calypso, John Patton asserts that "the rhetorical functions of calypso include the ability of performance to articulate and symbolize the thoughts and values of a particular audience, the dynamics of defining and redefining issues of central importance to the shared cultural world of performer and audience, and the development of critical cultural self-awareness and understanding that resonates after the immediate act of the performance has passed."[31] Patton identifies the reciprocity (using Victor Turner's definition) that is integral to (any) successful performance. At times, however, the transition from message to enactment fails to materialize, despite broad consensus on the obvious validity of the message and the apparent efficacy of its delivery. While such a performance may in general serve as "a critique . . . of the social life it grows out of,"[32] the prophetic calypsonian becomes something of a specialist who attends to what may be called the *mis*handling of history, which occurs when an agreed-on agenda is known but not followed, when its essence is heeded but not acted on, and when responses seem absolutely contrary to the grievances that cause them. This is eerily exemplified by the dire observations made in 1980 by King Austin (Austin Lewis), who warned of a world without its moral compass in "Progress." More than three decades after the song's release, Austin's observations of humanity's vaulting ambitions—ambitions run amok—raise questions about not only human limitations but also the degree to which the awareness of such shortcomings have failed to raise the consciousness of the people. According to Austin, "it is plain to see universally this land is not bountiful as it was."[33] Reminiscent of Marvin Gaye's "What's Going On?" (1971), "Progress" portrays the urgency of problems—social and ecological collapse—that not only outweigh the need for clever masking and wordplay but cancel that need altogether.

With respect to the genre as a response to the problem of inaction among the underclass, Rohlehr observes that not only has calypso become more aware of itself (and of its implicit contradictions as a public genre), but some calypsonians made a definitive shift from "assigning blame to politicians for the ills of society" and began "to turn their scrutiny upon the nation itself."[34] This brand of calypso signaled a shift from the messianic role of the calypsonian to a more jeremiadic mode in which members of the audience would be held even more accountable for their complicity in suffering *and* for securing the conditions of awareness and action that could possibly lead to their liberation; essentially, the shift entailed moving from an unrealistic hope in elevated leaders, wherein vernacular awareness was taken for granted, to the urgency of developing or reinvigorating meaningful vernacular awareness. The cause of society's troubles is society itself—that is, society in total, not only the leaders, the businesspeople, and the corrupt, but also the unwilling, the ones in willful declension, the ones *who don't hear.* Emrold "Brother Valentino" Phillip's indictment of enduring colonial attitudes in "Dis Place Nice" (1975) offers a prime example. After criticizing the merchant class and their political counterparts in earlier verses, Valentino redirects his frustration toward the audience more generally. Noting the irony of his audience members' tendencies to sing along to his choruses while seeming slow to enact true independence, Valentino likens their reception of his lesson to their singing "God Save the King." Regis notes that Valentino's audience was "unaware of his subtle mockery and his sober warning,"[35] but I am inclined to disagree for two reasons. First, Valentino was not addressing individuals unfamiliar with his strategy of using plain talk to amplify the folly of people's missteps. Highlighting the issue of broad malaise in the opening verse, Valentino provides an indictment: the "Carnival mentality" in Trinidad has become so synonymous with abandon that revelers far outnumber the "serious" ones, the "conscious" ones, making it difficult for him to convincingly commit to singing his own chorus of uplift and national pride.[36]

Second, the commentary is not at all subtle; it chastises the audience rather plainly, noting that the citizens of the postindependence nation not only have continued to internalize imperialist ideology but also tend to enact the contradiction as if it were merely an everyday paradox and not demonstrative of a problematic and potentially irreconcilable aspect of Caribbean life. To address this obvious incongruity, the calypsonian's use of the masque enables the display of a prophetic ethos (or an ethos of prophetic practice) that supersedes some of the more common characteristics of the genre: bawdiness, bacchanal, wit, wine, and wave. An examination of this evolution reveals a rhetor who is particularly astute at bridging key conceptual gaps—between tradition and innovation, the public and private, the sacred and the secular—for (and with) the audience. With Valentino, the "rhetorical question" (as it were) need not even be asked, for the answer is clear to the audience. Not only is Trinidad *not* a paradise (not that it ever could be), but the prosperity that true national awareness could bring has been displaced in favor of what Valentino sees as part of the legacy of colonialism: frustrating docility. Recall that the major imperative of Caribbean rhetorical activity is to counteract the debilitating effects of invisibility and silencing with strategies and practices that, through amplification, increase the probability of being seen and heard, an imperative that extends to an audience caught in a general state of declension and one for which the display is originally intended. This distinction suggests a recasting of the audience's "singing along" as indicative of mass complicity (and, possibly, mass participation) rather than abject ignorance. The audience members may be passive or even indolent in their responses, but they are *never* ignorant. This must be understood. According to Valentino, they only *seem* to be unaware of their sense of value as citizens of a still young nation, only *appear* not to know how to advocate on their own behalf.[37] In Valentino's view, then, while the "appearance of independence" may seem to eclipse the desire for it, the audience's failure to enact true independence is the greater point, one with which he believed his listeners would be unable to argue. My reading of "Dis Place Nice" allows me to claim that the prophetic impulse is prompted by audience members' apparent lapses in adherence to established phronetic and gnostic understandings that coalesce as tradition; that is, it emerges not as a result of popular forgetting per se but in response to seemingly willful complicity that the calypsonian will not simply wait to see be self-corrected.

The prophetic calypsonian is therefore put upon to say what needs to be said, not because those in the audience are unaware of what they ought to do, but because they may have failed to enact an agenda intended to serve their best interests. The explicit despair of "Dis Place Nice" clearly shows that the performer is attempting to safeguard his audience's interests, not predicting its eventual doom. Such efforts result in performances that rely equally on the piety of the audience members and on their potential incredulity—their willingness to respond to a rhetorical act or their refusal to do so. It was in the shadow of such regional and international discontent that David Rudder seemed to burst fully formed onto the scene, having gestated the previous decade as a mas man apprentice and singer-songwriter for Charlie's Roots, a brass band based in Lord Kitchener's calypso tent.

PLAYING MAS' TO CROSS THE BRIDGE ALIVE

After winning the Young Kings, Calypso Monarch, and Road March titles in 1986, David Michael Rudder was soon anointed by popular acclaim to lead audiences to the levels of critical consciousness from which they had either strayed or been distracted. His ministry, as it were, began with two songs: "The Hammer" and "Bahia Girl." In "The Hammer," Rudder pays tribute to the legendary pan arranger Rudolph Charles, a larger-than-life figure whose death prompts a frantic, grief-stricken search for his spirit.[38] The song is notable for the way it transforms its subject from a physical being to a series of disembodied objects and metaphysical entities that underscore Rudder's appeal to his audience's emotions and cultural memories: Charles is a man, a hammer, a legend, a Dragon, a Yoruba god. When the transformation is complete (and Charles's conversion from man to metonym is more fully articulated), Rudder makes an allusion that conclusively links Charles's spiritual transformation to the music and the people left behind. Charles becomes endowed with the power of Shango, the orisha of thunder. Sings Rudder: "Same time thunder roll, [Sister Sheila] bawl out, 'You see?' / He done start to tune a pan already!" "The Hammer" reminds the audience that the symbolic and material are inextricably (and purposefully) bound to each other. Using grief as an opportunity to offer critique, Rudder identifies a crisis in culture and tradition coinciding with a broader threat to the future of Carnival and Caribbeanness as a whole. Causing both grief and grievance, the loss of Charles, in Rudder's view, signaled the end of an era in Carnival, with reference to the disappearance of the traditional Dragon mas that roamed the streets, the decline of the carnivalesque, and the increased co-optation and corporatization of the "Carnival mentality." A principal feature in Rudder's work is the role of spirituality, the incorporation of Christian intrusions that defined not only the shape of festivals but also the face of worship in the Caribbean.[39] So he can easily be grouped with the cadre of performers, such as Calypso Rose, Brother Valentino, Leroy "Black Stalin" Calliste, Hollis "the Mighty Chalkdust" Liverpool, Weston "Cro-Cro" Rawlins, Maclean "Short Shirt" Emmanuel, Lutalo "Brother Resistance" Masimba, and Karega Mandela, who were already engaged in articulating a broad vernacular uplift at home and abroad.[40]

Nonetheless, Rudder's approach differed somewhat, for his work sought not only to chronicle the plight of disaffected Caribbean people but also to express what would be necessary to raise their collective consciousness and implicate them in the process of their own liberation. Refusing to conflate the spiritual and symbolic with the material solely as a result of historically situated cultural and religious influences, Rudder illustrates the role that a constant process of metonymic transformation takes in putting material objects, subjects, and their representative symbols to rhetorical work—or play—for a contemporary audience. Thus, his musicoreligious performances end up serving a larger symbolic function as a critical commentary on a people in search of its collective soul—a people that, of necessity, would need to enter into a state of heightened consciousness to not only endure current inequities but also aspire and work toward improved social conditions.[41] Rudder's prophetic vision foretells a specific future for his people expressed through the terministic screens of deeply democratic desires located in the vernacular epideictic traditions of lamentation, critique, and praise. In "The Ministry of Rhythm," for example, Rudder refers plainly to a society gradually unraveling, seeming almost to conspire against itself:

> What do you do in a land where
> there seems to be a charlatan on every corner?
> What do you do with a land that
> runs around like a chicken that's lost its head?
> What do you do in a time when
> you can't find the answers to simple questions?
> When the children choose to do a dance with the darkness,
> choose to walk with the dead?

His understanding of society's disquiet is obvious, and he shows deep awareness of the imperative to speak on behalf of the demonized underclass inhabitants of the disaffected post-Adamic ghettos across the Caribbean, the Americas, Africa, and Europe. In contrast to Stalin's "Burn Them" or Franz "Delamo" Lambkin's "Apocalypse," however, Rudder's "No Restriction," with the singer's defiant inclusion of himself "among the wicked ones," is intended to interrupt what otherwise seems to be a single-mindedly dystopian critique.[42] By doing so, he adds a measure of hope and an overt ethic of care into an uneasy conversation. Precisely because Rudder's commentary is intended for the uplift of the audience, his delivery is oriented toward healing rather than toward hellfire. It is, in fact, the guiding premise in "No Restriction." Following his identification with the people, Rudder sings:

> No restriction on the friction.
> I say we gonna work it out tonight
> Jah Jah people jamming up together
> And making everything alright
> . . . I say we gonna work, baby work, baby work, baby

Mass action in the context of the carnivalesque can be described, in Rudder's words, as "the last intimacy," an appeal to mass ritual as a means of achieving mass reconnection. As sacred as it is secular, the song entreats those in his audience to engage in some of the most basic communal activities: to congregate, to hold hands, hug, kiss, and dance with one another as a means of negotiating the things that they must face and endure.[43] Rudder does not avoid overtly Christian references—or, from time to time, the related preoccupation with damnation and retribution. "High Mas I" is a deliberate gesture in this vein. A revision of the Lord's Prayer, the song proceeds on the same premise, functioning as a minor repository for Rudder's prophetic discourse and evidence of his application of the vernacular mandate that forms the core of meaning for his own ethos and, by extension, his rhetorical delivery. Similarly, Rudder's preamble to "Pull Together" illustrates the singer's sustained attempt at audience implication:

> We have we have to use our biggest weapon. Too much division. Too much division. Anywhere you turn, every papers you open, every television set you turn on, the bottom line is division. Even in Trinidad where we boast about how we have so much "tolerance." Hm! Too much division. So we go be like a fisherman tonight, pulling, pulling the seine of, of togetherness home. The big fish of togetherness. Pull it together.
> [Singing] We got to dance together. Watch how you moving, brother man.

Rudder deliberately invokes Matthew 4:17–20 here. In that passage, Jesus Christ argues that people should repent because "the Kingdom of God is at hand." He subsequently enlists Simon Peter and his brother Andrew as his first disciples, offering to make them "fishers of men." I want to be careful here because, his mastery of religious tropes aside, the point is not to elevate Rudder, or any calypsonian for that matter, exclusively to the station of prophet. As I understand the genre, artists in the latter era of prophetic performance placed greater responsibility on the audience, whose members they typically thought to be in a state of moral decline, knowingly falling short and thus complicit in the circumstances that befall them. That said, to accomplish his objective in this example, Rudder connects the familiar biblical trope to the equally commonplace trope of "pulling seine," a traditional method of dragnet fishing along the shoreline requiring relatively few fishers to cast the net but many to pull it in. The obvious masquerades as a double entendre and is thus amplified: pull together to pull together—or at least to increase the probabilities of being pulled together. Not to be confused with preaching to the choir, this sort of exhortation implicates the audience but simultaneously endows it with the responsibility of engaging in a unified practice designed for the redemption of those who suffer most from the consequences of national disunity.

Rudder's music is saturated with the melodic dirges of the past—overlaid with the language of shipwreck, plantations, sugarcane, rum, oil, and blood—balancing elevated oratorical modes with the plain language of ballad calypsos that have been firmly rooted in Caribbean culture since the 1930s; it represents a confluence of contemporary musical styles that further articulate the arc of his humanism and widen the scope of those to whom he appeals as an audience, with every musical influence serving as a marker on the vast terrain of his project. "Calypso Music" does this kind of work, beginning with Rudder asking whether his audience members can "hear a distant drum bouncing on the laughter of a melody." They respond, "Yeah, yeah!" This exchange is key because it establishes that Rudder's performance is strongly predicated on the audience's awareness and acknowledgment of the drum as a nexus of historical, economic, and spiritual tension. As a consequence, the dialogic bonds that were established with audiences during calypso's formative years—when strategies of masquing, contingency, and re-presentation were already mastered—are allowed to reemerge as reliable "sites of memory," with the drum functioning as theme and exemplary text.[44] The drum, of course, survives as one of the instruments slaves on the Middle Passage used when they were forced to dance on the decks of slavers to stave off depression, suicide, and insurrection;[45] it endures as an elemental symbol of assertion and resistance, a common thread among the extant religions of the Caribbean Diaspora, which includes Spiritual Baptists in Trinidad and Tobago, Shakers in St. Vincent, Myal and Kumina/Pocomania in Jamaica, Big Drum and Beg Pardon in Grenada and Carriacou, Macoumba and Umbanda in Brazil, Santeria in Cuba, and Vodun in Haiti.[46] Be that as it may, Rudder's invocation of the drum raises several questions, including, among other perhaps more important ones, the following: How does Rudder actively demystify the complexities of everyday experience? How does he achieve continuity, bridging the distance between history and memory? And to what degree does he succeed? Where is his precedent, his source?

According to Atilla, the first calypso was based on a traditional incantation to the Yoruba sea god Ajaja, part of a longer chant that entreats a host of gods to "mount" attending dancers as part of a possession ritual:[47]

> La da de da da de da da dum-a
> Ah de de da da de de da da dum
> La da da da de de da da da
> Ah de de da de la da de da
>
> Ajaja oku ro
> Yea, aku ro sho aku ro sho
> (Chorus) Ajaja oku ro
> (Lion) Yea, aku ro sho aku ro sho
> Eh ku ro sho aku ro sho
> Ajaja oku ro[48]

I find this intriguing for a number of reasons. If we place stock in Atilla's speculation, the incantation functions as one of the earliest recorded articulations of the calypsonian's ethos, which emerges fundamentally as a conversation that is both oral (with the chorus) and aural (with the audience).[49] For me, it also illustrates a key principle in rhetoric—namely, that the symbolic act cannot be separated from its material consequences, which is to say that the greatest possibility for change occurs with acts of embodied consciousness that allow audience members to understand the signs made available to them by the performer. I must emphasize, though, that for people who rely on such a matrix of symbolic and materialistic interplay for knowing the world, their willingness to participate in a rhetorical act rests less on their being persuaded than on their being reminded of the spiritual equipment they already possess, equipment they will need if they are to endure and possibly change their social situations in meaningful (sometimes dramatic) ways.[50] So the prevailing hope—grounded in the prevailing desire—is that the performance is effective enough to implicate the audience, thereby increasing the probability of a desired outcome. The previously quoted verse of the incantation, taken from a version by the Roaring Lion, leads into a call by the performer and a response by the chorus ("Sababo!" "O-o-o-o-o-o-o!"), which signify the speaker's inquiry as to Ajaja's presence and the chorus's confirmation that possession had indeed occurred. As the song fades out, Lion intersperses his own chanting (in response to the chorus's repeated incantations) with a series of percussive vocalizations

> Goom doo dooom
> Guh guh guh mm
> Guh goom guh dooom[51]

By this point in the song, it is unclear whether Lion is mimicking the sound of the drum or the drum is possessing him. On the one hand, one can easily infer that the incantation works so effectively that the singer is possessed, moving beyond the impulse to dance and articulating the sound of the drum. Since he is a singer and not a dancer—a performer privileging the voice over the body—it follows that possession would manifest in this way, as a *materialized articulation*. On the other hand, one can presume a greater intent on the part of the performer; viewing things from this angle, I am compelled to resituate the ostensible "possession" in the context of an intentional series of exchanges between the mind and motive, the body, the voice that it houses, the sound produced by that voice, the instrument it invokes, and the audience for whom the performance is intended. This performance is an accurate demonstration of Glissant's idea that "in the pace of Creole speech, one can locate the embryonic rhythm of the drum. It is not the semantic structure of the sentence that helps to punctuate it but the breath of the speaker that dictates the rhythm."[52]

Rudder's invocations do more than just address the possible intersections that occur between history and memory, creating "sites" that enable us to see, "on the one hand, the decisive deepening of historical study and, on the other hand, a heritage consolidated."[53] They also provide the contemporary audience with a "usable past" that can be put to productive use. In other words, through Rudder's performance of tradition, a contemporary verse of a historical text coalesces—a calypso. As such, his music functions not as a mere nostalgic excursion but as a standing challenge to those in his audience to remember that they have always been calypsonians in their own rights:

> From the time the first bamboo cut
> And we dragged it down from up in the St. Ann's hill
> From the day the first
> Chantuelle leave the band
> The real jamming start
> And today we are jamming still still.
> Creating rhythms that could be deadly like Headly
> Only this time
> It's the spirit and the melody
> That's sending their souls to the boundary
> From the bongo drum

> To the roll of the tassa
> Well ever since Europe come and she make
> Bassa bassa . . . we are jamming it.[54]

While Rudder himself does not hesitate to call on the spiritual resources of tradition, his greater lesson is that of secular self-discovery and the evolution of moral practice. By deliberately invoking the primal equivalents of the contemporary carnivalesque, the Canboulay, and the steel band, he is able to sustain credibility throughout his repertoire, leaving him free to observe no significant distinction (or distance) between tradition and his innovation of it. Both aspects form the material and symbolic basis on a moral imperative that defines the calypsonian's project. For although Rudder expresses a deep suspicion of fundamentalism in the guise of religious piety, as in "Visions of Paradise," he himself is reverent of the ancestors, the saints and orishas who constitute the pantheon of his faith, and the practices they inspire. It is no coincidence, then, that by examining his music, we can come close to the point to which I alluded when this discussion began—specifically, the dynamics of *feeling* for an audience.

In "Bahia Girl," Rudder tells the story of an encounter with a girl from Bahia, Brazil. The literary framework of the song is that of an allegory, with the singer and the "girl" of the narrative standing as physical representatives and symbolic representations of their respective musical traditions. When the Trini and the Brazilian appear to consummate their union—with some "soca in she samba, samba in she soca" action, he taking off his shirt, she putting on a smile—she reveals that they have always been one and the same, with "the same vibration." Ultimately, though, he is forced to recount the story as an experience that defies and even vehemently resists explanation. Rudder sings, "She had me in heaven, she had your boy in hell. What that [w]oman do to me, I just couldn't tell. All I know is: she ring meh bell." The chanted chorus is predictably structured as call and response, but with the traditional roles inverted. The chorus (C) calls, and Rudder (R) responds:

> Refrain "1a" (01:02)
> C: pim pi lim pim pé bi di bam ba
> R: riggi diggi bam dama bi diggi bim
> C: pim pi lim pim pay bi di bam ba
> R: bing bang bi dum buh bé e nuka bing
>
> C: pim pi lim pim pé lé
> C: pim pi lim pim pé lé
> C: pim pi lim pim pé bi di bam ba
> R: e diggi diggi bum dé bé eka bam bé bé[55]

Undoubtedly, it is structured in this way to maintain the integrity of the narrative and underscore that he was responding to her. But there is also evidence of a more intricate dynamic occurring here. In the original encounter, he is *her* audience, and she is the original rhetor. Rudder, in response to the unchanging structure of the Bahia girl's vocalizations, offers a series of gradually improvised responses. Displaying an increasingly complex internal structure, these improvisations seem to go beyond mimicking, as Lion does in "African War Call." The song demonstrates Rudder's affinity for polyrhythmic representations—the drum (*diggi bum dé bé*) and other percussive instruments, including the bell (*bing*) and the steelpan (*pim*)—as fundamental material aspects of Caribbean subjectivity, rhetorical identification, and public performance. I will not attempt a translation here, but suffice it to say that the differences between the first chorus (1a) and second (1b) reveal subtleties (highlighted in the following quoted passage) that illustrate a gradual, though deliberate, move away from mimicking toward a more sophisticated form of rhetorical invention:

Refrain "1a" (01:02)
C: pim pi lim pim pé bi di bam ba
R: riggi diggi *bam dama* bi diggi *bim*
C: pim pi lim pim pay bi di bam ba
R: *bing bang bi dum buh bé e nuka bing*

C: pim pi lim pim pé lé
C: pim pi lim pim pé lé
C: pim pi lim pim pé bi di bam ba
R: *e diggi diggi bum dé bé eka bam bé bé*

Refrain "1b" (01:19)
C: pim pi lim pim pé bi di bam ba
R: riggi diggi *bim dimi* bi diggi *bam*
C: pim pi lim pim pé bi di bam ba
R: bing *bi muma nuba nubé*

C: pim pi lim pim pé lé
C: pim pi lim pim pé lé
C: pim pi lim pim pé bi di bam ba
R: —[56]

Soon the dialogic call–and-response structure of the song is temporarily suspended. Rudder disengages and launches into a monologic riff as the chorus repeats the refrain:[57]

Riff "2" (02:36)
bi bum bam bé bé
hing gung ka bang
brrring ibu ka bang bama
ibu kabang bé bé
ding giding bé bé
hing é bang hm bi dim bam
e digi ding ding bi bang bi
ding ding ding dmma
bi di bi ba ba ding buh bim bi bum a bam[58]

Refrain "3" (02:36)
C: pim pi lim pim pé bi di bam ba
R: —
R: —

C: pim pi lim pim pé bi di bam ba
C: pim pi lim pim pé lé
C: pim pi lim pim pé lé
C: pim pi lim pim pé bi di bam ba

The "last intimacy," then, is Rudder's acknowledgment of one of the earliest intimacies: the fundamental interplay of symbolic action and material production, the flesh-and-bones music designed to make the spirit dance. For Rudder, "every heart, every soul, is a drum."[59] But his numerous references to the materiality of the drum surpass mere nostalgia. For Rudder, as for all performers who rely on tradition as a bridge to progress, memory fuels the prophetic and attends the experience of self-discovery in which the engaged audience agrees to take part and hopefully resist total declension in the process—*Yeah, yeah*. Consistent with vernacular epideictic awareness, the improvisations in "Bahia Girl" strongly suggest that Rudder seems to anticipate the probability that the audience members will either misinterpret his meanings or (despite the urgency of the display) decline to act on his efforts to persuade them. That is, he appears to recognize that the commentary is as likely to achieve prophetic status *because* of the audience's conscious inaction. However, rather than simply chastise the audience for falling short, Rudder uses the vocalizations to transform *himself* into the illustration—leading by example, certainly, but more important, also drawing the audience deeper into a gradually complex matrix of expression and interaction. He reinvents himself for a more effective rhetorical display, turning, as it were, from symbolic representation to material representative, from metaphor to metonym, from messenger to text, becoming the message itself and challenging the audience to do the same. In a move reminiscent of the implicating dynamics of "African War Call," Rudder actively bridges the gap between hearing and feeling by *physically* traversing the liminal space between those of us *who don't hear* (demonstrated in the audience's rejection of a particular appeal, message, or agenda) and those of us *who feel* (exemplified in visceral reactions, the vibes, the tears, the bawling, the whining, or any other consequence of a performance that one not only hears but also *listens to*). The implication here is obviously that listening is an act. It is something we *do*. But what Rudder's reinvention suggests, furthermore, is that listening is also a physical activity—a *doing* that requires the commitment and constant involvement of the audience.

Rudder's performance constantly reminds the audience of the activities in which they are engaged and of their shared responsibility to traverse the poles of symbolic and material substantiation. Such performances resonate with audiences, most of all with those who see themselves in the representations of cultural heritage and practice and know what it feels like to get caught up in the performances. This interaction does not, however, ensure success or even suggest its possibility without work. For us Caribbeans, the *potential* for a better life, a life washed clean in the traditions of fragmentation and coalescence, depends on our ability to locate, examine, and interrogate some of the hitherto unarticulated aspects of Caribbean history, culture, and life to which we can collectively attest but often do not. We must, of our own volition, sound the depths of the Caribbean ethos for that chance to engage in a spiritual and physical "dancing of attitude."

Whether Caribbean music is approached in terms of global resistance to empire or a more narrow attention to the insular formation of Creole perspectives, the accountability of performers and audiences remains constant as a key conceptual factor, allowing them to respond to each other in ways that maintain the convergence of other factors.[60] Calypsonians such as Rudder, vigilant of this risk, compose with a definite prophetic agenda: to speak to the people, to pull them together, to implicate them in a project of individual awareness and collective uplift. Inherent in the relationship between Rudder and his *whole* audience is a mutual capacity for the exploration of a hope that something positive and even wonderful might result—or even something magical and materially wondrous that serves us better than nostalgia. In other words, the "brand new discovery" that Rudder proposes in "Calypso Music" is not brand new at all, not in the sense of being unknown. Rather, it is the critical recall that results when the tragic past is not forgotten but used as the impetus for transcendence to a higher reality by way of practical syncretic articulations of the nature of symbolic performance that rely on the deployment of ideas and the manipulation of emotions. The quality of Rudder's prophetic intention is exemplary, therefore, because it determines the quality of the message, directing and altering it on a visceral level.

To some, it will appear that the ethical paths laid out by tradition have largely been eschewed for nihilism in recent years, as have been the attendant responsibilities. This neglect, they might argue, has occurred in favor of mainstream market survival and at the expense of the people's interests, which these performers have been traditionally charged to uphold. As long as frustration among dispossessed people continues, however, there will be a need for the prophetic voice that will help shape it or at least disrupt the comfort of the social order.[61] Of course, with Rudder as with all other performers of the prophetic, the discovery may yield further tragic consequences. But the hope is generally that it will yield some good. Intractability is—has always been—a cause to work even harder to resist. And it is in such circumstances that the prophetic is most needed and, as an outgrowth of the carnivalesque, likely to be most effective. As people accustomed to various forms of struggle, we Caribbeans recognize that even the small probability of good is cause for fanfare and provides a raison d'être for the Caribbean vocalist concerned primarily with notions of the prophetic. The probable fulfillment of a shared hope and the subsequent recognition of potential that rises out of and reaches beyond the grip of tragedy, degradation, and apathy are justification enough for the attempt. Astute audiences know this and engage collectively on the strength of that hope when they are convincingly called into being because of it.

Recast in a more prophetic tone, even the most mundane of aphorisms can take on renewed significance, for if you do not hear, how will you be expected to feel? If you do not feel, how could you possibly know? And if you do not know, how could you reasonably be expected to tell? Further, while an audience may always choose to ignore the appeals, a rather easy counterargument consists in pointing out that even such a rejection would function reciprocally—that is, it could necessitate the calypsonian's role, elevating the performer's ethos over time and increasing the value of his or her performance. But jump high or jump low, with or without the calypsonian, a certain series of facts remain for us as an audience: who feels it, knows it; who knows it, tells it; who don't hear will feel.

CHAPTER 4

"We Is People"
EARL LOVELACE, ETHOS, AND A RHETORIC OF VERNACULAR FICTION

> Though Aristotle praises Homer for speaking in his own voice less than other poets, even Homer writes scarcely a page without some kind of direct clarification of motives, of expectations, and of the relative importance of events. And though the gods themselves are often unreliable, Homer—the Homer we know—is not.
> —Wayne Booth, *The Rhetoric of Fiction*

> Critical and imaginative works are answers to questions posed by the situation in which they arose. They are not merely answers, they are *strategic* answers, *stylized* answers.
> —Kenneth Burke, *The Philosophy of Literary Form*

> *Alone*, all a man could do is play a mas'.
> —Earl Lovelace, *The Dragon Can't Dance*

THE EPIC OF CARIBBEAN HISTORY and its long, literary stretch into contemporary times together signify an extended rhetorical situation, producing authors whose concern for their communities and constituents is founded on their desires for the authentic enactment of independence—that is, liberation and participation as recognized and recognizable members of society despite resistance from the ruling class. As I mentioned earlier, the French-inspired Carnival of the nineteenth century, functioning originally in jest as a temporary social leveler among the plantocracy, had become significantly less frivolous in light of an emergent Caribbean identity following emancipation. Jest had become mockery. Mockery had become scorn. Scorn had become threat. And the agenda for deliberate displays of vernacular motive began to coalesce with greater intensity. It is perhaps to the benefit of all Caribbeans—and the probable chagrin of our captors, colonizers, and governments—that there should be little difficulty in locating the exigence for a rhetoric of Caribbean fiction. In the unfortunate experience of being oppressed at various times in our histories, of being marginalized at others, and of being "granted" independence, our novelists have emerged, picking up the cause of self-definition that would in turn serve the cause of self-determination for people who may (still) be inclined to seek it.

Anyone who reads Caribbean novels peers not only into the Caribbean imaginary but also into the repertoire of expression, that is, the practice of expression and rhetorical (re)invention, the arrangement of features that give form and name to Caribbean experience. By telling the Caribbean story, the novelist implicates him- or herself in an extensive rhetorical project. It follows, then, that Earl Lovelace's agenda—exemplified in *The Wine of Astonishment* (1982), *Salt* (1997), and *The Dragon Can't Dance* (1979)—is not merely symbolic but also rooted in materialist concerns, with an explicit desire for praxis; that is, it functions as an endeavor designed to demonstrate potentially liberating motive and methodological application among members of a dispossessed vernacular class who strive to be recognized and to belong. Jennifer Rahim concurs: "At the core of these concerns is the primacy of people as the shaping resource and force of history; the necessity of safeguarding the values of freedom, dignity and equality on the individual and collective levels; and the propagation of respect for the place where people make their home."[1] To reiterate, the ultimate objective is not the construction of an ethos—literally, the character of Caribbeanness—that can operate only symbolically. That construction serves merely as a stage in Lovelace's process, an illustration of his vision and motive.[2] Having said that, I agree with Kenneth Ramchand when he observes, "It is not enough to notice that there is persuasiveness coming from the sympathy, sincerity and imagination with which the author comes to each character."[3] The important point, then, concerns far more than the obvious claim that Lovelace frames the activities of his characters as a tapestry of motives, displays, and outcomes that illustrate the discursive characteristics of tradition and the prospects of rhetorical choice among vernacular rhetors.

Following Ramchand's lead, and as I reflect on the epideictic role of masquing in these novels, I am inclined to consider how the author's rhetoric may be transmitted beyond the boundaries of his prose—leading, perhaps inexorably, to matters more prosaic and more typically Caribbean. I have concluded that Lovelace accomplishes this particular set of symbolic actions in a number of ways, most effectively through the strategic use of metonymy. In so doing, he deploys a method that emphasizes the fundamental contiguity of art, artifice, and audience, as well as his readers' awareness of the correlation between symbolic reference and material experience. That is, Lovelace's work exemplifies the author's implicit understanding of ethos as a form of embodied knowledge and meaning making that is not merely representative but *essential* to the group from which it emerges and that it is primarily designed to represent.[4] Additionally, Lovelace forwards his conception of ethos by using his characters as manipulable representations of the familiar, infusing them with the means and methods for arriving at a conscious statement of purpose in a range of situations. Lovelace is able to show how ethos emerges in response to material circumstances: inadequately at first, rising as a reflexive counterpoint to oppression and official apathy in *The Wine of Astonishment*; negotiated reflectively as a process of reparation in *Salt*; and then more successfully realized as a collaborative exercise in praxis and democratic involvement in *The Dragon Can't Dance*. In short, Lovelace's exploration of ethos, through the deliberat(iv)e construction of characters, is more than coincidence. His activation of dance as a major trope of embodied vernacular knowledge and his experimentation with characters as embodiments of that knowledge together form a metonymic bridge, allowing his readers to negotiate between the ethos that the author has imagined and described and the hopeful enactment of that ethos in different circumstances at different times among readers with whom these ideas resonate. The novels therefore serve as the masque that the author places on display, amplifying his theory of ethos for the benefit of the reader.

Before engaging wholly in my own "concept-spinning,"[5] however, I will begin with some preliminary framing centered on the texts themselves, providing a brief and intentionally simplified contextualization of each novel before returning to a more unified reading of their inherent rhetoricity and the author's efforts to demonstrate it as an explicit adherence to the tenets of the Caribbean carnivalesque.

EMERGENT ETHOS IN *THE WINE OF ASTONISHMENT*

As one of the foremost badjohns of the Lovelace novels, Bolo possesses a seemingly innate sense of resistance as a warrior fully trained in this tradition and thus perpetually primed for combat. The contentious battle dance of kalinda is the shaper of his nobility and thus the key to understanding his eventual breakdown.[6] Bolo is "the champion stickfighter, the king."[7] From his early appearance in the novel, his mystique as the fearless hero is apparent, fading only when he becomes a terror to the community of Bonasse. The narrator, Eva, recalls the undeniably heroic status of the Bolo she knew in the seven years before World War II brought U.S. troops to the island:

> The whole village talk 'bout him. They say that in the stickfight ring, the gayelle, it don't have a man to stand up in front of him. They say he don't fight just to win battles for himself, for him stickfighting was more the dance, the adventure, the ceremony to show off the beauty of the warrior. And he do it with love and

respect, more as if he was making a gift of himself, offering himself up, ... as if what he really want was for people to see in him a beauty that wasn't his alone, was theirs, ours, to let us know that we in this wilderness country was people too, with drums and song and warriors.[8]

Warriors indeed. Rohlehr describes the rhetoric of the batonnier within the kalinda tradition as "a formalized verbal prelude to a game in which manhood, status, identity within the group and on rare occasions life itself were at stake."[9] But Lovelace reminds us that when words fail in a given situation, the vernacular rhetor can resort to the nonverbal semantic of dance. Kalinda, for example, works as a cohesive, even centripetal, force of critical performance for disaffected rhetors and their sympathetic audiences. Beneath the tragedy of Bolo's personal disintegration, his madness and eventual dehumanization, and the inevitability of an unceremonious death are the rhythms of kalinda being beaten and sung, lived and witnessed, recalling and reinscribing among those present a rhetorical situation that emboldens Bolo to act (and act out): "Everything is ripe for battle," notes the narrator, "the drummers beating, and chantwells is singing this song that is to stickmen the terrible lamentation and anthem and invitation and warning."[10] The text thus shows kalinda to be a collective performance in which all performers must recognize the significance of their individual roles—as dancer, singer, drummer, or spectator—in order to effectively collaborate with others in their shared efforts to achieve the democratic ends suggested in the very performance of the dance. This imperative is eclipsed, however, by Bolo's inordinately egocentric vision of history and his response to it. Thus, in this novel, Lovelace conceives of a situation in which the kalinda would be a rhetorical display that maintains its relevance in contemporary society: Caribbean people, he notes, are "living in what can be called a culture on the defensive. We have to defend ourselves in what it means to be human. Affirming in order to defend."[11] But for Bolo, the disfranchisement he saw each day was a threat to his existence, such that the "rare occasion" of having to fight for his life in the gayelle had become an everyday hegemonic reality that precipitated the need to battle both in public and with the public.

Bolo clearly personifies the assertive power implicit in the kalinda; he is Lovelace's representation of an adamant and perceptibly indomitable warrior who seeks immunity from the social inequality of his day. His outrage, expressed in the context of a combative kalinda tradition, seems a justifiable reaction to the steady encroachment of matters rooted in historical precedent: sociocultural erasure and the community's apparently complicit role, exemplified by what Bolo perceives as its submission to the criminalization and subsequent silencing of religious worship with the Shouter Prohibition Ordinance;[12] the rapid, catastrophic social and moral decline brought on by external influences, specifically the U.S. military presence during World War II, the so-called new heroes engaged in a de facto occupation of the island;[13] and the added ineptitude of local leaders, such as Ivan Morton, in curtailing these effects. The nobility of Bolo's actions becomes harder to justify, however, when his aggression is juxtaposed with the fortitude we see in the community's religious leader, Bee, whose apparent tendency to vacillate in the face of oppression belies a level of patience that Bolo finds debilitating. While Bee appears unsure whether he should defy the ordinance and the added ban of Carnival celebrations that was instituted between 1942 and 1945, Bolo has already decided on the course of action he thinks the community should take: "We have to kill Prince" (a police officer charged with enforcing the bans, Corporal Prince serves as the local symbol of oppressive authority on the island, which can be traced all the way back to the British Crown, the seat of power for the region).[14]

When Bolo fails to kill Prince, however, the myth of his indomitability falls apart completely. He is, in terms of the carnivalesque, unable to assimilate to the societal shift and turn his symbolic kingship to actual material effect in response to the unyielding context of the status quo. We see instead a stickfighter whose obsolescent reflexivity brings him to the brink of erasure. A recalcitrant former champion facing the inevitable eclipsing effect of irrelevance. A deposed king, holding sway only in the realm of his solitary nostalgia. Following his imprisonment, an emasculated Bolo attempts to battle the ghost of history, mock fighting with a handkerchief instead of the unbreakable bwa, the poui shaft that was once the key accoutrement of his dance. This battle leaves him almost too bitter for words and definitely too bitter to exercise the dilatory and far more circuitous strategies of a trickster. He is no less rigid than his bwa, for he exhibits none of the flexibility, adaptability, cunning, and patience that would prove indispensable for his changing times. Pursuing such measures would just waste time, in his opinion, and too much has already been spent fruitlessly waiting for things to improve. Exigency, in Bolo's view, has apparently reached past its peak, and he has had enough.

Lovelace infuses Bolo with a great deal of the tragic heroic beauty emerging in postcolonial life and the colonial inheritance of struggle and oppression, cultivating in him an ethos of irrepressible resistance for which there can be no response but silence, no recourse but *to be* silenced. A scapegoat, it seems, from the very start. Predictably, his unwavering commitment to the unattainability of the past leads to his death:

> [His dying] didn't take away from us the burden that was ours and that is ours even today. His dying ain't solve no problem for us. It just give us the chance, if we so weak to take it, if we so dead to hold on to it, to put aside our human challenge and blame it all on Bolo, make him the victim and the sacrifice, make

him Christ . . . because it was easier . . . than for people to take upon their own self in their own life the burden that is theirs from being human in the world. . . . It just give us the chance to pretend that his death solve the problem.[15]

While Bolo is justified in his outrage, his reaction is ultimately misguided. Bolo's descent into chaos, performing madness by unleashing irresolvable personal aggression on the community, is certainly meant to be rhetorical—a display of masqued desperation intended to amplify the frustrations of the community and bring about an urgent, necessary change—but it only partially serves Lovelace's broader vision of a Caribbean identity that is representative, self-aware, and socially viable. Rather than be an apologist for Bolo's actions, Lovelace highlights the interactive dynamics of the kalinda tradition with the aim of illustrating Bolo's disregard for it. In short, Lovelace reveals the anachronism to be Bolo's particular expression of an individualistic ethos, not the tradition he ultimately disregards. So what does this mean for Lovelace's project more broadly conceived?

At the very least, Bolo's failure and death function symbolically as a foil that the author uses to frame the concept of an emergent ethos and its potential consequences. His dance is an articulation of the body dancing its affirmation of a defiant ethos forged in cynicism, almost overconfident in the hollowness of its rebellions. For a changing audience and a changing time, however, such a presumption tends to fall short of its intended effect. His ultimate offense—the kidnapping of Brother Primus's daughters—is, as Eva puts it, "the battlefield that Bolo bring the village to."[16] That is, he magnifies the exigence to a point they can no longer avoid, one that will prompt the actual work of reflection and their enactment of ethos. On the surface, it seem that the role of the badjohn is "to dead,"[17] as Fisheye puts it in *The Dragon Can't Dance*, or at least his role is to be unafraid to seek death. Recall that Eva says Bolo "don't fight just to win battles for himself" but does so "as if he was making a gift of himself."[18] But even though Marjorie Thorpe has argued that "the image of the black West Indian as courageous victim is superseded [in *The Wine of Astonishment*] by the presentation of the black West Indian as authentic hero-figure,"[19] Lovelace takes it a step further, using Bolo to strategically undermine the idea of noble savagery as a redeeming characteristic among the oppressed. For all its authenticity, urgency, and morally defensible justification, Bolo's kalinda ultimately fails to motivate praxis when the warrior becomes a tangible threat to the community, a flesh-and-blood representation of the systematized oppression that has loomed over its inhabitants for generations. In the end, Bolo is undone not just by the consequences wrought by his actions but by his own resistance to change, for in failing to adapt, he counteracts the basic imperative of collective ethos and the necessity of deep reflection. As a result, he is fundamentally unable to garner the support that could have actually protected him from himself. Bolo, who "wouldn't rest until he kill somebody,"[20] is not the exemplar of ethos for a changing world but a masque that magnifies the community's need for it. He thus represents Lovelace's critique of nostalgia as a bankrupt rhetorical strategy, the fate of one who is more concerned with "trying to dance back something that was going away" than with making adjustments for what exists,[21] as well as what remains to be seen.

Despite Bolo's personal sacrifice, however, and the narrator's awareness of its inherent nobility, members of the community are still obligated to assert themselves. The obvious implication here is that one does not get awarded an ethos simply by default, by forfeit, or in counterpoint. Lovelace reminds us that kalinda is not for Bolo to perform *alone*, for the absence of any element—body, voice, or drum—can render the performance benign and its rhetoric ineffective. In terms of its design, then, kalinda rests on an implicit principle of cohesive engagement with the audience: *the whole thing is one*, and its success is predicated on the sum of its parts. This means that even for members of the audience, to witness the performance is to participate directly in the assertion of an ethos that has taken shape under pressure. To witness is to identify. And when the matrix of involvement among performer, audience, environment, and context is disrupted and the centripetal force of the performance diminishes, when nothing comes of the drumming and chanting, energies lose their focal point and collective purpose, and identification becomes a virtual impossibility; appropriately, this is also the point at which the metaphor crumbles to reveal the discursive core: there is no *carnivalesque* without the people who gather to create it, those who must not only implicate themselves in the drama but also immerse themselves in its outcome.

Rather than allow Bolo's death to satisfy the requirements of an emergent ethos through force and tragic sacrifice, Lovelace casts ethos as a form of reflective self-discovery, as something each individual must take personal responsibility to realize so everyone can consciously practice it—that is, as a bona fide aspect of a culture and a people who understand it. The contexts of the persecution and prohibition these characters have been made to endure supply a fitting—if not strategically overt—precedent for reading the development of ethos purely in terms of the omnipresent risk of rhetorical failure. But I want to emphasize that Lovelace does not situate the exigence for ethos in the insufficiency of Bolo's heroism or the futility of community activism; rather, he locates it in the community members' self-assertion that must occur despite all these factors. Lovelace further uses this standpoint to provide his conception of ethos as a critical alternative to the reflexive version we see in Bolo, thus establishing reflectivity as the more effective rhetorical choice, one that encourages participation in the realization and practice of a potentially equitable life. Lovelace, taking opposition as that which is always already present, enables the coalescence of an ethos that exists at the very heart of recuperative social action.

NEGOTIATING THE LIMBO SILENCE IN *SALT*

In *The Wine of Astonishment*, ethos is not posited as a quality that grows primarily in opposition to certain actions. By taking opposition as the always already present, however, Lovelace suggests that ethos forms in the context of self-discovery *in response to* oppositional social forces. Self-conscious inquiry thus increases the chances of progress amid the carnival of complex life experiences. Such inquiry is evident in *Salt* as characters labor for a sense of self in shifting contexts and, in the process, find a way to *get through*. In this novel, Lovelace takes up the issue of reparation. But he avoids the beaten track of demanding that empire foot the bill for the cost of a people's oppression. Instead, Lovelace focuses on the degree to which reparation refers to the subject's acquisition of self-awareness and self-determination, the reflective practice of attending to *one's own repair*, even preceding that of restitution from an external entity. Reparation is not granted, in other words, so much as it ought to be practiced. For Lovelace, the issue of reparation unfolds "more along the lines of an individual relationship, a human relationship," leading to an intensely personal gesture of self-reflection that will allow "a starting over, an effort to acknowledge the wrong but trying to continue with the knowledge of injury by both parties."[22] Bango, the narrator's uncle, makes a critical distinction in this vein, contextualizing the struggle and reprioritizing exigencies for the reader:

> "Understand from the start," he said. "I ain't come here to make the Whiteman the devil. I am not here to make him into another creature inhabiting another world outside the human order. I grant him no licence to pursue wickedness and brutality. I come to call him to account, as a brother, to ask him to take responsibility for his humanness, just as I have to take responsibility for mine. And if you think it is easy for either one of us, then you making an error. This business of being human is tougher than being the devil, or being God for that matter. And it doesn't matter whether in the role of brutalized or brutalizer."[23]

Bango's words constitute a declaration of independence that masquerades as a concession, a statement made specifically for those who have ears to hear and eyes to see (for) themselves. Rather than place the sole responsibility on the oppressor, Lovelace repeatedly suggests that the oppressed—including, by extension, his readers, probably most of whom have inherited the legacy of oppression—are complicit in their suffering. As such, he implies that we need to relearn what it means to look inward, reconnecting more elementally with the humanity we seem to have forgotten. The onus for achieving reparation, in other words, falls primarily on the ones in need of repair. Taking into account Bolo's misapplication of the kalinda in a rhetorical situation that has outmaneuvered him in *The Wine of Astonishment*, I propose the following: if we are willing to accept the terms of Lovelace's overall argument here, including its exposition in passages where he uses Bango to express it, then we should simultaneously be inclined to locate the author's articulations of *how* we ought to face the inherent challenges of getting through and of productively (if not always successfully) engaging and negotiating with those challenges. Let me put this differently. What are the available means by which members of a vernacular class can break through to the other side? A limbo sensibility, in my view, is most fitting.

From its beginnings as a ritualistic dance performed at wakes to its contemporary secular performances on street corners and at "cultural" festivals, limbo goes beyond the literal contortion of the body wherein dancers bend over backward to negotiate a pole that lowers with every successful pass.[24] *Salt* signifies the author's efforts to describe a strategic method that demonstrates an implicit vernacular awareness of liminality, one that designates the *space between* the pole and the ground (and other permutations of the metaphor) as a site of encounters between symbolic elements and material consequences that are fundamental to one's spiritual development, to the more subtle operations of ethos in the physical plane, and to the critical awareness of tradition as a strategy of negotiation and empowerment. More important than simply being in a situation defined solely by strict social and political limitations is the vernacular tendency to transcend those limitations—indeed, the necessity to do so with performances that take place primarily in the service of one's own best interests.[25] And though its pronunciation might suggest a more Dantesque reading, a basic point is that one does not *stay* in limbo, for though the spectacle may be based on the dancer's ability to respond physically to the insistent refrain ("How low can you go?"), the true feat consists in completing the maneuver and rising. According to Sonjah Stanley-Niaah, "the dancers . . . emerge on the other side, as their heads clear the pole, as in *the triumph of life over death*."[26] In other words, the logic of the dance dictates that the dancer must *go through* in order for it to be considered a complete maneuver—that is, reflective of "the whole cycle of life."[27] A limbo sensibility operates on the same logic; that is, it expresses not only the fundamental impermanence of situations and experiences but also the inherent connections created as rhetors move from one stage of awareness to another to realize a greater potential. This aligns with Molly Ahye's attempts to link the limbo to ancestral Kongo cosmogony: the significance of passing below the bar may portend "disruption on the earth plane, the struggle and suffering in order to gain rewards." She continues, "Also, by this interpretation, the passing under of one instead of two emphasizes the individualization of the soul of man."[28]

Similarly, in the rhetoric of Lovelace's fiction, we can recognize that the ability to endure life—literally, to get through it—is undergirded by an awareness of impermanence and completion, both of which, when balanced, aid the rhetor in accepting the challenges that come with living a whole life. Systemic constraints notwithstanding, the challenges that vernacular rhetors are bound to experience also occur on a subjective level, as an internalized process of self-awareness that they must undergo to reconcile *with themselves* and, in so doing, increase the probabilities of a meaningful resolution to personal conflict—even if that resolution means coming to terms with their own mortality. This is best demonstrated in the articulations of a subject who is deeply self-aware, portrayed in the following example as an elaborate limbo as the reader is introduced to the protagonist's mother, Miss May:

> [She] parted the curtains at the front door of the wood house on top of the hill, *gathered up her strength and stepped down into the speckled sunlight filtering through the overhanging branches* of the immortelle tree, her small black Bible gripped in one hand, a *finger between its pages marking her place*. And with the laborious delicacy choreographed by her pains *eased herself down* unto the step where the sun was brightest and rested there, *her eyes shut, her breath inhaled*, the metronome of her mind keeping time to the rhythm of her distress, trying to find within the music of her pain *a space in which to breathe*. And when she did, she *opened her eyes* sparkling with gratitude to chuckle with reproachful admiration for the pain, saying softly, "Like is kill you really come to kill me," in her mind glancing at it sidelong, as at an acquaintance sitting there beside her.[29]

The novelist's deliberately activated limbo sensibility functions as a recognizable trope of existential ambivalence, an articulation of social survival that influences the way his characters—and his audience—are able to engage rhetorically with their world. Lovelace relies on this limbo sensibility to frame the gesture of a vernacular rhetor's emergence into the light. He suggests, furthermore, that such an abstract sensibility would be rooted in the rhetor's ability to decipher meaning from everyday experience, such that what is gleaned from that experience can directly influence the rhetor's approach to life. In fact, this sensibility—this deep experiential awareness—comes so firmly embedded in the everyday that hardly any reference to even the most mundane process can occur without invoking it. For instance, as part of the reader's indoctrination into the "aimless ease" of the vernacular discourse community of Cunaripo, where the novel is set, Lovelace describes the experience of "looking beneath each phrase spoken or sung for its other meanings, running the gauntlet of ridicule to emerge toughened to an indifference that made it fun for them to tease the cripple and mock the weak."[30]

In carnivalesque terms, limbo satisfies a more specific function in this novel, something more than just the symbolic action of a shared cultural consciousness that far exceeds the limits of emancipatory and Shrovetide festivals in terms of time, space, knowledge, and intention. In addition, it serves as a representation of the machinations of rhetorical choice faced by individuals engaged in a struggle to get to a point where they can define themselves in their own terms, albeit within the context of unyielding situations. What results is the symbolic and material suspension of rhetors in a space that requires from them the ability to negotiate the choices they face as part of a rite of passage that can lead them to increased self-awareness. Life is hard, and these tensions often conspire to separate performers either from their communities or from the actualization of their desires. This tension manifests in the novel (and in many of our own lives) as the familiar dogged pursuit of education at the expense of tradition; rhetors who experience the tension in this way, whether through immigration, island scholarships, or studying and living abroad, endure a deep ambivalence when negotiating between the pull of a tradition that is coming more into its own and that of a life separate from it. For instance, when speaking of a section of the island where "the only part of the oil [the residents] get" is the oil drums that they "take and fire and shape and beat to make a music to coax into the daylight,"[31] the narrator reveals his awareness of these foundational tensions as he recalls the misguided (though unfortunately typical) escapism that emerges from a familiar frustration:

> My mother thankful to her God that we not living next door to them [Africans], not by those drums that would giddy up your head and full you up with a power African and useless that point you back to a backward people that can hardly help theyself, far more help you, can only make you shame, can only drag you down deeper into the dark.
>
> To her the *onliest* thing to save *us* is the education that she begging me to learn.
>
> Because without it you *have* to dance below the Limbo pole. You *have* to bend low and flex your spine and bend your back and *try* to come out on the other side of the stick without your knees touching the ground.[32]

The juxtaposition is clear. The choice, apparently an obvious one for the narrator's mother, is to go to school or to end up with no recourse but to struggle, to contort between intractable conditions and systemized constraints that thrive on their tendency to overwhelmingly hamper people's progress.[33] Beyond the mother's expression of a relatively simplistic resistance to the dance's exoticism and spectacle, limbo resonates as a site of (trans)formative resilience, sometimes to tragic ends, that is recognizable as a space in which rhetors can actively engage various social pressures.

Jojo, one of the quasi-ancestral characters in *Salt*, is in the midst of dealing with such pressures. He represents a new native who does not have the luxury of nostalgia for a distant mainland to which he can no longer return; instead, he must recall and (re)fashion his traditional rhetorical skills in order to go through the process of *becoming* Caribbean. He has to "put aside the depth of this loss . . .

and *find a way in his mind* to claim this new world."³⁴ Faced with the unyielding reality that he has "lost track of the exact place he had come from," Jojo is compelled to revisit the modes available to him so that he can place a meaningful claim on the place he has come to know as his home:

> He had to learn how to conjure power out of his situation of powerlessness. He learnt the power of parody, of ridicule, of double entendre, of grand charge, of mamaguy, of pappyshow. He learned to divine the degree of vulnerability of a person. He learned the songs, the dances, beating drums and singing at wakes and at estate games. . . . [He] presented himself as a freeman, going through the most elaborate stratagems to get himself off work gangs, managing by his own luck and cunning, . . . his unconquerable spirit, his trickery, his flattery, his sham, his dreams. . . .
>
> He had to think and work things out. He had to find meaning in his captivity, his enslavement, his enduring, to re-examine his relationship with women, his role as a man, he had to think of power, of what it was, of what must be its function. He had to think of the world, of life, what was it, was it a matter of domination by the strongest, what was man, what was tribe and people and race and country? He had to re-examine all the old questions, to look again at the old songs, the old sayings, the stories, —the meanings.³⁵

In a situation that will either force his capitulation or motivate escape as the only viable contingencies for survival, Jojo (re)constructs an ethos that can allow him to deal dialogically with his circumstances and thus get through. It is a process that begins when Jojo shifts his focus from ruminations of *who he could be* and, at least if it is to succeed, can end only with an acceptance of *who he must actually become*. His adaptability is a rhetorical response that results from his examining the consequences of his current circumstance, as well as performing the skills he recalls. One can see how he avoids getting stuck between the challenge of the situation and the potentially debilitating hope of surviving it. In practical terms, the promise of success that the skills provide cannot replace reflecting on and applying them.

Like Jojo and the rest of the community, the main protagonist, Alford George, knows he must endure this process before he can realize the full potential of identity: "We do not know who we are. And we will never know until we see ourselves with new eyes." The "new eyes" Alford imagines are really not so new at all, only forgotten. Similar to Jojo's, Alford's aspirations for greatness are reprioritized, making considerations of *who he is,* not a preoccupation with *who he could have been* or what society has made him, serve as the impetus for action. He is driven to confess this when, after being shamed by a coconut vendor for being nothing more than a pretender, a "pappyshow," he relents: "I have forgotten my mission. I have become part of the tapestry of pretence at power. I who ought to have been disturbing this numbing peace have now become keeper of that peace. I have joined the gang of overseers that help to keep this place a plantation. Thank you, brother man. Thank you." But this is how it must go—not as part of some entirely abstract order but through the insertion of experience in our most profound moments of reflection—so that when we are exhausted and called to reflect on the causes for our exhaustion, we must stop. Alford concedes, ultimately, to what he has always known, something to which we as an audience might be inclined to agree when it comes to recognizing a strategic reservoir from which we can collectively sip: he "had to find his way back to the people from whom he had stood apart from the beginning, from whom he had tried to escape. He had to embrace his shame, to claim his outrage and so lay claim to a future of dignity. He had been *too long underneath* the Limbo pole erected for him to pass under *in order to be admitted* to that other world that for too long had been the world."[36]

Alford's mask is inadequate, aiding only to illustrate the insufficiency of self-imposed exile. That is, the mask develops when Alford is apart from the community—in it but not of it. To realize his place and role, he must remove the mask, return to the community, and face, with new eyes, the demons he perceives. As one might expect, the manifestation of these demons bears a strong resemblance to Bolo's: political corruption, complicity, wasted opportunities, pride, and shame. Lovelace charts Alford's getting through in parallel increments that include the childhood dream of leaving his world behind for a "world that was elsewhere,"[37] the disdain he holds for the students he feels forced to teach, his disillusionment with political office, the misplaced idealism of a hunger strike, and the trials that lead eventually to humbling himself to his lover. The sensibility that attends such rhetorical situations and choices is embedded in the text as a strategy on which each character is able to rely in times of necessity: the ability to struggle, persevere, and *hold strain* amid encroaching social pressures in order to get through. But it also indicates a more essential(izing) practice of inquiry into Alford's identity: what he must go through in the search for himself. It is a generalizable quest.

For instance, harking back to the experience of rupture and resultant accretion of retained African—that is, proto-Caribbean—traditions while simultaneously reinforcing the contemporary ability to survive the frustrations and limitations of African diasporic life, Wilson Harris characterizes the limbo as reflecting "a certain kind of gateway to or threshold of a new world and the dislocation of a chain of miles."[38] Limbo, in this context, is an invocation of memory as a preparatory activity for encountering trials, as a method for negotiating the virtually irreconcilable tension between survival and liberatory ambition in contemporary times. The process, done in earnest, leads to what Harris calls a "renascence of a new corpus of sensibility" that places the enactment of Caribbeanness in conversation with a larger, more diverse "architecture of cultures."[39]

For Lovelace, too, the invocation of memory is intended to achieve a deliberate purpose. According to its author, *Salt* involves "a retracing of steps, returning to emancipation and its effects on Africans and the Caribbean and coming forward" from within the framework of an examined culture, identity, and politics.[40]

Part salvation, part debilitation, the limbo sensibility as methodology is innocuous when it comes to providing resolution; that is, it never resolves this tension for members of the audience or pronounces any judgment but rather calls on them to resolve these issues for themselves. They are left to choose or change their minds. Lovelace suggests that a vernacular approach to rhetorical choice must be fashioned anew from the ability to productively negotiate the traditional and the contemporary, to rely on what they know to help shape what they envision, to manage the past and prepare for the future by going through the present. The unavoidable present. To crystallize the point, Lovelace reminds us that a limbo sensibility relies fundamentally on the authentic approach to tradition—literally, as a legacy of knowing and remembering. This realization makes Alford's return the poignant completion of a rite of passage. Alford relies on tradition that is infused with a contemporary experience of having personally traversed the liminal space of knowledge, ambition, success, and failure. His own mother had been warned to do the same.

When, as a growing child, Alford's ability to speak was hampered, his mother made her way back to the Spiritual Baptist faith for a cure, or a resolution, from Mother Ethel. Intertwined with self-righteous rebuke, a simple pronouncement was issued: "Nobody ain't tell you you have to come home to your nation?"[41] The subtext here is that nobody can tell you to "come home." You have to do it for yourself. Try as one may, no return—of memory, conversion, or any other kind—is possible without the self-conscious willingness to undertake it and the knowledge of what one must go through to get there. Lovelace suggests that engaging in limbo is a rhetorical choice, one solely the individual's to make. There is no special invitation to struggle. And while the choices one makes will undoubtedly yield consequences—as with the choice to painfully sequester oneself from family for the pursuit of the world's other offerings, training one's gaze away from vernacular tradition and into the tradition of book learning, or with the choice to return from self-exile, humbled and hopeful, to the people, immersing oneself in the tradition—Lovelace articulates ethos here no less explicitly than he does at the beginning of *Salt*: go through to get through, but in the midst of going through, remember/*re*-member yourself along with what you are made of and all that has made you. Remember, or you will be left with no recourse but to struggle on the other end with who you are, to contort between the intractable conditions and systemized constraints of an anonymous life, another life, or a sensibility that is, in the end, less *Caribbean*. A limbo that remains unresolved is no limbo at all.

DAEMONIC TRANSFORMATION IN *THE DRAGON CAN'T DANCE*

In *The Dragon Can't Dance*, Lovelace explores how the process of self-awareness can be put to rhetorical work by having Aldrick, the protagonist, evolve from being a man behind the mask he uses for Carnival to being a rhetor who uses masquing to negotiate the carnivalesque. The tenuous position of the individual in search of a self-awareness that emerges in *Salt* also resonates strongly with Lovelace's hero in this book, an "aristocrat in this tradition . . . of Idleness, Laziness, and Waste."[42] Lovelace is most explicit in this novel about the vernacular rhetor's negotiation of rhetorical outcomes, highlighting the crucial difference between two forms of play—pretense and performance—such that "playing a mas" is formally developed as an ethos needing to come into its own, and "making a mas" becomes a more deliberat(iv)e demonstration of ethos. Lovelace's plotting and subsequent playing out of Aldrick's ethos gives us a way to read evolving practice as rhetorical method. Like Alford in *Salt*, Aldrick wears a mask, a literal one in the form of the dragon costume he assumes each year for Carnival. We can, for that reason, take the use of symbolism as de facto, understanding that Aldrick's basic conflict is illustrated in the choice to give up the mask and instead bring his *self* into public view. This frees us to ask more pertinent questions. How much is mas and how much is man? Where, on the continuum of expression, do Aldrick and his fellow characters land? What forces the conflicted individual to choose the authenticity mandated by the faithful subscription to ethos rather than contrarily pretend to play the role he has taken great pains to craft? Most of all, and most relevant to my purpose, what is at stake in the choice—for Aldrick, his community, and even ourselves?

Aldrick's performance of the Dragon—and of the Diable-Diable, or devil, which spawned it—harnesses the terror of the underworld with the symbolic performance of breaking out of that underworld and into a better life. This imperative directly aligns Aldrick with the general democratizing aspects of the carnivalesque: because the space created by the carnivalesque is mutual, intended to be neither owned nor inordinately monitored, it is also primed for rhetorical possibility in which an individual's sense of identity can flourish in the presence of and in cooperation with an audience that is implicated in the act by means of vernacular witness. In addition, the intricate construction of particular sites of carnivalesque expression that enable the revisioning of a potentially democratizing practice is repeated every year in the ritual of Aldrick's preparation for Carnival, pointing to a methodology that can be applied more directly and generalized as an approach to public rhetorical performance:

> In truth, it was in a spirit of priesthood that Aldrick addressed his work; for, the making of his dragon costume was to him always a new miracle, a new test not

only of his skill but of his faith: for he knew exactly what he had to do, it was only by faith that he could bring alive from these scraps of cloth and tin that dragon, its mouth breathing fire, its tail threshing the ground, its nine chains rattling, that would contain the beauty and threat and terror that was the message he took each year to Port of Spain. It was in this message that he asserted before the world his self. It was through it that he demanded that others *see* him, recognize his personhood, and be warned of his dangerousness. . . . He worked, as it were, in a flood of memories, not trying to assemble them, to link them to get a linear meaning, but letting them soak him through and through.[43]

The devotion Aldrick pays the process of mas making and the tendency to "[work] it all into the latticework of this [present] dragon, into the scales and threads, the exodus [of his relatives]," serve as an appropriate illustration of the symbolic convergence of history, memory, and the possible motives that are required for a particular rhetorical situation to take form and through which a subject can more clearly see and be seen. However, he is also obliged to face the limitation of symbolic representation, ultimately providing an alternative analysis that emphasizes the importance of self-conscious performance and suggests that the sufficiency of meaningful rhetorical practice is achieved through the additional convergence of motive and action among those involved. His approach implies a desire for agency, recognition, and justice, the fulfillment of which is contingent on an implicit understanding of the way rhetoric operates among the folk who form the society, as well as those whose rhetorical agency has been largely ignored or fundamentally misrepresented. His project is circumscribed by "the symbol of an unyielding and triumphant martyrdom, . . . that sense of escape, . . . mud in the Spiritual Baptist church, . . . [and] the growing story of lives of miracle and manness and faith . . . entangling him like Shango drums that he was already fated to dance to."[44] From the vantage point of anonymity, and despite being equipped with a critical lens shaped by tradition, the masked performer is constrained as much by the costume as by the social and political limitations he or she faces.

Through Aldrick, Lovelace's project is fundamentally rhetorical because it suggests a designed attempt to raise and breathe new life into the collective consciousness of his readers by portraying aspects they recognize and remember—aspects of themselves that, in the course of living, may have atrophied. By extension, the methods he uses to achieve his literary ends, as well as the agents he puts into play, are configured for reception by a contemporary audience. Once dressed as a dragon—that is, armed both materially and symbolically with the mask—Aldrick erupts as a mas man, fully equipped for a turn in public. At least, this is what Lovelace leads us to believe. Now dressed, Aldrick dances, and the transcript of his nascent ethos is put on display, along with that of the people who "scrimp and save and whore and work and thief to drag out of the hard rockstone and dirt to show the world that they is people."[45] He dances the Dragon, assuming his role as "human trope" to represent his audience,[46] showing their frustrations and their complicities back to them, putting his conception of performance in practice for them despite the mechanisms of official power that bind them:

> For two full days Aldrick was a dragon in Port of Spain, moving through the loud, hot streets, dancing the bad-devil dance, dancing the stickman dance, dancing Sylvia and Inez and Basil and his grandfather and the Hill and the fellars by the Corner, leaning against the wall, waiting for the police to raid them. He was Manzanilla, Calvary Hill, Congo, Dahomey, Ghana. He was Africa, the ancestral Masker, affirming the power of the warrior, prancing and bowing, breathing out fire, lunging against his chains, threatening with his claws, saying to the city: "I is a dragon. I have fire in my belly and claws on my hands; watch me! Note me well, for I am ready to burn down your city. I am ready to tear you apart, limb by limb."[47]

Lovelace implies that rhetors are exposed as authentic to their audiences only insofar as their performances will allow. We cannot fail to note, for example, the contentious, boastful affirmations reminiscent of the Midnight Robber's speeches, which I discussed in chapter 2. Evident also is the symbolism of escape from the hellish life of despair and dispossession. These tropic maneuvers (including Lovelace's interlectal maneuvers) are particularly noteworthy because they illustrate the breadth of applicability involved in these performances. Being seen, however, often heightens the individual's responsibility to sustain his or her *display* or repeat it (even to the point of obsolescence) for the benefit of the audience. That is, the preoccupation with seeing and being seen, which Lovelace posits as his protagonists' fundamental enactment of a rhetorical vision, constitutes an epideictic that the performer can use to bring about potentially democratizing circumstances against the onset of what Harris refers to as a "self-confessional blindness, blindness to self-destruction and the destruction of others."[48]

Lovelace constructs Aldrick as the Caribbean rhetor at a critical stage of pragmatist development, one in which he begins to understand that only the true face of the masquer will suffice. Recall that the process of the Caribbean carnivalesque is founded on an ethos that allows for the conscious enactment and reception of emancipatory assertion that privileges display (and actually resists the tendency to mask, or hide, its appeals). Moreover, the distinction that Crowley observed between performance and rhetorical practice speaks directly to strategy as an integral component of the repertoire, or rhetorical skill set, that constitutes the collective assertion of a Caribbean ethos. Because Aldrick opts for performance rather than pretense, affect is ultimately achieved not through hidden appeals but through direct ones that are symbolically conceived and materially performed. The point is not that the mas Aldrick plays is irrelevant or unimportant. It does have its liberatory uses as a symbolic outlet, a scapegoat representation of the people's collective desire to escape (which of course forestalls actual escape). In fact, according to Ramchand, "Lovelace recognises the necessity of veils but points to the saving virtue of being conscious of one's veils as veils, as well as the dangers of allowing the veil to become the permanent mask."[49] Thus, from the perspective of the rhetor—especially one who so clearly needs, as Aldrick does, an actual awakening—any mechanism or activity that results in the concealment of his or her motives and expressions is a liability. To miss the contemporary relevance of such a practice is to miss the rhetorical significance of a recuperative project in liberation and democracy that takes place for the individual as well as the community: the unfolding future, into which Aldrick enters as the newly conscientized Caribbean subject, must be confronted in terms of a masque tradition rather than be masked as tradition. At stake, therefore, is the crucial need to perform as oneself, as a rhetor engaged not in pretense but in the deliberate display of ethos—"making a masque" rather than simply "playing a mas'."

The compromise Aldrick makes to play the Dragon actually forestalls meaningful confrontation with the realities and materialities of his personal situation. A crucial turning point in the novel occurs when, in protest, Aldrick refuses to dance the Dragon so that he can "catch a breath... to see what [he is] doing... on this fucking Hill."[50] His annual battle with the history that has circumscribed his identity is ultimately realized as an inadequate preparation for times in which apathy and social dispersion prevail and for which the deliberat(iv)e efforts of a conscious rhetor appear most necessary. The regret of purely self-serving actions that ultimately undermine meaningful reflection, which we can see in Alford's epiphany in *Salt*, leads Aldrick to recognize the exigence that would justify a more authentic dance:

> You see me here, I is thirty-one years old. Never had a regular job in my life or a wife or nutten. I ain't own house or car or radio or race-horse or store. I don't own one thing in this fucking place, except that dragon there, and the dragon ain't even mine. I just make it. It just come out of me like a child who ain't really his father own or his mother own.... They killing people in this place, Philo. Little girls, they have them whoring. And I is a dragon. And what is a man? What is you or me, Philo? And I here playing a dragon, playing a masquerade every year, and I forget what I playing it for, what I trying to say. I forget, Philo. Is like nobody remembering what life is, and who we fighting and what we fighting for...[51]

When the social situation reaches a critical point where rhetorical performance must be reconfigured for meaningful effect, the nature of the dance is under pressure to change. The performer's *only* recourse—if he or she is true to the relevant ethos—is to change the nature of the performance altogether. For Aldrick, the tension with the community is especially heightened in his encounter with materialities beyond the purview of the festival that possesses him. In the novel, a failed coup is the main example—a grand dragon dance, replete with a Jeep, a pistol, a trial, a conviction, and a "prison dance." Aldrick and his compatriots attempt but fail to truly possess the moment. It is a pretense, no different from what Aldrick has performed year after year during Carnival:

> Indeed, their efforts at rebellion was just a dragon dance. In jail the first thing Fisheye said with a kinda pride, kinda justifying to himself the seven years' sentence, was: "I can't say they jail me for nutten; we play a mas', eh? We really play a mas'. We really had them frighten. We had them wondering if we was going to shoot down the town or what. We really play a mas', eh, Aldrick? You couldn't play a better dragon."[52]

Along with his accomplices, Aldrick is symbolically and materially implicated in the rhetorical moment, physically inscribed as a site of display and circumscribed by the constraints of his subject position in the broader society. When it comes to providing a greater clarity for the performer, however, the limitations of the mask become glaring: even though Aldrick is an accomplished mas man, his skills of invention are inadequate because they are initially reserved for the mask he prepares. Noble though his efforts may be, then, if such a reservation—a limitation, really—succeeds as the status quo, one is led to ask not only whether liberation is possible but also who will liberate the liberator from the inadequacy of his method. For Aldrick, the answer is ultimately very simple: no one but himself. This is the spirit in which he responds to Fisheye's compliment:

> "Yes, we played a mas'," Aldrick said. "We played a dragon."
> And it was many months later, by which time Aldrick had grown accustomed to being in prison, to the food, the guards, to his own silence, and he could see in perspective those two days without the regrets, the disappointment, the feeling of waste....
> "You know, we coulda play more than a mas'."

The dragon dance, like the others, is biographical or even autobiographical. Its effectiveness, Lovelace shows us, is based on the fact that it consists of a human being attempting to be human—fighting, in a sense, to practice that humanness and have a better view of self. What remains for Aldrick, however, is the realization that the ethos he seeks in the people, one evinced in the need to "show the world that they is people,"[53] is also the ethos he himself requires if he is to effectively understand and articulate his place in the world, among the people, and in their service. It is only when he is immersed in the true process of carnivalesque invention—that is, in the cycle of the creative energies that feed the stages of self-construction, self-destruction, and eventually self-conscious reconstruction—that his tension can be resolved, enabling him to do the work of making a *real* mas—his masque, his own self-conscious display.

DANCING THE CONCEPT

Aligned no doubt to an overarching philosophy of having and not having, or wanting and not getting, which interpellates subjects primarily on the basis of their economic material deficiencies—the absence of things and the ironic normalization of that absence—Lovelace's argument relies on an approach to materiality that begins with the body, with the subject's growing self-awareness.[54] We do this "not because we own anything," as Aldrick argues, "not because we have things, but *because we is*."[55] Thus, the novelist's take on performance as a conscious dancing of attitude clearly articulates the Caribbean ethos as it prepares the rhetor for a life in the mainstream. Dance is practiced as an act of both seeing and being seen, and the vernacular reliance on it and its inherent element of display result in an attempt at ontological leveling, an opening of democratizing space and the (re)claiming of an opportunity to disrupt what Wilson Harris calls a "tautology of tyranny."[56] Literally, dance enables the dancer's body, as well as those implicated in the dance, to negotiate the materiality of enduring tyranny, its causes and consequences, by calling attention to the situations that necessitate the performance of the dance. For example, in *The Dragon Can't Dance*, as the Carnival season approaches, Lovelace has the omniscient narrator articulate (or extol) the dynamic found at the epistemic core of his project:

> "Dance! There is dancing in the calypso. Dance! If the words mourn the death of a neighbor, the music insists that you dance; if it tells the troubles of a brother, the music says dance. Dance to the hurt! Dance! If you catching hell, dance, and the government don't care, dance! Your woman take your money and run away with a nother man, dance. Dance! Dance! Dance! It is in dancing that you ward off evil. *Dancing is a chant* that cuts off the power of the devil. Dance! Dance! Dance!"[57]

An examination of the dance as rhetoric and rhetorical trope reveals what is true of all rhetoric: that persuasion is never a foregone conclusion and that the dance itself contains no inherently persuasive element that will ensure change for the assertive individual or for anyone witnessing the performance.[58] As rhetoric (or counterrhetoric), dance must involve the audience as much as the dancer, requiring the establishment and maintenance of the psychosocial bonds necessary for the performer's dialogic interaction with the audience—in essence, a call by the author and a potential response by his or her audience. The default inclusiveness of dance therefore allows rhetorical exigence to be manifested and maintained in the context of a shared experience; not surprisingly, the lines of distinction between performer and audience, while theoretically easy to maintain, are less clear when we see how lived experience disrupts order in favor of an evolving, organic practice of a rhetorical tradition.

The ability to dance—that is, to live or *perform* in one's best interests and in the shared interests of one's community, implicating members of the community at different levels—is thus essentially a rhetorical reference to the dancer's awareness of, and negotiation with, an evolving responsibility to his or her audience. This is no panacea. But whether the act itself succeeds, stalls, or fails, the rhetorical underpinning of one's responsibility to the community (as primary audience) is implicit in all aspects of a performance. Rhetorical practice, in this sense, must of necessity resist an uncritical dependence on the past, threatening instead to subvert the futility and anachronism of mere recall or nostalgia. To address this, Lovelace relies on formative and transformative practices that enable audience members not only to recall the legacy of emancipation but also, and more important, to equip themselves for broader, more productive inclusion in contemporary democratic life while simultaneously negotiating the constant threats of erasure that such participation might entail.

The author posits an idea of ethos that is filtered through the terministic screens of vernacular tradition and society in order to address an array of negotiations that have, in great measure, been designed to respond to and counteract the legacies of malaise, marginalization, and disfranchisement that undermine more productive understandings of Caribbeanness. Endowed with vernacular sensibilities, these negotiations serve as critical points of entry for the reader who is interested in the way the author relies on these and similar aspects to meaningfully articulate everyday life.[59] Lovelace describes this further as "a New World challenge" that his fiction is intended to address, which I take as a redoubling of his lifelong effort to develop a "literature of independence" and, subsequently, to describe an ethos that is under pressure to *begin* to be practiced on its own terms in what Burke might call an elaborate dancing of a Caribbean attitude, intended to highlight the author's awareness of "the correlation between mind and body."[60]

"The major theme in Earl Lovelace's work," according to Daryl Cumber Dance, "is the quest for personhood, . . . which [Lovelace] describes as '*man's view of himself*, the search as it were for his integrity.' Frequently, however, this quest is threatened as his characters encounter the impersonal, dehumanizing world."[61] I have shown this fundamental conflict throughout the preceding sections. In the specific context of his stated agenda, the rhetorical impetus for his work appears to be well served by Emilian Kavalski's notion that "the postcolonial narrative . . . presented itself as an in-between space, a metaphorical bridge between the dystopia of existence and the utopia of imagination (probing the liminality of its own narrativisation)."[62] Nonetheless, according to Kavalski, "the postcolonial symbol of the imagination acts as a transcendence of the material objectives of everyday life" that eventually coalesces in the context of an imagined, even utopian, sense of unity—that is, as an alternative to the experience of disunity that was the postcolonial norm.[63] This seems to contradict what an author such as Lovelace sets out to accomplish. In fact, the characterization of the postcolonial (and postmodern) imagination as a mode of escape inevitably leads to an all-too-familiar conclusion: that the myth of Caribbean unity, or a unified sense of Caribbeanness encapsulated in the phrase "all o' we is one," signifies the pinnacle of a historically marginalized people's desire for a viable, federated sense of their own Caribbeanness.

Rather than imply that these desires can be realized, say, in the form of actual performance and material consequences, the approach to "postcolonial narrative" conspires against the author and the audience, creating a situation that is tantamount to the concealment of those desires in the imagination. This relegation runs contrary not only to the masque as a rhetoric of display but also to rhetoric in general. If Lovelace's imagination does indeed give us a better, clearer sense of the Caribbean ethos as this author understands it—exemplifying what Kavalski describes as the "ideas-churning locus that urged the people in the Caribbean to be more resourceful in the creative interpretations of their immediate conditions of existence"—then it would behoove the author to invest in the actualization of efforts that conclude not with an imaginative demonstration but with an enactment of the ethos that he has imagined.[64] And the author would be *ethically beholden* to demonstrate this investment as a critical part of his revolutionary work.[65] This is highlighted, for example, in Lovelace's rejection of the "postcolonial" identity and his subsequent critique of its (mis)application in the context of the hollow masquerades of nationalism. In fact, according to Lovelace, "the whole idea [of a postcolonial identity] has to be looked at afresh. We need to clear the ground for a new beginning. There is the sense that once free from colonialism, I now become a finished project. None of us is the finished project. We are all unfinished projects. We need to envisage a communal project: what is it to be truly human. We were always involved in that but colonialism got in our way."[66]

The ethos represented in Lovelace's fiction is no tabula rasa, however. Despite its humanist vision, it does not elide the tragedy of the past. Still, though it may bear the stain of colonialism and history, this ethos is foregrounded by the impulse to strive for self-definition. In other words, Lovelace treats history and its hypocrisies not as determinative preoccupations but as events from which the progressively oriented eye must turn, a dream from which Caribbean people must wake if anything is to be accomplished beyond the mere imagining of it. The characteristic vernacular responses to pressures and problems that ensue in the course of living emerge, therefore, as an extended argument in which Lovelace attempts to recontextualize history in terms of its practical application by privileging the individual and collective will of the people.

It would require relatively little, even at this point, to conclude that the author's articulation of the individual's view of him- or herself, the search for personal integrity, and the overt negotiation of the process and its pitfalls all constitute a larger, ongoing attempt to construct and theorize the elements of practice as a performance of embodied knowledge—in short, a *vernacular ethos*. Indeed, this is a role to which the West Indian novelist in general has traditionally been linked. Regarding such novelists' engagement in specifically rhetorical work, for instance, Lamming observed that "the West Indian novelist did not look out across the sea to another source. He looked in and down at what had traditionally been ignored. For the first time the West Indian peasant became other than a cheap source of labour. He became, through the novelist's eye, a living existence, living in the silence and joy and fear, involved in the riot and carnival. It is the West Indian novel that has restored the West Indian peasant to his true and original status of personality."[67]

At the same time, we must contend with the point that though Lovelace acknowledges limitations with respect to the nationalistic staging of episodic treatments that are representative of a (proto)typical Caribbean ethos, the underlying humanist conception of that ethos, not to mention the obvious sociological movement of peoples in and out of the region, is subject more to the limitations of practice than to those of place. Lovelace makes clear that his main audience consists of *Caribbean* people, not just those in Trinidad, where each of these novels is set, and in terms of a rhetorical project that reaches far beyond the shores of archipelagic nations, the setting of these narratives is incidental; people "from Martinique and Grenada and St Lucia and from wherever they bring them" all augment the essential Caribbean identity Lovelace brings to form.[68] In fact, Rahim emphasizes that "to name Lovelace a national writer is not to imply that his investment in writing the nation does not simultaneously entail an embrace of the transnational and, for that matter, the universal. In short, his vision while concretized via an ongoing exploration of his native Trinidad and Tobago does not suffer from the malady of parochialism in the worst sense of the word."[69] I agree with the point and, on the heels of it, want to emphasize that Lovelace also consistently subscribes to the carnivalesque notions of fragmentation and coalescence, particularly to the extent that they can serve as a justification for minimizing jingoism and nativity in favor of more pressing matters of social (in)justice that are common to all Caribbean peoples.

That said, the sustainability of a "nation" is not a topic Lovelace tries to avoid. In fact, the realization of nationhood is key as a contextualizing feature. That is, the quest for personhood is part of the cultural milieu of postindependence fervor and failure in which the region's writers, poets, dancers, and musicians made significant attempts to define a sustainable Caribbean ethos that could effectively counteract the apparent tendency to forget what is really at stake: self-determination. So it makes sense that Lovelace would root his novels in such a theme and time. His position serves as the available platform on which to stage his project in dramatic recuperative self-assertion. As Rahim observes: "[The] natural consequence of this belief in the opportunity history has provided the region is the emergence in [Lovelace's] thinking of the nation as the primary context for *refashioning the future*. The nation is the place or ground of human endeavour, where people of various backgrounds, persuasions and gifts, by their investment in the landscape, make democratic claims on belonging and ownership."[70]

The argument central to these texts is not an argument for denying history, for without history, no tradition would exist for us to discuss. Lovelace nevertheless engages in a reordering of priorities necessary to more effectively support and promote conditions for achieving greater awareness. History is to be not escaped but rationalized, managed, understood, and reconfigured as aspects of experience that can be tapped as a reliable source of reference for a given audience. This has the added effect of priming members of that audience for the contemporary experience of being engaged as citizens in a vast transnational community. To be Caribbean, then, does not suggest a particularly exclusive preoccupation with place or jingoistic singularity in these texts or, for that matter, in any meaningful conception of Caribbeanness.

As I have shown, the significance of the dance, in particular the rhetorical purchase that it can ensure, transcends the individualistic pursuits of the dancer, moving beyond the dusty rings, broken sidewalks, or graying asphalt. Lovelace's overall approach to the notion of ethos as a fundamental characteristic that precedes practice in neighborhoods or nations emerges from a point of self-definition, not simply as an argument against history to satisfy a narrow definition of nationhood, but as a critical, subjective response. It is conceptually akin to the familiar axiom that every pot should sit on its own bottom, except that once the stewing of one's own ethos is complete, the community can be fed and can thus benefit from the yield. And the more practiced we are in aspects of the tradition, the clearer the message it embodies, the more visceral its effect, the closer we are to the ethos of the tradition. But there is still—always—more work to be done. At every point in the dance, the individual must deal with hard choices on the way to self-discovery, taking pressure, making sense out of nonsense, working through history and memory, and fighting erasure. Lovelace, explicating a notion of praxis that evokes Thomas Farrell's discussion of the idea, insists that "when we think about culture, we have to think about cultivation.

One cultivates culture through practice; it's a *lived* experience."[71] We can, the closer we are, *feel* the tradition working on us because we identify fundamentally with it, having accepted and internalized it as being meaningful to us and meant *for* us. We bring our identity, manifested in the practice of a Caribbean ethos, to bear in the face of social tensions.

For Lovelace, the carnivalesque is not a fossil that should be examined through a fixed lens of history but an evolving methodology for rhetorical display on which symbolic performances of rhetorical appeals are based. Its significance consists in the role it plays in the individual's preparation for a changing world and the levels of implication that consequently become possible. The mechanism for that change is the masque. Adaptability to that change or set of changes constitutes the rhetoric with which I am most concerned, and it is in the effectiveness of consequent adaptations that I believe the case for rhetoricality in Caribbean fiction can best be made. As an audience, we subsequently gauge effectiveness by measuring and comparing related probabilities, desires, and consequences, which are all undergirded by intention, (re)invention, and critique. Concurrently, Lovelace's manipulation of the carnivalesque as rhetorical practice, occurring beyond the veneer of celebration, equips us as rhetors for the possible transformation of unequal power relations.

The point is not merely that the ethos is carnivalesque—that is, in flux, adaptable, contingent—but that its realization prepares the vernacular rhetor to negotiate the dynamics of a situation not necessarily in his or her control. Lovelace's work exhibits the presumption and subsequent articulation of what I believe Caribbean authors have sought from the beginning: an answer to the question of where we find ourselves and how memory, history, imagination, and foresight all combine to facilitate the conscious transmission of knowledge and a contingent tradition among rhetorical bodies.[72] The basic imperative is to foster discourse that undermines the existing limitations of hegemony, nonpossession, and inequality. The Caribbean author's symbolic action, as a part of that practice, not only engages the audience in a generic communicative act but also establishes a particular relationship that is saturated with the characteristic motives, actions, and reactions of all of those involved. It is a relationship predicated on the development of and response to the stages of emergent ethos, negotiation, and authentic change. Through the successful interplay of these dynamics, the vitality and efficacy of carnivalesque concepts are able to unfold and be sustained as a rhetoric of Caribbean fiction.

CHAPTER 5

Inhabiting the Digital Vernacular
THE OLD TALKERS, THE CARIBLOGGERS, AND THE JAMETTES

> Hello Kevin I am Making a Email For You. I Love You. I Hope That You Are Fine.
> —Layla Browne, personal e-mail correspondence

> Nothing is more lively and more feminine than deviation.
> —Jane Sutton, "The Taming of the Polos/Polis"

> I'm going into Labor and Jamaica's Prime Minister is speaking out for gay rights; #talkaboutmotherfuckingmiracles
> —@staceyannchin, Twitter post

FOR CARIBBEAN PEOPLE, WHO HAVE emerged collectively from a history of fragmentation and coalescence, the notion of a "virtual community" ought to be passé;[1] at the very least, it ought to be fairly easy to conceive, if only because they have traditionally had to contend with presuppositions about their ability to cohere on a complex vernacular level while devising alternative means of expression to ensure that kind of activity. The way Caribbean users conceptualize and articulate their online activity thus relates closely to the frames and features they employ in everyday offline contexts. Relatedly, the texts they produce are undergirded with a familiar carnivalesque logic. Indeed, the operation of Caribbean-ness online belongs among other oppositional consciousnesses that have provided what Chela Sandoval refers to as a "methodology of the oppressed."[2] Despite the obvious boundaries—the global, social, and democratic divides that are far too well known[3]—Caribbean practitioners are nevertheless equipped to define and refine what they can do online, testing the elasticity of the borders they encounter to make space where their familiar discourses can flourish toward the gradual achievement of material ends. This is not to eschew the very real issue of limited access and de facto marginalization among whole populations but rather to investigate what those with access do and the degree to which their performances solidify the vernacular impulses I have previously discussed.

As the Internet continues to open up to more varied communities, practitioners log on with their own varied traditions, mores, and sociolinguistic codes, bringing them to bear in a space where those identities can possibly flourish. Online, normative conceptions of traditional social practices are not only challenged but also redesigned according to evolving conceptions of Caribbeanness. Given a Caribbean cultural presence operating in this context, I wonder what kind of work this online activity can achieve, despite the persistent effects of marginalization that occur within mainstream technologies. For me, the overarching questions are the following: How do Caribbean people strategically apply the dynamics familiar to them (e.g., orality and masquing) while making more public use of mainstream technologies? Put another way, how do they allow themselves to evolve online while simultaneously resisting the tendency to be "conditioned" by the technologies at their disposal?[4] How are Caribbean users able to Twitter, Facebook, Google+, LinkedIn, and "reply all" their way into a culturally, linguistically, and rhetorically indeterminate space without fully giving up what they hold fundamentally as their own culture, language, and rhetorical tradition? The answer is largely one of priority.

With respect to the three genres I will examine—chatting, "cariblogging," and video sharing—these activities are largely underwritten by a carnivalesque imperative, an impetus that compels the rhetors to attend primarily to achieving visibility *in direct resistance* to the experience of invisibility in what I call the "digital public" of cyberspace. This ontic activity involves the deliberate deployment of countermeasures that thrive on the indeterminacy of the medium and on the attendant opportunities rhetors have to perform their identities in those environments. For these rhetors, the digital public is limbo space where the materiality of pole and ground has been supplanted by virtual factors of "global surveillance and personal alienation."[5] Additionally, the resulting cybercultural activities serve as key demonstrations of rhetorical (re)invention among those who engage technology as part of an implicit inquiry concerning the Caribbean user's desire for and participation in global citizenship, calling into question not merely *who* we are online but also *where* we could be and *what* we can do while there.

My contention is not simply that technology allows Caribbean users to interconnect multimodally on various social levels, maintain contact over long physical distances, and share information relevant to the survival of cultural practice as a whole, though all these consequences certainly occur and can easily be observed in the abundance of culturally specific sites that represent specific islands or the region in general. We can see, for instance, that oral, literary, and visual practices on social networking sites—including WordPress, YouTube, Twitter, and Tumblr—enable the continuity of traditional forms of vernacular consciousness, agency, and activism. The particular virtues of such media, however, may seem to lie in providing opportunities to conceal oneself from the public, whereas my observations suggest that many users are invested in declaring their participation in an authentically Caribbean presence. These vernacular practitioners, as well as the audiences who identify most closely with them, are obliged to subscribe to an overarching sense of ethos rather than a situational one in order to realize an enduring legitimacy online, beyond themselves, and long after they have disconnected.

ETHOS AND THE DIGITAL VERNACULAR

Acts of online representation (including the roles of practitioner and audience/conversant) and the unrelenting sense of identification and identity that gives rise to, connects, and maintains them suggest that the ethos of the users has survived the process of inteconnectivity intact. In 1994, a year before the National Science Foundation Network (NSFNET) was decommissioned and the Internet was fully commercialized, there was the calypsonian Winston "the Mighty Shadow" Bailey's song "Gossiping." In an age characterized by the obsessive compulsion to share information, this song, about the local macos (gossips) Rosemarie and Eunice, rings familiar. In this case, Rosemarie's impulse to disseminate information as widely as possible presumably leads to universal knowledge of Jack and Imelda's apparent transgressions, regarding which Rosemarie is compelled to tell and tell and tell, "till she forget who she tell."[6] The efficiency of the macocious act is undeniable, with an effect that is recursive rather than conclusive. I will not go so far as to insinuate that Shadow's characterization is prophetic or that the song functions as a primer of any kind for Internet users. Shadow is not describing the Internet, but if his evocation of the pervasive nature of oral activity is at all indicative of a familiar vernacular practice, illustrated in the characterization of gossip as a rhizomatic activity that quickly proliferates throughout the community, it is because he is aware that these practices maintain (and are maintained by) the vitality of that community. That is, the key here is not that Imelda and Jack have their private business aired but that there is a deep familiarity with the gossiper's role in the success of a social network. This is already the case with Caribbean Internet users, many of whom refer colloquially to their social interactions in related terms. Facebook, for example, is rather unflatteringly referred to as *macobook* or *fastbook*, both references to the performance of publicizing one's own business and minding everyone else's.[7]

These connotations suggest that the practitioner and audience are engaged in a continuous narrative that includes a vernacularized awareness of technology in the process of rhetorical (re)invention. Often, they subscribe to predetermined codes of "old talk" (or "shit talk") that are then enacted as a negotiation of what Karel McIntosh refers to as the "brazenness and transparency of the social media environment."[8] Consider an example from a chat conducted on Facebook where two users (I will call them "Brian" and "Peter") engage in some old talk. This particular conversation revolves around a central topic of free will in the course of human activity that unfolds as a complex prophetic commentary. Supplementary discourse strands are strategically deployed throughout the discussion; these strands touch on religion, impropriety, government, oppression, the paradox of church and state, sexual deviance, pop culture, hegemony, and retribution.[9] Each subtopic is used at various points to initiate, frame, posit, exemplify, rebut, and concede aspects of the argument:

> Brian: in fact he allowed us to have free will so he could be entertained
>
> Peter: me too. but, assuming there is no intention of separating the two (church and state) where does the accountability lie?
>
> Brian: accountability is only to appease the masses when water get more than flower padna
> is like the cowboy x story on sesame street
>
> Peter: i dont know if i buy the god-as-voyeur narrative (a la George Carlin)
> lol
> i hear yuh
> but it could also be like black bart, tho
> also sesame st
> you recall bart was, in fact, repentant, at the end of the skit
>
> Brian: accountability is a temporary condition to appease the people and distract them from the greater ills that continue to blight them
> cowboy x wasn't tho, he keep fucking up the town, but the people were happy[10]

Despite the opportunities for synchronous interaction between Brian and Peter, the example shows that traditional turn taking is replaced with a more dynamic form that benefits from an asynchronous transcript (and the apparently diminished need to recall every detail of what was being discussed). This underscores their facility with the informality of a less constrained social interaction that leaves the conversation to go wherever the participants please, unfolding organically—which is why we are able to join them, relatively seamlessly, in the midst of an ongoing discussion. When Brian gives his initial opinion of the paradox of an omnipotent God who creates beings that, having free will, remain outside his control, doing so simply to amuse itself, Peter's response immediately following bears no reference to it. In fact, Peter's response to Brian's initial statement of the paradox is actually delayed for some time. Peter's first comment is aligned with one of Brian's earlier points and uses that common ground as a platform to initiate a question of "accountability" with regard to "church and state." Brian's first response is to Peter's question of accountability. Following the newly introduced tangent, Brian remarks at first:

> accountability is only to appease the masses when water get more than flower padna
>
> is like the cowboy x story on sesame street

Brian then follows another reference to the fallacy of accountability with a further explanation of the "cowboy x" reference as a metaphor for the capitulation to hegemony that occurs in lieu of actual liberatory action:[11]

> accountability is a temporary condition to appease the people and distract them from the greater ills that continue to blight them
>
> cowboy x wasn't tho, he keep fucking up the town, *but the people were happy*

Appearing a few lines (and minutes) later is Peter's response: "i dont know if i buy the god-as-voyeur narrative." The inherent skepticism of the comment is temporarily bracketed, as Peter opts to respond to Brian's earlier *Sesame Street* reference instead of expanding on his opposition to God as a voyeur. Fair enough.

But what sets this exchange apart from other, non-Caribbean ones is that it affirms the vernacular character of an interconnected relationship that contextualizes the exchange and makes successful authoring and coauthoring possible. To maintain a basic continuity and interrelational logic, users such as Brian and Peter deliberately employ authenticating measures, orthographic displays that are often based on creolized (and some phonetic) spellings, as well as syntactic choices that exhibit the rhetor's familiarity with and membership in the virtual community. To maintain the authenticity of the exchange, both Brian and Peter use numerous orthographic features, as illustrated in table 5, to replicate some of the oral (syntactic and phonetic) features of creolized language variety, doing so even though their performance was originally intended as a private interaction that, presumably, would obviate the need for an authenticating performance.

Neither their interaction nor the text they produce is a static practice; this example, like all similar others, provides only a glimpse, a screenshot of an active, evolving discourse. As a matter of fact, Brian and Peter move back and forth along a familiar sociolinguistic continuum, relying on their familiarity with acrolectal, mesolectal, and basilectal linguistic features for effectiveness—though, as the conversation goes on, they more often choose basilectal features (which can be distinguished, say, from typographical errors). For example, at one point they use highly creolized discourse to emphasize their outrage, giving

TABLE 5. Orthographic features used in Internet chat

Orthographic feature	Examples (including their standardized equivalents)
Interpellations	*Padna* (partner, friend), *my brother*
Zero copula	*is like* (it's like, it is like); *he keep* (he keeps)
	i letting (I'm letting); *water get* (water gets [to be])
	i go leave (I'm going to leave, I will leave); *you right* (you're right)
Inflectional spelling	*bun* (burn)
	kyah (can't, cannot)
	madda (mother)
	ah (I, of)
	yuh (you)
	mah (me, my)
	de (the)
	dem (them)
	dey (they, their, there)
	dat (that)
	dis (this)
	they (they, their, there)
Nonstandard subject-verb agreement	*priest molest, water get, dey kick*
Maxim and exclamations	*When water get more than flower*[a] (when things are out of balance, out of sync, or out of control)
	Is fire for all ah dem (It's fire for all of them)
	Bun dem (burn them)
	well yes (exclamation, formulaic signaling beginning or conclusion of exchange)

[a]This is sometimes presented as "water get more than flour."

the conversation a deeply apocalyptic tone and discarding the relatively abstract, quasi-esoteric fragments in favor of concrete metonymic examples, such as the 2008 fall of the insurance giant American International Group (AIG), to justify their critique:

Peter: i mean, is 6 of one, 1/2 doz of the other, so we dont really need to split he=airs on this
Brian: maybe becase we put more weight on accountability tto God
Peter: is fire for all ah dem
Brian: but yuh right . . . condemn de lot ah dem
Peter: i go leave the condemning to the master, but they go get what they have to get, tho
Brian: well i letting de master kno now dat ah support de condemnation
Peter: indeed! a little black stalin vibes
        bun dem!

They arrive at a point of total agreement ("is fire for all ah dem" and "yuh right . . . condemn de lot ah dem") when a specific mode of retribution is put forward. Though Peter initiates this segment of the exchange, Brian later substantiates it with his own anecdote; Peter responds in kind:

Brian: dat is why dey kick mih outta confirmation class
        ah wouldn't yield
Peter: they kick me out after
Brian: but from young ah question dey bullshit
Peter: and i didnt care
        some shit just didnt make sense to me

This reflective moment plays a more important role than does the classic pop cultural reference to *Sesame Street* characters of the 1970s. Using specifically Caribbean creolized features to identify and authenticate their exchange, Brian and Peter authorize each other to take certain liberties in the ensuing discussion.[12] In truth, while this exchange reveals little about the two on an interpersonal level, it illustrates how vernacular language, culture, and worldview enable forms of active and evolving negotiation. To me, the transcript suggests they are encouraged by a history of adaptability that has served those who have had to find a way or make one when none seemed available. They boast about it, in fact. That adaptability in turn accentuates the malleability of their discourse. Their activity demonstrates collaborative critique and contributes directly to the evolving performance of Caribbean expressions in mainstream contexts. The interaction, as well as the efficiency with which their performance is likely to be understood, thus illustrates an ethos that many Caribbean users deploy online. It is carnivalesque, furthermore, in that it enables a dramatic (re)enactment of social opinion, with Brian and Peter relying on their shared understanding of ethos to determine the credibility and sustainability of their respective positions. Using common vernacular experience as the critical lens, they indulge in a conversation that works pragmatically—that is, as a counterweight to given topics, concepts, or histories in need of critique. They express and engage with situations of general dissatisfaction, producing a collaborative text that culminates in a statement mutually intended to demonstrate their raised (or revised) awareness:

> Brian: well yes padna . . . thanks for the intellectual stimulation and dis course . . . ah could rest easy now
> Peter: knowing yuh not alone
> look for me, men, i here
> Brian: fuh dat
> Peter: but i going and sleep, tho
> Brian: definitely, we go pick up
> Peter: yeah, my brother
> Brian: yeah padna, bless up
> Peter: laters

Old talk may be redefined in the online context as technologically enhanced cultural commentary that recognizes the limits to access but also builds on available opportunities for participatory practice. Such activity thereby influences the effectiveness of what participants see and read. From the vantage point of this kind of technologized activity, we are better prepared to discuss the implications of key themes in Caribbean discourse—such as access, masquing, and representation—that produce and support agency among practitioners. More than a method of sharing information, old talk includes familiarizing aspects that have a suasive function transferable to online contexts. It not only reinforces the many social and interpersonal bonds that exist in their familiar communities; it also helps define the paths that a virtual community may take to move through its digital confines, to endure them, and to embrace their divergent influences. In this community, rhetor, act, audience, context, and consequence are all made to inhabit a space that can invite or repel morality, offering the option to participate, whether passively or actively, to those present.

ACCOUNTS OF OURSELVES IN THE "CARIBLOGOSPHERE"

Another key factor in gauging the overall authenticity and probable effectiveness of a rhetorically inflected Caribbean text is the degree to which it is public, the degree to which it may be considered accessible to a public that can see, read, and respond to it in the context of a shared or perceived Caribbeanness. This goes beyond the need to make things and texts available for readers to maco. An ethos, of course, whether Caribbean or otherwise, is not created in a vacuum, nor does it emerge from one. Instead, it results from activities that plainly demonstrate the deliberate construction of personal and public character; it takes form as a result of the rhetor's abilities to deliberate on given issues, to articulate his or her position through dialogic interplay, and thereby to inspire trust among members of an audience.[13] But the audience is circumscribed in the previous example. Although Brian and Peter's discursive mode(l) exhibits oralized features, it faces a major limitation with respect to accessibility for an outside audience. As a private text unlikely to become public, an activity of this kind will probably accomplish little for a broader audience. Short of its inclusion in this book, for instance, the exchange might never have been read by anyone but two interlocutors. They are anonymous; their exchange is partial. Public though the exchange may be—that is, to the extent that it exists encoded as ones and zeros in a cyberspatial realm—the respective authors still presume a certain degree of privacy, which is provisionally afforded by the format of their chosen forum.

Blogs, on the other hand, are a more public genre. Whether by eliciting judgment, censure, censorship, or critique, they allow more extensive rhetorical work among wider audiences in ways unavailable to private chat sessions. As the following examples illustrate, this comparatively more effective public availability depends on establishing an ethos that will sustain productive interaction among Caribbean authors and their audiences. By satisfying some of the familiar tenets of discourse in public spaces, their efforts lead to the following results: a declaration of terms and issues contributing to a sense of the common good that can be fostered among them; the reconstitution of images and representations of Caribbean people in public; and the establishment of shared (and shareable) codes that can aid in framing these issues and images, resulting in the (re)enactment of social opinion by an engaged Caribbean audience. Such efforts thus stand out as examples of the carnivalesque impulse of (re)invention—the pragmatist self-definition and adaptability discussed in chapter 1—that endows users with techniques for establishing and sustaining a Caribbean identity online.

Although Technorati.com's "State of the Blogosphere" does not include statistics on Caribbean blogs, Sharon Meraz suggests that what has come to be known colloquially as the "Caribbean blogosphere" began to take shape around 2001.[14] Nevertheless, even though no conclusive list of active Caribbean blogs yet exists, we can qualitatively identify them by their expressions of Caribbeanness used as deliberate statements of self-representation. The texts offered here are by no means paradigmatic (or rigidly definitional beyond their obvious subscription to carnivalesque sensibilities); they are instead meant to serve as representative examples of what Amy Tracy Wells says early adopters of the Internet generally sought in that medium: a *"channel* to an available and authoritative source" that could facilitate but not necessarily dictate communication. Wells found that many of these early adopters chose "the channel that could link them to the most people and sources, or literally the most 'social' selection," according to their interests, values, and beliefs.[15] But there is more to it than that. While indicative of a general trend, the evolving role of the "cariblogger" can be somewhat more elusive when viewed with as generic a lens as the one posited by Wells.[16] And attempting to pinpoint a specific role for a vernacular audience in the vast indeterminacy of cyberspace can produce more confusion than clarity. Conceding to the limitations of the means available to me at this stage, I want to call attention to features that illustrate a more overt rhetorical subscription to a vernacular ethos, as well as to the ways in which those features may be activated for an audience with access to them.

On the surface, some caribloggers can seem to differ markedly from the traditional Caribbean speaker; that is, they may not necessarily claim to be entrusted with the specific narrativistic role of spreading the word about issues relevant to Caribbean people, or of letting them know what is going on, or of keeping the talk (that is, the subject at hand) in constant circulation. Some, with the support of microblogging and short-form applications such as Twitter, even revel in the performance of an ethos of self-appointedness if not a sense of playful self-importance. That is, the cariblogger can sometimes assume or attempt to enact an individualized ethos, whether as solipsistic complainer or as critic, rather than one developed specifically for the benefit of the audience. At other moments, however, the dynamics are resolved with the organic development of publicly reflective discourse practices, the approach to and awareness of the body's materiality *and* the materiality of the text constructed to embody an author's references to it, and increasingly overt subscriptions to a discernibly vernacular ethos that promote effective interaction between bloggers and their audiences.

For instance, explaining his rationale for blogging in a seemingly conventional format, Taran Rampersad admits that "every writer has a story. Something drives them to write—to share their perspectives"; he adds: "In my case, it was a need to document things really *for myself.*"[17] Rampersad, a self-described "reserved blogger,"[18] implies that if, as is likely, his perspectives and documents evolve—either growing into a more extensive commentary or diminishing to a skeletal series of salient details—the message will retain the essence of what it was intended to communicate because it was intended *primarily* for him. In this configuration, where the individuality of the cariblogger is privileged, the risk of misinterpretation by an audience remains minimal because the potential effects and responses will be moot. Additionally, Rampersad's comment implies that the subsequent (mis)interpretation by a disembodied audience—which Rampersad neither sees nor interacts with directly—does not erase the basic expression of self-interest but, on the contrary, confirms it. In other words, the virtual absence of an physical audience—or the presence of a virtual one—emphasizes the author's subjectivity and elides even the desire for an audience. That is, while Rampersad suggests that there *may be* some degree of responsibility to the audience that undergirds the message itself, he also implies that he can easily avoid the responsibilities of that role by reserving the right to invoke a desire for monologue over dialogue. It follows that in electing to blog, Rampersad is privileging egocentrism as a default, attempting only *secondarily* (if at all) to balance what he produces with what would be intended for audience consumption. This kind of activity suggests that, in terms of motives and otherwise, the cariblogger may not be so different from many mainstream bloggers after all. As a matter of fact, the appeal of a blog like Rampersad's may be measured in the degree to which it can mimic the genre instead of challenging its norms.

This may be the case, but I am not entirely convinced by the rationale behind Rampersad's disclaimer—just as, I suspect, the rest of his audience is not—particularly as it contradicts its author's awareness of a growing Caribbean presence online. To begin with, no kind of blogging can be so easily dismissed as the innocuous rantings of a single author writing for him- or herself alone, the virtualized equivalent of a talking head in a hi-fi echo chamber fitted with an upgraded soapbox. Access to a global audience all but dispels the myth of navel-gazing once a post has been uploaded. In fact, when bloggers post, it is highly likely that some people will read; when they posit, some people are likely to engage; and when they suggest, some people may, as a matter of course, respond. However, rather than suggest that Rampersad is just "bumping he gum" as part of a self-centered "grand-charge," I argue that his relationship with his audience is deliberately inflected with a Caribbean subjectivity. The gesture—specifically, the suggestion of a strong *monologic* impulse that actually results in an increased probability of *dialogic* exchange—also exemplifies a consciously vernacular approach to dialogic online activity. It aligns with (and thus aids in the articulation of) a strategy that is modified for deployment in cyberspace. Indeed, the gesture is somewhat reminiscent of a dragon dance, an allusion that reframes the disclaimer as a masque: a performance that masquerades monologically but is amplified for display and, in actuality, depends completely on the implication, reception, and active participation of an audience to determine its relative success or failure. In the following excerpt, Rampersad acknowledges his role as an individual, but one who is also situated within the broader ethic of a vernacular expressive practice: "As I learn more, my focus shifts, and as my focus shifts, I end up writing about more. Typically, I write what *I think*, and try to explain it to others. Not everyone does that. But if everyone in the world was like me, the world would make sense and I would have nothing to write about."

As Rampersad continues to explain his composing process, his focus shifts to a more pointed methodology for achieving what he thinks ought to be at stake in the development of an effective Caribbean and global inquiry. Notice that his argument is based on the premise of a collective awareness of motives among authors and audiences that will determine the nature of the texts produced: "I think everyone who is writing on the web from the Caribbean needs to consider why they write what they write, and why they read what they read. In fact, I think that on a global level, people need to consider these things." After having posited a general set of guidelines that readers and writers ("they") ought to follow, he takes a series of steps to advance his argument and highlight the importance of his recommendations. This allows the reader to interrogate the validity of his ethic *and* the viability of his method. First, however, he reemphasizes his individuality: "As far as myself—I'm all over the place. I *don't* really have a focus on issues; I just write what I know or what I don't know and want to know." Notice that the suggestion of a conscious methodology is brought into even greater relief by Rampersad's attempt to distinguish himself as a separate individual: "Weblogs are participative, and the quality of the people who participate by leaving comments really defines a weblog to me. But I'm not claiming to be a good example of what a weblogger should do—in many cases, I am not." By deliberately *contradicting himself*, Rampersad emphasizes and demonstrates the logic of his argument that "everyone needs to consider why they write what they write, and read what they read." The contradiction serves to moderate the relative inefficiency of his method as it stands in contrast to his more general(izable) recommendation to Caribbean users. He realigns his original motive to meet what he perceives as the audience's revised expectations. The move clinches his argument, which amplifies his concern for readers who are critically conscious of their engagement online, as well as their role in the collaborative creation and performance of public(ized) texts.

Like all other forms of rhetorical activity in Caribbean contexts, these performances are oriented toward the possible coalescence of a sustainable discourse community, whether virtual or real. So despite the playful pretense, I think it is fair to assume that Rampersad imagines an audience whose ethos operates parallel to, if not fully in concert with, his own conception of a cariblogger's role as a producer and consumer of text. Regarding his readers, he notes, "The audience typically comes back and tells me what is on their mind, and that feedback can really be worthwhile—if you have quality people participating." The topics and discursive features produced in these texts are recognizable not because bloggers privilege technology but because they identify with and practice an ethos that is definitively Caribbean. As a result, they are able to establish a clear set of terministic screens that can be effectively applied in a range of discursive contexts. Take the following post, entitled "Dear Rihanna." In it, the cariblogger Attillah Springer comments on the 2009 incident in which the pop star Rihanna was battered at the hands of her boyfriend, Chris Brown:

> Pardon the intrusion in your personal affairs. I expect you are used to it, by now.
> Your love life isn't my business. In truth I didn't care to know the details of your life at all until I heard about what Chris Brown did to you.
> And I don't know if my words will have any effect on you, but I feel like I have

to say it. Not just for you, but for myself and for all the young women out there who are your fans, who enjoy the entertainment you have chosen to share with us....

This scares me, Rihanna. Especially since women like you are role models. The epitome of this bizarre construct called modern woman. You, the post feminist self-determined Barbie, who have money, a top career, men the world over who practically worship you and thighs to make the rest of us women die of jealousy. You who are all these things can't possibly accept such behaviour from a man.

I fear that the news of your return to your abuser sets a bad precedent to all the Caribbean girls becoming women who admire you, your rise to fame, your spectacular claiming of Hollywood. *You, a regular Bajan girl that could be any regular other girl from any regular other island.*[19]

While the currency of her critique consists of legitimately feminist overtones, Springer's work operates firmly within an economy of expression that marks her project as characteristic and critical of Caribbean identity. It is clear from the very outset that Springer never really presumes any privacy between herself and Rihanna and that her letter is intended as a public address to women who "would rather take the occasional licks than lonely nights or trying to find someone else to love us." In this instance, masking as a viable strategy of concealment is out of the question. In fact, the blogger goes to some effort to implicate members of her audience as active collaborators in her rhetorical endeavor.

First off, Springer attempts to redirect the audience's focus away from Rihanna's body, opting for a wider, more inclusive focus on more abstract topics such as "love and power and sex and if we will ever figure out how to balance them all." This measure lets Springer redefine the scope of her interests, the manner in which she intends to weigh in on the scandal, as well as the point on which she believes the audience ought to focus. Springer's choice to decentralize the obvious speaks to a more general issue, for even though she counts herself as "fortunate to say that no man ever put God out of his thoughts to raise his hand to hit" her, her thesis hinges on the fact that *any* woman, including herself, could suffer the same fate as Rihanna's at any time and *as easily*. Rihanna's reputation as an internationally successful pop icon is soon jettisoned in favor of her potential respectability as a "regular Bajan girl." In addition, Springer implicates herself along with her audience in the discussion and its outcome: "My fear is that I am part of a minority of women. That there are more women out there who have experienced some kind of physical abuse at the hands of someone who allegedly loves them." The resulting identification with the audience is designed to operate viscerally (that is, on a "regular" vernacular level), allowing Springer to launch her critique on behalf of "regular other girl[s] from any regular other island."

Ultimately, Springer pushes for a more critical approach to Rihanna's ethos as a role model, as well as the likely benefit of that approach for the audience in question. She concludes with her own recommendation for balancing love, power, and sex, factors that seem to exist solely in the context of de facto intransigence; embedding it in the address to Rihanna, she makes a much broader appeal, one that implies that a change would be possible if Rihanna and women like her could "negotiate around and past the problem of abuse and add your voices and your strength and your ideas to women who don't have the resources or the confidence in their own voices to break themselves out of cycles of violence."

It is difficult to make the point any more succinctly than Springer does. But what, in the way of rhetoric, are we to conclude from it? Springer's commentary exemplifies rhetorical masquing because it centers simultaneously on the overdetermined inscription of social values on bodies that have been publicly claimed by a vernacular audience and a critical approach to the body that relies on what the audience may be willing to presume (about those values as part of a broader sense of Caribbeanness). By virtue of their shared knowledge, the audience is always already implicated in the discussion, but in exchanges such as these, participants are especially invited to either identify as Caribbean or demonstrate that their sympathies and sensibilities align accordingly in order to effectively participate in the gradual development of a public opinion. Springer's effort to divert explicit attention from Rihanna's body thus doubles as an effort to acknowledge the vulnerability of "regular" unprotected bodies and the representation of those bodies as overdetermined texts on constant public display and subject to public consumption in a culture that is unable (or unwilling) to satisfactorily and decisively resolve the problem. The critique thrives on the presumption that there is a moral imperative—possessed by the author and presumed of the audience—to be taken on abstract but no less familiar terms: love, power, sex, and their related dynamics. This imperative is expressed in the vernacular identification with the "regular other" and thereby surpasses the singular limitations of individual motives, bodies, and performances.

MASQUING THE BODY PROVERBIAL

The aforementioned criteria for identification help underscore the point that cariblogs succeed rhetorically only to the extent that their respective authors can identify so well with their audiences that they are able to produce extensive interpretations of particular displays relying solely on the deployment of features the audiences are willing to take for granted. In other words, a blogger who has established a viable discursive bond with his or her audience increases the probability that the persuasiveness of a given rhetorical act will hinge not on explicit evidence but on what the audience is able to infer from well-placed allusions to implicit—even insider—knowledge.

On the cariblog *Cheese-on-Bread: From Barbados to the World*, for instance, Bajegirl participates in the Rihanna–Chris Brown battery scandal with a commentary that, like Rampersad's and Springer's, is designed to establish and ensure a dialogic exchange that privileges recognizably vernacular sensibilities. Like Springer, Bajegirl demonstrates an awareness of material realities—that is, the connection of symbolic discourse to the bodies that motivate, produce, or respond to discourse. But Bajegirl takes the issue a step further, such that we may even consider her approach comparatively more inclusive and comprehensive, flourishing in a way Springer's example does not. Predictably, she relies on shared knowledge and identification that goes beyond a narrow focus (here, Rihanna's body) and typifies vernacular activity aimed at achieving a more general sense of identification with an audience. In this instance, Bajegirl sets the parameters for relevance among a fairly specific audience. Unlike Springer, however, she broadens her discursive focus not by diverting attention but by calling attention to Rihanna's image, her body, and what it could provide when subjected to critical vernacular scrutiny. To accomplish this, Bajegirl transforms Rihanna's body into a symbol far more workable for her purpose: a parcel of land. As the second reason listed in "Six Reasons Why Rihanna Would Marry Chris Brown," she writes: "*She's really pregnant.* Well, time will tell soon enough 'cause as we Bajans say, *you can hide and buy land, but you can't hide and work it.*"[20] In the discourse of empires and enclaves, land is perhaps the most elemental currency of power. It is a conspicuous feature of vernacular life, serving as a representation of historical injustices and contemporary norms. There is nothing more visible than land, nothing more ubiquitous, and few things are more prized. Even a symbolic reference to land evokes the natural world, including its flora and fauna, its sugar, spice, bauxite, and pitch. At the same time, it further evokes commerce and nostalgia; homelands, nations, and plantations; the lack of opportunities for ownership among the underclass; being bought, sold, and sold out; and escape, economic survival, negotiations of poverty, and freedom.[21]

In contrast to Springer's enthymematic activity, which implicates the audience by leaving gaps they would probably fill if they were inclined to engage in the discussion, Bajegirl relies on the conventional wisdom of a proverb to make her argument conspicuously self-evident. By doing so, she actively frames her critique within an economy of display and materialist awareness, making the constitutive factors (orality, materiality, the vulgarized body) conspicuous, even unavoidable, to her audience. The body is recast as an object that can be bought, sold, walked on, worked over, beaten, fucked, and fucked up at the hands of a "lover." In this particular context, Bajegirl uses the proverb to initiate a critique of male dominance and complicity, which she views as inadequately addressed in discourse of the everyday. The author strives to make an implicit reference to pervasive sexual politics explicit for the audience: using the audience's familiarity with the symbolic reference, the author contributes directly to the possible formation of public opinion and public consciousness. Her efforts result in a text that has the potential to spur meaningful action rather than simply entrench cynicism and malaise. It thus serves as a public indictment of persistent misogyny and overwhelmingly masculinist discourse that positions the female body anachronistically as a naked commodity subject to arbitrary transfers in ownership and the whims of its owner. Bajegirl's symbolic reference to land, however, does more than just express the abstract intersections of domination and sexual overtones; when connected to the materiality of what may be perceived in the world, as well as the related effects of what may be conceived, it also orients the audience toward more localized—even nationalized—considerations of what ought to be done in response. It resonates so effectively, in fact, that the same proverb is evoked by one of Bajegirl's readers, Khaidji, in an acrostic poem entitled "So Confused."[22] Taking her cue from Bajegirl, Khaidji attempts to connect an identical symbolic consideration of material effects located offline. She is no doubt aware of the abstract concepts contained in proverbs and maxims and their integral relation to material causes, so her use of the same proverb in her poem further substantiates the central point of Bajegirl's critique: the transferable body, while animate(d), is ultimately at risk of being seen as passive, receptive, and without agency in the occurrence or consequence of violence done to it.

The crux of Bajegirl's methodology in her persona as a cariblogging critic is located in her choice *to write about the traditional talk about materiality*; that is, the rhetorical deployment of the proverb implies the author's recognition of a "starting point" that could lead to possible material change rather than to the discursive stagnation of a "forced poetics" that Glissant has described.[23] This is an important distinction because it anchors Bajegirl's material awareness in both orality's transferability into literate practice and the literal reference to oral practice. As a consequence, members of her audience are invited to collaborate with her to deconstruct the complexity of the proverb and are implicated in the consequence(s) of broader considerations of the probable material consequence of her discussion. This is achieved through a process of recognizing and striking a balance between localized particulars, acknowledging their rhetorical applications, and explaining their broader social implications.[24] The fulcrum of this process is located at the intersection of symbolism and materiality.

Rather than merely deploy inexplicable complexity with little or no desire for consequence, Bajegirl exhibits a degree of rhetorical awareness that extends further than the reliance on shared knowledge. It is, in fact, an awareness that undergirds the author's deliberat(iv)e efforts to unpack linguistic codes, particularly since her motive is geared toward the activation and explanation of principles embodied in a traditional proverb. This increased awareness becomes more apparent when, a few weeks after presenting her initial list of reasons, Bajegirl reintroduces the scandal in the context of an even more serious discussion of domestic violence, social complicity, and the murder of Sophia Phillips by her boyfriend:

> Yet another Barbadian woman lost her life to domestic violence. . . .
> I have lost count of the number of women who have died in the last five to 10 years at the hands of their husbands or boyfriends. One beat his wife to death with a piece of wood in front of their children; another abducted his girlfriend from her workplace and killed her. Yet another stalked his ex-girlfriend mercilessly all over the island, finally catching up to her and murdering her near the home [at which] she was secretly staying.[25]

The effect of the composite masque (frivolity, light gossip, and proverb) that appears in her previous post is compounded by the deeper tragedy of Phillips's murder and the heightened urgency of an enduring danger women face. Together, these qualities form a reconstituted masque that further amplifies Bajegirl's outrage, as well as the need for redress among members of the broader community offline. Having already established the shape of her critique by deploying the proverb about land, she goes on to explicitly invoke a sense of shared responsibility, choosing to shame her audience into action by relying on the strategic reactivation of related everyday vernacular practice: "How many more women are going to die before the authorities and all of us take this issue of domestic violence seriously? Almost daily many of us *see and hear* women being brutalised by their partners, yet we're reluctant to get involved because 'we don't want to get involved in other peoples' business.' Since when do Bajans don't want to get involved in other peoples' business? Only when it matters, it seems."[26] Bajegirl does not end with the sensationalistic treatment of Rihanna's misfortune as an abstraction. On the contrary, the episode helps publicly reinforce her own understanding of community responsibility, not to mention the counterintuitiveness and counterproductivity of "not getting involved," which she sees as anathema to a familiar vernacular grounding. Thus, instead of merely marking her commentary as a purely solipsistic one, or localizing her critique for an audience of Bajan girls (other "Bajegirls" like herself), Bajegirl uses the exigency of a scandal to masque her critique of audience members who share a central role in the prosperity or failure of their communities:

> One survivor of domestic violence, Liesl Daisley, is saying enough is enough and is doing something about it, and we all need to follow suit.
> As tired as I am of the Rihanna/Chris Brown saga, the upside of that sad chapter is that the seriousness of domestic violence is being discussed worldwide. But we have to back up the talk with action as well—the courts, police and

we citizens have to band together and fight this social scourge. Ladies, today it's someone else, but tomorrow it may be your mother, sister, best friend or you.[27]

Of course, the success of Bajegirl's appeals depends on whether her audience will have access to them; obviously, limitations in access decrease the likelihood that the message will take root among a larger audience, despite its rhetorical potential. Ironically, it is the very fragility of such rhetorical exchanges that fuels the imperative to engage, driving the agenda and shaping both opinion and consequence among caribloggers and their audiences with every transmission, post, or reading. To reiterate, then, a productive online presence is based not only on the practitioner's discourse but also on the fact that the practitioner and audience choose and are permitted to take part in a sanctioned, potentially self-regulating exchange that relies equally on globalized assumptions and the presumption of traditional, localized values in the digital public. Nonetheless, while vernacular rhetors depend heavily on a familiar catalog of rhetorical features when working online, they do not necessarily attempt to replicate offline experience; they no doubt recognize the two realms as distinct. Still, bloggers such as Rampersad, Springer, and Bajegirl demonstrate that having access satisfies only part of a more elaborate agenda: having a meaningful, sustainable presence online. They show, in fact, that a more comprehensive Caribbean presence depends on an intricate stirring up of shared understandings and the conscious enactment of expressions that are designed to elicit a particular audience response. To the extent that caribloggers such as Bajegirl choose to be representative and credible sources communicating publicly on their audiences' behalf, with their audiences responding in kind, there is a constant negotiation with respect to the implicit expectation that the narrative will evolve into understanding among the audience and the larger discourse community or that it will not. And though its expression may not immediately be clear to others, this "understanding" is nevertheless probable because it falls under the rubric of traditional motives, expressions, and responses that function among rhetorically astute practitioners who deploy orality as a key feature of their cybercultural presence.

DE/EN/CODING THE DIGITAL JAMETTE

Similar to other contemporary public displays—fêtes; dancehall performances in clubs, backyards, ballrooms, and basements; and the expressions of desperate self-liberation that emerge in Caribbean music, novels, and Carnival celebrations—the amateur videos of young women on YouTube represent what Carolyn Cooper refers to as the "embodied knowledge of female authority." This designation endows these women with a particular ethic: it allows them to orient the unquestionable potency of their sexuality to serve a more complex rhetorical purpose. Cooper suggests that, for the dancehall performer in particular, "exhibitionism conceals ordinary imperfections . . . [and provides a space where] old roles can be contested and new identities assumed."[28] She describes this sort of performance as "a dancehall affirmation of the pleasures of the body, . . . an act of self-conscious female assertion of control over the representation of her person. Woman as sexual being claims the right to sexual pleasure as an essential sign of her identity."[29] This point can certainly be observed in many videos in which women routinely engage in erotic displays. Not surprisingly, conventional Caribbean sensibilities still tend to resist erotic, out-of-season displays of the body, an unshakeable consequence of a legacy of internalized shame. And the typical response to the act of wining up a body in front a camera for everybody to see hinges on whether the actor has any "shame" or "decency." This is a fundamental source of contention between traditional expressions in public spaces and the imposition of mainstream notions of female respectability, a liminal space within which the jamette is undoubtedly poised to elicit responses to texts that can leave the neat, static expectations of convention upturned.

"We are all little filmmakers," says Jessica Helfand, "directing on a pathetically small screen—yet broadcasting to a potentially infinite audience. This in itself is conflicting (not to mention corrupting), but more important, what are we making? What are we inventing? What are we saying that has not been said before?"[30] The same basic questions arise when certain texts are produced, viewed, and critiqued through a lens specifically oriented for Caribbean audiences: practitioners similarly exhibit themselves and deliberately attempt to unsettle established precepts, making them exemplary practitioners whose strategic displays serve a key purpose of self-representation and rhetorical (re)invention. These practitioners end up producing texts that are controversial enough to ruffle the normalized gaze and sensibilities of a traditional—even conservative—Caribbean audience, which can place them at odds with their audiences and their communities of origin. By opening up the expression and exchange, they provide their viewers with an opportunity to observe alternative discursive strategies, or "newer ways to mean,"[31] that rely on the jamette's negotiation of fluid subjectivities in the digital public. Furthermore, by opening up her constructed self for the simultaneous pleasure, consumption, and critique of a public audience, the jamette turns the gaze into a carnivalesque dialectic wherein both tradition and innovation are used to thrash out divergent issues of the status quo and change in the context of a discourse of virtualized self-definition. It is from this point that I embark on a more extensive discussion of the jamette, whose videos foreground the importance of the dancing body not merely as a text but as an object that is integral to the *audience's* discourse of everyday vernacular desire. As such, these videos can be thought to constitute rhetorical displays of erotic carnivalesque negotiation and implication.

Inhabiting the Digital Vernacular   147

Having originally been invited to leave comments to the videos they see, members of the audience were drawn into the exchange. Once engaged, however, most of them actively set out to appropriate and manipulate its tone with a grammar of masculinist motive, thereby disrupting the original set of values that defined the jamette's sense of decency. In one example from a poster named 5MANGEMENT155, while some commenters offer fairly mild compliments—"nice whining btw . . :)," "very nice," and "nice vid effects what software did u use?"—others attempt to manipulate the authenticity of the exchange deploying familiar creolized language features: "yo my gurl ur fukin greeezy you bom bom bom bloodclawt sell off yah fuk . . . . drop dead my gurl fukkkkkkkkkkkkkkkkkkkkkkkkkkkk kkkk!!!!"; "ENERGY MASH UP DI PLACE SELLOFF."[32] To achieve some degree of identification with the author, breezzoo issues a series of recognizable features that range from a textual representation of an oral gun salute—"bom bom bom"—to tonal semantic features intended to mimic and authenticate breezzoos awe and appreciation for the display, "fukkkkkkkkkkkkkkkkkkkkkkkkkkkkkkk." Additionally, breezzoo includes the expletive "bloodclawt" (i.e., blood cloth), a reference to sanitary pads and menstruation that is used to express surprise or anger. The possibility of a genuine compliment notwithstanding, these comments betray breezzoo's veiled attempt to place an implicit claim on the "fukin" body in motion.

Though such exchanges use linguistic features similar to ones in Brian and Peter's previously quoted exchange, the dynamics of interaction between jamettes and their critics differ significantly from Brian and Peter's, for the critics deploy these features not to frame a relatively equitable interaction but to *encode* the jamette according to a specific perspective that privileges vulgarity, further adding to the perception of the black dancing body as a taboo, hypersexual, and oversexed object of illicit desire. While the "real" author of the video is relatively protected, having somewhat removed herself from the act by placing an avatar—a virtual representation—to perform symbolically on her behalf, the responses generated by these performances nevertheless add a provocative dimension to the rhetorical act. For example, even though she set a standard for commentary on her videos, the content of comments that 5MANAGEMENT155 receives illustrates a fundamental disregard for what she has established as acceptable codes of interaction: "you pretty damn sexy mah"; "BAD ASS FUCKIN' VID!! i LOVE THE FX, YO!!! LOVE THE WAY U DO IT LIKE DAT!!"; and "shawty, where u at? I wanna grind dat up like coffee then beat it down like Ali!"[33] These comments contradict the desired type of interaction, for members of the audience proceed to enact a degree of entitlement constructing themselves as coauthors not only of the exchange between themselves and the jamette but also of the *jamette herself*. In an apparent reversal of roles, the audience members (now fully empowered and authorized to denigrate the video in creole) engage in a concentrically designed/targeted performance of offensive speech meant as an effort to place a mark on the body *as offensive* (vulgar, slack, dirty, sexy, fukin greeezy, etc.) and, by extension, to demarcate or delimit what the author, the video, the body, and its motions actually *mean*.

Despite efforts to marginalize her authority, however, the jamette is still able to control the dynamics surrounding her performance. About a month after posting her video, "NO INTRO NEEDED," 5MANAGEMENT155 responded to the overt objectification and suggestive violence of the comments that bigrayray11, babyboi3000, and LordBlacknWild posted to her video: "tek time badbwouy"—that is, "take your time, bad boy."[34] Back up. Slow your roll. The videos posted by performers such as mslikklebit and flexio7 similarly illustrate the dissonance of author intent and audience interpretation, as well as the respective authors' attempts to manage that dissonance. For instance, while mslikklebit maintains a greater degree of anonymity on her YouTube channel (opting to direct viewers to her MySpace website, which advertises her professional occupation as a dancer), she does offer justifications for the quality and content of some of her videos, the stated motives ranging from boredom to insomnia to practice. These bear the rhetorical intent of deflecting harsh criticism and critical efforts to define *who* the jamette really is.

The woman who posts as flexio7 is more forthcoming than mslikklebit, doing more to differentiate her personal identity from the virtual one she presents online. On her channel's homepage, she lays out her criteria for performance and critique, which bear quoting in full:

> First of all im not much of a dancer ... Lol everybody keeps saying what are you talking about but honestly i do all this for fun. To be honeast i didnt really know how to dance so im mainly doing these videos to see my progress and to get some critism (about my dancing not about my character) my dancing has nothing to do with my character i dnt wlk around half naked of the street lol. How i dance in my videos is basically how i dance in a club and i dont care what anyone has to say about it. I was born in Jamaica and came to england when i was very very young so sooo slightly diluted but i will still tell you where to go suck out if you come pon di page and try start up stupid internet arguements i dont have time for haters! you will be blocked, deleted, cursed out etc. Im here to have a lil fun and share my talents Hopefully people can pick up a few moves or learn somthing off me or maybe i can learn sumthin and i would like to here some feedback off some Jamaicans Cos back in the day i didnt know how to dance and i wanna make sure ive got it on lock. Any requests or comments is cool got to here the good with the bad just not the negative vibes.[35]

The justification flexio7 offers may lead the casual reader to categorize her intentions along the lines of self-improvement or even a public service, offering examples from which others can "pick up a few moves." This would establish her as a humble though highly qualified amateur dancehall queen who bears no ill intention. The humility with which she introduces herself is short-lived, however, for she directs a more aggressive tone to a specific segment of her viewing audience, the "haters" who, as it turns out, have already set a precedent for offensive commentary. As a countermeasure, she draws on the effectiveness of carnivalesque implication—the masque—wherein the audience is deterred from harsh insults and "negative vibes" by being *invited* to provide commentary of a certain type. Even though flexio7 purports not to "care what anyone has to say about it," she clearly attempts to protect herself against attacks from a hostile audience. For instance, she takes a self-deprecating stance as an amateur with much to learn, despite the accolades she has received from "everybody." In the event that the reader is not so inclined, she engages in a bit of preemptive posturing—her own grand-charge. In anticipation of the possibility that commentary on her performance might be outweighed by persistent misogynistic claims on her digitized body, flexio7 switches to a fully creolized dialect so she can issue an explicit warning to her potential audience, promising to tell them "where to go suck out if [they] come pon di page and try start up stupid internet arguements." *Fuh real.*

As I showed with Bajegirl's use of proverb, the act of masquing involves calling attention to known practices, amplifying given topics, and making them plain(er) for the audience. In a virtual context, the dynamics take on an even more complex rhetoricality. The probability of rhetorical negotiation increases because the performance inhibits audience members' abilities both to fully subscribe to the ethereality of desire for a virtual(ly unattainable) subject and to fully relinquish their grounding and responsibility as materially complicit actors. The jamette's performance therefore has a delimiting function that supersedes the audience's efforts to define her. So audience members are implicated in the display to the extent that they are able to reflectively examine the interaction as it unfolds *in relation to* the performance and the intentions of the author.

It is worth noting here that, despite the apparent dissonance in these exchanges, the jamette's masque relies on a presumption of sustainable degrees of identification between jamettes and their audiences. So while aspects of the display may possess shades of deliberate misrecognition and a fundamental disjointedness between the jamette and the audience, they are still connected by means of a shared ethical underpinning. These masqued articulations therefore not only confirm the idea that "*saying* is also a *doing*" that produces consequences but also highlight the efficacy of rhetorical intention and relative positionality demonstrated by savvy practitioners who seek to set the terms by which they wish to be addressed.[36] Thus, for jamettes, the masque of their dancing bodies functions as an expression of motive and of embodied wisdom made available to the dancer and the audience through the effective repetition and innovation of vernacular codes and sensibilities: a process of deliberately calling oneself into being that runs rhizomatically through the vernacular tradition. For a literary prototype—or at the very least, an analogue—of the activity we see in grainy, low-res YouTube clips, recall Lovelace's depiction of an identical display of rhetorical (re)invention with Sylvia in *The Dragon Can't Dance*:

> She was dancing still with all her dizzying aliveness, dancing wildly; frantically twisting her body, flinging it around her waist, jumping and moving, refusing to let go of that visibility, that self the Carnival gave her; holding it balanced on her swaying hips, going down and coming up in a tall, undulating rhythm, lifting up her arms and leaping as if she wanted to leap out of herself into her self, a self in which she could stay for ever, in which she could *be* for ever. He watched her dancing into the insides of the music, into its notes, its soul, into every ring of the tall ringing iron; her whole self a shout, a bawl, a cry, a scream, a cyclone of tears rejoicing in a self and praying for a self to live in beyond Carnival and her slave-girl costume.[37]

Like Sylvia, the jamette is driven by the imperative to define herself in/on her own terms, thriving on the indeterminacy of the medium to engage in what Pramod Nayar calls "the recursive identity formation of cyberculture."[38] The resulting activity may be thought of, in this latter context, as a willful virtualization of the self: the transformation from subject to object to a virtual representation of that object, from performer to performance to text. By making her self subject to virtualization, the jamette has produced an image of her self that retains its fundamental materiality while simultaneously requiring less energy to modify, manipulate, or (indeed) to *share* her ideas (of herself) with an infinite audience.[39] The real question, then, is whether any rhetoricality is lost in the transference. The answer is no. If anything, we stand to gain from what such a transference can provide as a public expression of notions and opinions that are (too often) privately held. Even though much of the critique the jamette receives is rife with potentially abusive tones that can reset discursive parameters of language and meaning, her own masqued negotiations in such a public forum demonstrate a degree of self-assertion that can disrupt the power of the abuse. In her discourse on the "embodied freedom" of dancehall performances and other feminist counterpractices, Mimi Sheller offers the following apropos observation: "The mere exercise of sexual agency . . . may enable some forms of maneuver, negotiation and exchange. But crucial to such bodily negotiations of freedom is the ability to drag them into the public sphere, in effect to make public the pubic. Against the privatization of violence, abuse, and terror within the household, the workplace, or the closed community, diverse forms of sexual agency in contemporary Caribbean and African-American popular cultural forms—and feminist readings of these forms—engage in public with these intimate embodiments of power."[40] Following Sheller's lead, we can posit that the jamette not only is beset by language and other systems of domination but also has the means and the implicit responsibility to handle how these systems can be used—by her and on her. Thus, while her performance may provoke criticism, it may also elicit affirmative assertions, for jamettes such as flexio7 display themselves publicly as bodies *on offense*, making it clear that attempts at domination will be resisted. Consequently, their refusal puts them squarely in place to trouble, critically address, and enact hypotheses of subjectivity that go against the sensibilities of the status quo. The great irony of the contemporary Carnival narrative—as allowance and sanctioned revelry—is thus disrupted by the ethos of the practitioner who uses the indeterminacy of cyberspace to provoke the "repressed" fantasies of the audience and evoke the kind of critical dialogue that makes the carnivalesque such a central framing device for Caribbean rhetorical tradition.

Curwen Best, in his study of the politics of Caribbean cyberculture, claims that "the question of access is in many respects central to debates about competitiveness in the still-emerging world of real and virtual relations. But to conceptualize the debate concerning cultural power relations, technology, and development only in terms of access to hardware and software is limiting." He goes on to note that "given the enhanced role played by technology in the twenty-first century Caribbean, the question of how technology is perceived, implemented, utilized, applied, and appropriated is crucial to an understanding of how society, culture, and state-of-the-art begin to 'reason together' in the digital dispensation."[41] On these points I agree, but our ideas diverge when I consider the inherent dynamics that lead to the production of certain cybercultural texts. Best's idea that "Caribbean society up to the present continues to grapple with working out the relationship between the facsimile and the real" is particularly intriguing,[42] but not because it implies that Caribbean people have only recently emerged from a technological dark age and remain half-blind because they have been mystified by the light of a monitor and its peripherals, trapped, as it were, in an infinite loop of primitive Promethean gratitude. Rather, it presents a false binary, suggesting that the "facsimile" (for me, the "virtual") and the "real" are at odds and require reconciliation. They *are* reconcilable, he suggests, but Caribbean society has yet to figure out the relationship between the technologies and their inherent notions.

From the perspective of rhetoric, such distinctions need not be made, not least because symbolic actions cannot be meaningfully separated from their material causes and consequences. For example, even if we concede that the enthymematic and metaphoric approaches espoused by Springer and Bajegirl are effective, it would be something of a stretch to presume that either of them would consider their symbolic actions—no matter how complex—to be *termi-*

nally symbolic. That is, both eventually try to work their way back to and settle on the possible material outcomes, directing their opinions and possible effects toward "regular other girl[s]" and the need to "back up the talk with [the] action . . . [of] citizens."[43] In cyberspace, the constancy and reliability of the vernacular practitioner provide opportunities for social cohesiveness that are as flexible as they are grounded. I am thinking, specifically about hubs such as Caribbean360.com and, even more specifically, Code Red for Gender Justice, a feminist collective of men and women that describes its methods as "an innovative mix of the traditional and creative."[44] Indeed, that group's subsequent activity is a recursive expression of a people's resistance through rhetorically inventive means, each related post an example of the functional, critical, and rhetorical literacy of rhetor *and* audience.[45] It is, furthermore, the expression of a people's attempts to evolve, redefine, and reframe the dimensions of its narrative, both individual and collective, instead of being forced to jettison one narrative for another. Caribbean rhetorical activity, put another way, is symbolic *and* material, a rhetorical practice reflective of a people's extended desire for self-determination and subjectivity.

The jamette has shown that the relationship between the symbolic and material stands to become even more entangled in cyberspatial contexts—and more generative, too.[46] What are we to make, for instance, of Caribbean360.com's reporting that protests in Guyana forced Chris Brown to cancel his concert three years after the incident in which Rihanna was punched and choked?[47] When the audience's recall of Rihanna's battered face inspires such outrage, what kind of rhetorical power can we ascribe to the regular girls, the jamettes, or those who wish to advocate for them, whether personally or in principle?[48] As I look ahead to the inevitability of the ever-deepening immersion of vernacular participation in technological discourses, I wonder how else we are to negotiate processes of virtualization and the representations of body, texts that imply a deliberate disembodiment on the part of the performer followed by what appear to be deliberate inscriptions. I understand what is at stake with this suggestion—namely, a deep consideration of what is to be gained or lost when the process of rhetorical (re)invention is attenuated to the point of appearing to remove the body *altogether*. But it is a risk worth taking if the payoff is understanding the intricacies of a Caribbean presence and activity in cyberspace. It remains to be seen whether digital jamette texts, with their deep subjectivity, will be included with other, more traditional texts in the consideration of embodied counterpractices of Caribbean sexual citizenship, erotic agency, transnational representation, and political economy. But just as the performance of dancehall functions as "a site for the activation of and struggle over sexual citizenship and embodied freedom,"[49] these texts, archived the instant they are produced, may turn out to have as much rhetorical staying power as other expressions of freedom embodied in more conventional forms.

At least, this is the hope—not a fool's hope, but one that I situate firmly in the virtues of vernacular tradition. Plus, if it is true, as Nayar suggests, that "the task of cyberculture . . . is to shift focus away from the individual subject that initiates conversations to the social and material conditions in which various subject positions become visible and possible,"[50] then perhaps it is in the virtualization and critical *reembodiment* of the subject that the actualization of a truly democratic text has the greatest chance. Perhaps it is in this process that the material subject will be most able to demonstrate the scope of an author's ethos. I am not certain on this, but Pierre Lévy does argue that "the virtual is an infinite source of actualization,"[51] which I take to mean that, among other things, the process of virtualization, as a form of *conscious* disembodiment, enables the vast range of Caribbean users' motives to be displayed on a wider, more amplified scale, as part of an elaborate masque. In other words, while the performance of the jamette may not be singularly *physical*—that is, embodied in the flesh and bones of the author-rhetor—she is nevertheless *material*. Digitally embodied. Virtual but no less real.

It may come down, in the end, to an analysis of the range of means available to us, as well as to a working knowledge of what we are willing to do to pull ourselves together and participate more fully in the creation of public discourse. That is, an act of "convergence" that is comprehensive and culturally relevant, a reflective and collective practice that could lead to productive Caribbean rhetorical activity, successful deliberation, and social action.[52] With that said, I want to conclude by reiterating that the point of this chapter is not to claim undue exception—as part of some "we does be online, too" action—but to begin to illustrate examples of Caribbean interaction that are generative rather than reductive. Similar to the chat session between Brian and Peter, the particular medium employed by caribloggers is, in and of itself, innocuous. Rampersad argues, for example, that "[his] aspiration is not to be labeled by the technology [he uses] to write with."[53] It is, rather, the deliberate insertion of values and meanings that determine the character and effectiveness of their transmissions. The point, in other words, is that online activities do not simply *resemble* rhetorical activity as cultural analogies; they are themselves *cultural* and represent ongoing attempts at pulling together in the interest of achieving collective praxis. Like Caribbean culture itself, the online realm faces strong tensions that threaten to undo much of the interaction and collaboration there, particularly in the kind of texts we create, use, and sometimes *are*. But it is to be hoped that continuing efforts to frame orality, textuality, and physicality as inclusive discourse will go a long way to bridging discursive gaps between the marginalized and the mainstream. A major constant, though, will be the influx of rhetorical choices that authors and audiences make to achieve these and other "public" outcomes in the transition from private to civil/civic discourse.

In the context of Caribbean cybercultural activity, the greatest actualization possible would result in the text's being used as a lightning rod for the collective democratic desires of the audience—that is, the text would help audiences develop a clearer sense of what it means to enact their Caribbeanness toward a collectively beneficial end. For as Lévy suggests, "when these interactions are capable of enriching or modifying the model, the virtual world becomes a vector of collective intelligence and creation."[54] Indeed, as we look forward to the growing possibility of a post-Caribbean ethos, it appears that the action is here, with the virtual.

CONCLUSION

Or, Reprise for the Carnivalesque

> Sing from your own hymnbook.
> —Anonymous, Tobago, December 2007

> Looking forward and looking back, nah.
> You could finish now.
> —Rene Farrow, Frankie's Bar, April 4, 2009

> Time to cut the thread. Just make a loop 'round yuh finger an buss it wit yuh teeth!
> —Lesley Ann Capolino, April 23, 2012

LABOR DAY. CROWN HEIGHTS, BROOKLYN, 1999: that memory of myself in blue—with fork and horn and tail—brings with it a nagging question. What is the value of intuition without inquiry, and what merit is there in remembering if action is not forthcoming? This was a call to which I could have provided only a partial response. I quickly decided that the time for critical reflection was not in the midst of a bacchanal. The memory is still a good one—if also a bit sad—but was it just a dragon dance I was dancing? Perhaps. All the Carnivals I have missed since then cannot be reclaimed, and while it is tempting to remain in that moment, replaying the nostalgia still somewhat fresh in my head and heart, it is not enough to just remember it. Nostalgia that turns only inward yields little of use for a project in rhetoric; it is selfish. The carnivalesque as the rhetorical perspective that I have described in this book counteracts the tendency to subscribe to a nostalgic view of a people and their practices, thrusting the practitioner into the present. In so doing, it allows us to move past the inexplicable sense of loss and the cognitive dissonance between past and present that can too easily forestall pragmatist approaches to consequence by coloring experience solely in romantic, exotic, or purist terms. Yet I wonder: if it is reasonable to presume that nostalgia is potentially debilitating, as I have alluded elsewhere, then is it not just as reasonable to presume that items of culture and cultural expression can masquerade as nostalgia and (more important) that the sentiments embedded in their performances can be effectively activated for rhetorical work?

For the vernacular rhetor, success hinges on the commitment to a single criterion: practice. The practice of looking backward and forward at the same time to revise aspects of the past and equip ourselves for changes to come. The practice of critical inquiry in real contexts for real effects. The practice of a vision of democratic participation that is shared across oceans and differences. Together, these points of practice have been my signposts for navigating this project and making sense of its complexities. More importantly, they have helped me forge a path to further inquiry. It is fitting, therefore, that I draw on these practices to underscore the depth and significance of the Caribbean carnivalesque, the relevance and timeliness of its deployment in transnational contexts and its capacity to implicate the audience in the rhetorical act, and the vast range of transformative consequences such interpellating acts permit. Practice in this modality begins with the acknowledgment that the Caribbean carnivalesque operates on an imperative of social commentary that is publicly displayed, whether for praise or blame, compliment or critique. In contemporary times, it involves the recognition of a rhetorical imperative that emerges from the circumstances of everyday life and sustains us Caribbean people in our encounters with the constraining effects of mainstream discourse and institutions. Furthermore, the articulation of this imperative in such terms allows us to identify the possibilities and implications that follow from the *deliberate* practice of Caribbean tradition and to use that tradition as a means of rhetorical negotiation with others. Can there be praxis after all? Or are these examples of Caribbean popular culture—the oral, the visual, the literary, and the digital—only the exaggerated manifestations of my neuroses unfolding in a public I have yet to know? The answers, I think, are in the question. I acknowledge the profundity and move on.

Labor Day. Crown Heights, Brooklyn, 2012: a black woman stands, legs apart, arms spread wide. She is tall. She is smiling. She wears a headdress fitted on a "dark Caesar" haircut. Her hair is bleached gold. She wears sateen gloves and a rhinestone garter above her left knee; both are adorned with pastel-colored feathers. Around her neck, a stylized *caracol* (snail) necklace. A bikini top made of a thin fabric and white studded straps covers her round breasts. A patch of the same fabric covers her most private parts, the material barely held in place by fishing line tied on each side to chains that hang from the bikini top. Black, five-inch-heel leather boots reach high. Christian Louboutin zip-back over-the-knee, if I were forced to guess. I imagine they go much higher, though they seem loosened now. The Eastern Parkway is a trek, after all. All eyes, except her own, are transfixed on her—an entire audience embarrassed but refusing to look away. She is, from the looks of her spectators, as repulsive as she is seductive, and she seems to revel in this very fact. She is smiling. *Watch me, nah!* Stop. Look. She is, as my mother put it, "practically naked." This is not the mas of my mother's youth. This is different.

Practically naked. I do not take the pun lightly.

Though I concede that it is impossible to presume her intentions, when the fundamental imperative of the vernacular rhetor is self-definition—to be seen and heard on his or her own terms—it is difficult to separate motive from the need to display it openly. It is reasonable, then, to view one alongside the other and to claim that the display is intentional. That said, there is a fundamental practicality in her almost nakedness that evokes the epideictic function of the masque: the success of this display is predicated on its capacity to simultaneously shock, please, disturb, entertain; the motives embodied in the display extend outward from the rhetor and into the society that has sanctioned it, drawing spectators in, implicating them in the display and its outcomes; and the display highlights the ubiquity and invasiveness of dominant discourses and the patent absurdity of our efforts to conceal the effects of the imposition or our resistance to it. At the very least, these factors provide the basic lens with which anyone so inclined can view and critique such displays, as well as recognize how they amplify the complexity of everyday life. What more to make of this performance? What are the intents and purposes to be gleaned from it? What to do with similar expressions of abandon that evoke visceral responses among audiences, ones that they feel deeply but often can put to rhetorical use in their everyday lives only with great difficulty? What does an almost naked masquer have to do with trade unions, transnationalism, education, or foreign policy in and beyond the region? Once in the public eye and noticed, does this previously invisible and marginalized vernacular rhetor have the responsibility to educate her audience, seeking *in situ* to establish a balance between the impulse to emerge in the midst of a bacchanal and her willing immersion in its processes and trappings of excess? Or are the spectators meant to do the work of understanding their complicity in the gaze? Are they to make sense of the competing symbols, their turnoffs and stimulations, reconciling the terms that define their voyeuristic interactions? What is the value of an individualized declaration—a broadcasting of the self—to a fragmented people? What does it offer in terms of strategy? I do not yet know. Not every herculean task will include a Hydra, but here, I suppose, I am likely to find mine. But as more (and more) questions emerge, my hope is that I will not have to engage them alone.

As a rhetorician, I am obliged to choose contingency over providence as I consider available means, rhetorical methods, and their applicability in given circumstances. As a rhetorician, I am also compelled to consider how the ordering of these circumstances and people's characteristic responses to them demonstrate the endurance of more particular sensibilities—specifically, whether these sensibilities contribute to (or detract from) a shared sense of democratic deliberation in the context of a Caribbean ethos. Despite the sometimes overwhelming limitations we Caribbeans face as a people, the ritualization and revision of traditional practices enable us to override the tendency to capitulate when situations seem to be at their bleakest and exigence is high: when chirren doh have no milk to drink and drag hunger and underperformance behind them like a ole mas that everybody know they too young to play; when rent and cell phone bill cyah pay; when water more than flour; when lights gone; when we cyah vote; when yuh struggling; when a country's murder rate can be read with the same nonchalance as a cricket score: 550 all out, 99 for 3;[1] when the dialectical flexibility cyah flex we out of socioeconomic depression; when the times we live in are not just interesting but *hard*, and we must take it without giving a thought to the fact that our island nations resemble the hyperextended vertebrae of a spine in perpetual limbo. "Banga Season," some call it. Others, "life." How do we rely on the lessons and performative aspects of the past to envision and put into practice the motives that make different forms of liberation probable for us *now*? We must not only manage multiple and often conflicting discourses that can be dissected and analyzed as disembodied texts but also incessantly work to establish, demonstrate, and maintain knowledge among practitioners through careful attention to our languages, our expressions, our ideologies, and our embodied wisdom. In an attempt to ameliorate the inevitable challenge of answering these questions, I have taken the preliminary step of describing examples of a tradition—or a set of traditions—that coalesced, at least in part, as a response to the imposition of other traditions of power and culture (indeed, in response to traditions of rhetoric as well). If I miss the point from time to time, it is because my reading has been shaped and delimited by my own point of view as a rhetorician. In the quest to understand and articulate Caribbean rhetorical activity, I face the risk of being perpetually distanced from my people. Shunned, as it were, for not having a clue and for sharing more than a methodological kinship with the writer, the critic, the sociolinguist, or the ethnographer. The difficulty, and the danger, will likely endure.

As a Caribbean rhetorician, though I remain fully engaged in the struggle to articulate the mysteries of motive, expression, and outcome among my people, there are moments that strain explanation and remind me that I have so much further and deeper to go. At these times, I am grateful to be reduced to a familiar Caribbeanness that is only slightly less intimidating than it was before I started this work. I write from that place when I say that there is more to this woman's performance than the obvious, and understanding that I may veer more into speculation than toward some empirical certainty, I am compelled to leave off of theorizing at this point and take to thickly describing what I see in the plainest terms possible.

This woman has brought my theory back to its roots. Back to its beginnings, with the completion of a circle that has, at times, been wide enough for me to doubt what I have seen, heard, felt, or known in the course of my inquiry. To me, her display is more than that of a dancer at whose feet I can pile the confluence of metaphors—conquest, eradication, assimilation, desire—that have served me along the way. There is a hint of providence in it, an awareness of some personal sovereignty. I see in her pose a self-consciousness I have longed to see: the self-assured aliveness of a vernacular rhetor, the deliberate (re)invention of a jamette claiming her visibility with arms spread wide, smiling. I see Lovelace's Sylvia come to life, "refusing to let go of that visibility."[2] She dances herself off the page, out beyond the digital boundary, and into being, talking back to the drums that talk to her: every drummed syllable a bass beat, every bass beat a bumper, a "Bahia Girl" who desires to be bound only by her flesh. And the Maroons are invoked. I see Bolo's redemption and Alford's revelation, their kalinda sensibilities and limbo silences resolved, finally, in what she portrays. The gayelle has disappeared. The limbo pole burned to ash in the memory. I see my mother, pregnant with me during Carnival, coming up Coffee Street. And I see myself, almost catching power at my grandmother's wake, parang playing loud, and my aunts saying, "Watch him, eh. Watch him." *Watch me.* They are all coming to pass in her dance, performed not as a hollow dragon dance but as a conscious movement of limbs that leaves to the imagination only that which cannot be seen with the naked eye.

There is in her *Watch me, nah!* a deliberate and unapologetic concession to a basic vernacular logic with which we can all identify: when the expression of freedom is circumscribed by regulations that curtail the realization of these freedoms in everyday circumstances, then the expression is not of freedom at all but of the desire for a freedom that has been denied, one that, despite all the hustle we hustle to make ends meet, has failed to materialize. In short, her dance is a dance in protest to the legacy of emancipation. Canboulay. Cannes Brulées. The burning cane. She stands to face it, smiling. I feel like I know this woman, like I see her every day. Everywhere. In all things. Her dance is the reality to which my ideas aspire. In her display is the antecedent to every genre I have examined and a prophecy of their validity come to pass. The literal embodiment of the carnivalesque.

For all it is, this display is only partly who we are—condensed, potent, but ultimately an abridged expression of who we wish to be. That is, with all she brings to this project, I am unable to satisfactorily clothe her in a theory of my own design. I am likewise unable to impose my latter-day cynicism onto her or allow my perfunctory forays into feminist discourses to collect on her skin, like powder or glitter, even as I refer to the subtle consummation of symbol and material. The sublime and racist firestorms that flare up in the aftermath of these displays are not hers alone to consider or defend.[3] I know she is dancing her own dance, dancing for *her own self*, trading on her own economy of pleasure. She does not weave magic with the sway and roll of her hips. She is neither muse nor neurosis, only a Caribbean woman, dancing her tradition. This, I know.

And yet I am unable to shake the feeling—to which I have committed myself here and in the previous chapters—that every instantiation of the impulse embodied in this woman's performance will bear the mark of a vernacular rhetoric that waits on the awareness of its practitioners who wait poised on the cusp of tradition and (re)invention. Those who know that every fête, lime, cooler party, breakfast party, bashment, wuk up, jump up, and Jouvay will bear this potential. Everything that start late and get shut down early will bear it. And whether we wear makeup or mud; tallow grease, tar, or feathers; short pants, skirt, or shirt and pants—however we masque it, as long as the expression of freedom occurs solely at the behest of municipal, national, or foreign governments that mean only to tolerate our presence and the ephemerality of our spectacles, while curtailing our full empowerment, we are bound to show that we desire the opposite of that. Bound to show that *we is people*, just like we bound to talk the way we does talk, and act the way we does have to act, all to the ridicule, bewilderment, or frustration of our audiences.

CODA

So it comes to this. Every act is bound to the history in which it emerged. It gives me no pleasure to note that the consequences of enslavement and emancipation—specifically, the formation of a rhetoric that helped breed carnivalesque strategies to deal with the realities of an emancipation into poverty, homelessness, unemployment, and disfranchisement—manifest similarly today and in the different sites where Caribbean people and their Carnival celebrations end up settling. They are the common denominators of a familiar hustle, the hustle of the dispossessed. Despite the history we have inherited, however, our rhetorical traditions did not develop as systems of practices that were intended to be performed *solely* in the margins. I am not disputing that protocarnivalesque sentiments were originally developed among the underclass, or that the fragments of retained cultures and languages had initially coalesced almost completely outside the view and comprehension of the ruling class. The emergence of these sentiments as public display coincided with the assertion of Caribbean identity, and the Canboulay demonstrations were evidence that the original Carnival was not a Caribbean one; rather, it was a colonial subscription to hegemony that only gradually sanctioned the public behavior of an emergent vernacular class. Catalyzed by emancipation—that is, emancipation not as freedom by any means but as a lightning rod to charge the intentions of those who would be free—those in the urban underclass embraced the stigmatization levied on them and brought their subjectivity to bear as members of a *culture* in which everyone ought to have had a stake.

Of course, all performances remain, to some degree, subject to hegemony. This is a fact, and in our performances, we Caribbeans are no exception. At the same time, however, the onslaught of these discourses prompts the development of counterpractices and counterdiscourses that resist homogeneity through the conscious practice of difference. Thus, the democratic impulses in Caribbean rhetoric bespeak a desire among vernacular rhetors and their communities to exist and be recognized as part of a transnational citizenry. There is an implicit danger, however: ignorance, the rock against which the force and formlessness of an idea is always likely to crash. And I am forced, through inquiry, to weigh what I think I know against what I understand and struggle to articulate, only to arrive at this: inquiry is driven as much by the terror of ignorance as by curiosity, a phenomenon of rhetoric that many of us who choose to study it understand intuitively. Our questions tap into our intuition, raising memories and bringing what "we *know* we know" into sharper relief, revealing more of what we do not know. This, according to Plato, is a gamble even Socrates would have been cautious to make,[4] for any project that results in an effort to legitimize its own internal logic by closing a circle—ending, as it were, at the beginning—ultimately reflects a fundamental insecurity in the author's ability to adequately encompass and account for the immensity of the idea he or she has pursued. At the same time, the gesture suggests that there is more to do. As is to be expected, a project such as this one faces certain inherent limitations. Any project that seeks to identify activities and modes will fall short of accurately representing those who use them, the circumstances under which they are deployed, and the range of consequences they produce. No attempt was made to cover the vastness and depth of Caribbean culture or to fully account for its rhetoric. Nor have I attempted to provide a complete catalog of expressions. Though I think some of the more key aspects of Caribbean rhetorical activity will be easier to detect, if we were to consider the study of our tropic tendencies in terms of icebergs, this would undoubtedly be only the tip of it. A framework has been constructed. And even though I have attempted to scrutinize some representative examples of Caribbean rhetoric as extant practice, the scope of rhetorical work I envision for and with Caribbean people would make this effort inadequate if I were to end here. (This is a masque, of course: the caveat of this project's incompleteness serving as the opportunity for me to promise to do more, an authenticating humility that serves as a staging point for my scholarly ambition. I do of course hope that the holes will be filled by those inclined—or intrigued by the inadequacies—to join in the conversation, supplementing what I have attempted here with even greater substance and proceeding with even greater vigor.)

What should not be in doubt is the fact that Caribbean rhetoric exists, that the Caribbean carnivalesque is real, and that the masque as its major device is sufficiently effective to bear the strain of our histories. Consistent with the tenets of the carnivalesque, however, this project in Caribbean rhetoric is only the first stage, an introduction to cultural, linguistic, and religious inheritance, interpretation, and expression on the vernacular level. Like the carnivalesque, it acknowledges the trauma of our past but does not remain there. The Caribbean ethos will continue to evolve and be performed in contemporary times, out of which we can detect and discern significant rhetorical strategies. We perform out of a history—or, more accurately, a memory of history—that has shaped our identity. Identity, in turn, infuses our performances with particular rhetorical weight, enabling collective subjectivity to be practiced wherever our numbers are significant enough to support it or our social conditions serious enough to demand it. Embedded in *every* rhetorical exchange is an ethos on which the conversants rely in order to make their interactions not only comprehensible but meaningful, convincing, familiar, and authentic. Thus, an approach to culture that pays serious attention to the tradition and to the deployment of symbols in producing specific rhetorical effect can help us better understand the personal significance and broader sociocultural implications of a ethos recognizable particularly to those of us who make up the representative group and feel an increased need to engage in the cultural displays of that group. Those of us, that is, who know that all o' we was never one in the way that was intended by the West Indies Federation. Yet we are more effectively so when our lives mesh beyond the mutual intelligibility of our tongues, and we are forced to bend over backward together. A clearer conception of this activity can facilitate more effective and productive discussion of the relatively undertheorized topic of Caribbean rhetorical practice, but at stake is the (re)configuration of recognized aspects so as to secure a meaningful place and role for the Caribbean individual in contemporary society—whether one can hold one's own, as it were, singularly *and* as part of an increasingly global scene.

The development of an ethic that encourages belonging on a global scale is key, particularly as I flirt with the possibility of a transnational or even post-Caribbean identity. Rex Nettleford, for example, has claimed that Caribbean people "do not (or they no longer) conceive of a 'mainstream culture' outside of what they themselves have to offer to human civilization. They see themselves as part-determiners of that mainstream and not as outsiders to be let in."[5] What remains to be seen, however, is the degree to which our related performances will embody collective forms of vernacular criticism or activism in our publics.

Conclusion; or, Reprise for the Carnivalesque

The implicit threat of passivity and the continued fragmentation and distance from home communities can certainly be addressed with an agenda for participatory culture that not only encourages and creates collective intelligence and collective meaning making for our collective benefit but also inquires about the use to us, in these times, of a tradition of struggle, dissatisfaction, accountability, and critique that has sustained people in decades past but now seems to have run aground amid the obstacles of contemporary life. I am brought all the way back to consider C. L. R. James's prophecy on the liberatory potential of the Carnival. Writing in 1959, James noted:

> Once the people are convinced that the effort that they are being called upon to make is worth making, that it is for a good cause, and is led by people they can trust, then we can be certain that the energy, the creativity and the capacity for independent organisation which they show in Carnival will very easily be transferred to another object. We can see in Carnival the possibility (we do not go any further than possibility) of such a national mobilisation, as would put shame to all efforts that have hitherto been made in industrial and social activity.[6]

"How we fête is not how we party," argues Rudder.[7] Maybe. But the possibility does set the mind ablaze. What if we, in our millions, demanded to be heard and plainly seen? What could happen then? What indeed? What if, in addition to seeking redress for calls among law enforcement agencies to let us "kill each other," the millions on Eastern Parkway were participating, hands in the air, in a peaceful protest of the New York City Police Department's "Stop and Frisk" campaign? What if the specters of "self-deportation," transvaginal ultrasounds, and "legitimate rapes" featured prominently among these millions? What if they stood in solidarity with refugees from the Congo to protest the plunder of its minerals? And what if these enunciations spread, with the conviction of an Arab Spring, beyond the savannah and the parkways, from nation to nation, and across the region we call home? Caribbean exceptionalism activated, finally, in the course of a major change? A political party amassed in response to the politricks and charlatans who (with masks of their own) celebrate our exotica, as if our identities and concerns were tourist destinations? Once we are seen and heard, what do we say? Do we amass our outrage internationally against the beating of gay men in Jamaica, or secretly revel in it, identifying instead with a crowd that clamored for an opportunity to take part in such brutality?[8] Even silence can be a form of brutality, can't it? More questions. More will come. When they do, the likelihood that the Caribbean carnivalesque or the masque—my own or anyone else's—will be transformative will rely as much on courage as on urgency, awareness, and identification. The emphasis will therefore be on the authenticity of performances that (we convince ourselves) resonate deeply with us and those with whom we identify. They will serve, in the end, to maintain the relational and rhetorical ties in our ever-expanding experience of community and will be the flexible frame on which an enduring and evolving narrative will be constructed.

My repeated attempts to frame this activity as rhetoric should not only demonstrate my preference but also, and more important, suggest a breadth of applicability that may be of use for Caribbean people specifically and others in general. When we are forced to operate within the normative constraints of societies of which we seek to be a part, then the performance of rhetoric is not simply useful as a form of practice; rather, it becomes *necessary*, if only because these performances counteract the onset of overwhelming normativity by provoking witness, inquiry, and critique.[9] Ultimately, though, the success of this or any project in Caribbean rhetoric will result from an engaged dialogue occurring at the various points of intersection and flourishing in the context of constructed meanings and events. Such dialogue can foster a propagation of exigencies that could help us take into fuller account the social, political, economic, material, spiritual, and linguistic conditions in (and under) which we exist. Such dialogue may even help us become the kind of agents who are compelled to reevaluate our cultural production in greater numbers for the specific purpose of uplift, recognizing that we have significant rhetorical power and are obliged to use it expressly for our benefit. If this seems too much like wishful thinking on my part, then I welcome the label. After all, what is theory but wishful thinking that goes in search of practice to legitimize it, a flight of fancy in need of some grounding?

Sooner or later, we may come to find that everything is indeed everything. Until that time comes, we are behooved to distinguish, to recognize differences in the resulting distinctions, and to draw our similarities from whatever may be left. And if, in our classifications, we come upon similarities with greater ease than we have come to expect from the drudgery of a life experience with which we can all identify, we should count ourselves lucky that we have had a moment of clarity, a moment of connection to the civic mystery of our shared humanity. But when the party done, we know the intoxicants will take their leave, taking with them the euphoria of discovery and the uninhibited vulgarity that can punctuate the monotony of our days. In their place, a sobriety to which, for better or worse, we will have become accustomed, a sobriety with which we hope to face all things. I am reminded by Patricia Mohammed that "the Caribbean's centrality in the construction of modernity has waned." Left to our own devices, she suggests, we are busily engaged in understanding the eccentricities of our identities.[10] This is the hope: continued engagement, demystifying the things we know. For me, that hope lingers in the quiet as I look ahead for something else to do. I have gone some distance from wishing I did not have to do this work, but I am so much more tired now than I was after the rum wore off and the blisters set in at my ankles, heels, and toes. Lactic acid seeming to have pooled in my thighs and hamstrings. Road rash swelling on my knees. Neck and shoulders sore from whoever was up there in the frenzy. So, as I scramble to finish this book and try to get out ahead of the coming obsolescence, I am forced to go in search of exigencies that have yet to reveal themselves. I am forced—again, as always—to trust my people to be for me what I will try to be for them.

NOTES

INTRODUCTION: A *Jour Ouvert*

1. Lamming, *Pleasures of Exile*, 107.
2. Walcott, "The Antilles," 70.
3. Ibid., 69.
4. Burke, *Philosophy of Literary Form*, 1.
5. Ibid.
6. Farrell, "Practicing the Arts," 87.
7. For my purposes here, I consider democracy to have the following characteristics: it ensures the right to be heard as members of the citizenry and helps legitimize the collective expressions of an immigrant social group in the public sphere; it provides access to policy change (the act of voting, for example); and it is not limited to native or naturalized citizens but extends to all the members of a nation, even if that nation is made up of distinct communities. Democracy, then, should function as a means of participating, allowing people to partake in whatever opportunities are available in their society, including economic, political, and educational opportunities. In the absence of these opportunities, democracy makes space for subversion, transgression, protest, or acquiescence to take place in the interest of justice at various levels of society—family, community, classroom, and the interstices—be it Caribbean or otherwise. The manifestations of those rhetorical practices in the society are viable objects of study.
8. By Caribbean, I refer primarily to people of African descent from the anglophone nations of Jamaica, Trinidad and Tobago, Guyana, Barbados, Grenada, Antigua-Barbuda, St. Lucia, St. Vincent, Dominica, St. Kitts, Nevis, Anguilla, and Montserrat, including those who have spent a significant part of their lives outside the region. I also include in this group the children of Caribbeans who have spent all or the majority of their lives outside the region but who self-identify as Caribbean (and who may strategically switch to, say, an "African American" identity as the situation demands).
9. Bryce-LaPorte, "Introduction," 229.
10. I think it is important to note here that I employ a deliberate, albeit somewhat hybrid, understanding of the "rhetorical situation" as originally forwarded by Lloyd Bitzer ("Rhetorical Situation") and then refuted, in a sense, by Richard E. Vatz ("Myth of the Rhetorical Situation"). Vatz's argument—that the ascription of empiricism to

necessarily organic happenings is reductive and that imperfections are in fact modified by means of discourse—does not elide the overarching circumstances and contexts, which may not be subject to the control of all practitioners involved. The goal in my use of it is to suggest an awareness of context and of the interplay that takes place between events and the practitioners involved.

11. John, *Clear Word and Third Sight*, 2.
12. Fabre and O'Meally, *History and Memory*, 7.
13. McKerrow, "Critical Rhetoric," 451.
14. Harris, "The Limbo Gateway," 378, 381.
15. I am relying here on Carole Blair's preference to "hypothesize as a starting point for theorizing rhetoric that at least one of its basic characteristics (if not its most basic) is its materiality" ("Contemporary U.S. Memorial Sites," 18).

Chapter 1. *Mas Rhetorica*: A Brief Discourse on the Caribbean Carnivalesque

1. "Across Two Oceans," *Illustrated London News*, February 25, 1888, 205.
2. The Slavery Abolition Act (1833) was followed by emancipation on August 1, 1834. This was partial, however; slaves could be kept but not bought or sold. Full emancipation came four years later, in 1838.
3. Cassá, "Economic Development of the Caribbean," 7.
4. McKerrow, "Critical Rhetoric," 451.
5. Conquergood, "Performing as a Moral Act," 9.
6. E. Hill, *Trinidad Carnival*, 21.
7. Benítez-Rojo, *The Repeating Island*, 306.
8. Ibid., 307.
9. Ibid., 306.
10. Cowley, *Carnival, Canboulay, and Calypso*, 72. These types are not unique to one location, having counterparts on every island with a high percentage of emancipated slaves.
11. Cudjoe, *Beyond Boundaries*, 176.
12. Ibid., 176, emphasis added.
13. Benítez Rojo, *The Repeating Island*, 307, emphasis added.
14. Aching, *Masking and Power*, 15.
15. Blair, "Contemporary U.S. Memorial Sites," 19.
16. Metonymy is classically defined as "the figure which draws from an object closely akin or associated an expression suggesting the object meant, but not called by its own name" (*Rhetorica ad Herennium* 4.32), while metaphor is thought to occur "when a word applying to one thing is transferred to another, because the similarity *seems to justify this transference*" (4.34, emphasis added). The former is thought to operate (along with synechdoche) in terms of contiguity, and the latter (with irony) is thought to concern similarity. Roman Jakobson explores metonymy further in *Fundamentals of Language* (92), situating it between the decline of romanticism and the rise of sym-

bolism, though being opposed to both traditions. For my purposes, I rely primarily on the definition of these tropes as they appear in *Rhetorica ad Herennium* to underscore the continuity (universality) of expressive categories. Twelve in all, they have been gradually pared down to four in modern times and then paired (metonym/synecdoche, metaphor/irony) for their related applicability to aspects of contiguity and similarity, respectively.

17. The picturesque emerged as the eighteenth-century tourist's ideal for visual representation; adherents to it sought to straddle the beautiful and the sublime by representing life as it was rather than life as a stylized creation or, worse, an inexpressible abstraction. This genre included not only depictions of fields and trees, or ruins on the English landscape, but also representations of the suffering, poor, and otherwise marginalized members of society who had also faced ruin. In the nineteenth century the practice became normalized as an expression of visual imperialism, what Patricia Mohammed has called "the absolute conviction of European superiority and right to control" (*Imaging the Caribbean*, 137). "To determine what is picturesque," she writes, "is also to prescribe what is and is not aesthetically pleasing to the viewer's eye, implying a discrimination in taste and that such taste is universal" (290).

18. In the closing chapter of *The English in the West Indies*, the British historian James Anthony Froude mused on the nature of public opinion, claiming that "we live in a new era, when public opinion is king, and no other rule is possible; public opinion, as expressed in the press and on the platform, and by the deliberately chosen representatives of the people. Every question can be discussed and argued, all sides of it can be heard, and the nation makes up its mind. The collective judgment of all is wiser than the wisest single man—*securus judicat orbis*" (323). Needless to say, Froude limited his conception of "public" to his compatriots—colonizers, not the colonized—who were by nature of birth endowed with the right to engage in discourse at such a level. Froude's concluding chapter comes on the heels of a lengthy treatise opposing the push for self-rule and federation in the West Indies.

19. Hauser, *Vernacular Voices*, 14.

20. Ibid., 11.

21. Shotter, "Creating Real Presences," 275.

22. Howard, "Vernacular Web," 492, 493–95.

23. Ibid., 496. The vernacular system is doubly hybridized, for Howard describes "an economy of empowerment and subordination where the vernacular emerges as a hybrid of the institutional" (491).

24. Some characters, such as Dame Lorraine (a traditional eighteenth- or nineteenth-century French aristocrat) and Negue Jadin (the name is patois for "field slave"), were particularly popular among whites, perhaps giving them a sense of virtual anonymity as they began mingling in the streets: the former was usually played by masked women of the planter class, and the latter was portrayed as the total inverse of white aristocratic subjectivity, a black field slave. Other masques had their origins among slaves and were

reserved exclusively for use by the diametre; these included representations of the devil, demons, and assorted imps.

25. Barthes, *Mythologies*, 143.

26. Froude, *English in the West Indies*, 70.

27. Crowley, "Traditional Masques of Carnival," 194.

28. The need to "re-emancipate" operates as a commentary on the inadequacy of the official gesture of the 1830s. In "The Emancipation-Jouvay Tradition," Earl Lovelace notes that these now former slaves experienced the irony of emancipation that "sought to mock the idea of liberation by 'emancipating' people to nothing" (193). There was no infrastructure in place to support these people, who now had to provide for themselves in a society that had previously taken their labor for free. "Emancipation" was thus designed as a negative reinforcement, with the condition of continued enslavement being the better option for the survival of a people unaccustomed to the challenges of freedom. The strategy failed.

29. Aristotle, *On Rhetoric* 1358b3.

30. Sheard, "Public Value of Epideictic Rhetoric," 773.

31. Kennedy, intoduction to *On Rhetoric*, 7.

32. Aristotle suggested, rather problematically, that, "epideictic style is most like writing, for its objective is to be read" (*On Rhetoric* 1414a5). According to Kennedy, epideictic rhetoric was originally viewed as an "oratorical contest," as Isocrates describes it in the *Panegyricus*; later, Cicero (in *De Oratore*) linked it to history and Quintilian (in the *Institutio*) tied it to poetry. During the Renaissance, it was further broadened to include poetry, prose, painting, sculpture, and music (Kennedy, 48n77).

33. Oravec, "'Observation' in Aristotle's Theory of Epideictic," 166.

34. Perelman and Olbrechts-Tyteca, *The New Rhetoric*, 51.

35. Hyde, *Ethos of Rhetoric*, xiv.

36. Ibid.

37. Hall, "Negotiating Caribbean Identities," 283.

38. As opposed to Scott's notion that "the *hidden* transcript of subordinate groups, in turn, reacts back on the public transcript by engendering a subculture and by opposing its own variant form of social domination against that of the dominant elite. Both are realms of power interests" (*Domination*, 27, emphasis added).

CHAPTER 2. Structure, Strategy, and Rhetorical Parameters in Caribbean Expression

1. Abrahams, "Introductory Remarks," 148.

2. He notes that "as the call for a particularistic ethnography of experience has come together with a thorough tryout of the dramatistic metaphor used to describe observed life, it has seemed important for folklorists-ethnographers to become involved in the project" (Abrahams, *The Man-of-Words*, xxx).

3. Abrahams, *The Man-of-Words*, xxx–xxxi.

4. Glissant, *Caribbean Discourse*, 49.

5. Roberts, *West Indians and Their Language*, 16.

6. The latter differences may involve consonant clusters (*t*ing instead of *th*ing, *d*at instead of *th*at, wanti*n* instead of wanti*ng*, or learni*n* instead of learni*ng*) and vary more from territory to territory than do other syntactical features.

7. Burnett, *Penguin Book of Caribbean Verse*, xxiii.

8. I have identified these modes building on sociolinguistic categories suggested by Smitherman (*Talkin and Testifyin*) and Roberts (*West Indians and Their Language*).

9. The use of "visual" in this context is meant to refer to physical expressions—gesticulations, demonstrations, etc.—that occur predominantly *in conjunction with* oratorical delivery.

10. *Circular Despatch from the Secretary of State*.

11. Ibid.

12. Thomas's efforts were substantiated further by his critique of antireformationists like Froude. In *Froudacity* (1889), Thomas systematically refutes Froude's claims.

13. Thomas, *Theory and Practice of Creole Grammar*, iv.

14. Rickford, *Dimensions of a Creole Continuum*, 2.

15. Alleyne, "Caribbean Linguistic Perspectives," 158.

16. Brathwaite, *History of the Voice*, 262.

17. Rickford, *Dimensions of a Creole Continuum*, 3.

18. For more on the Creole Bible Translation Project, see the organization's website, accessed March 5, 2013, http://jamaicanbible.org.

19. Devon Dick, "God Understands Patois," *The Gleaner*, September 29, 2011, http://jamaica-gleaner.com/gleaner/20110929/cleisure/cleisure2.html.

20. This is borne out on the organization's blog, which includes a brief catalog of recent articles that take opposing views on the issue; see "The Jamaican Language Debate Resurfaces," accessed April 17, 2013, http://jamiekanbaibl.blogspot.com/2011/04/i-indicated-that-debate-re-place-of.html.

21. Fanon, *Black Skin, White Masks*, 17–18, emphasis added.

22. Bennett, "Dry-Foot Bwoy," 65–66.

23. Bryan, "Proletarian Movements," 141–73.

24. Carew, *Black Midas*, 26.

25. Prospero: Abhorred slave, / Which any print of goodness wilt not take, / Being capable of all ill! I pitied thee, / Took pains to make thee speak, taught thee each hour / One thing or other: when thou didst not, savage, / Know thine own meaning, but wouldst gabble like / A thing most brutish, I endow'd thy purposes / With words that made them known. But thy vile race, / Though thou didst learn, had that in't which good natures / Could not abide to be with; therefore wast thou / Deservedly confined into this rock, / Who hadst deserved more than a prison.

Caliban: You taught me language; and my profit on't / Is, I know how to curse. The red plague rid you / For learning me your language! (Shakespeare, *The Tempest*, I.ii.505–19).

26. Lamming, *In the Castle of My Skin*, 154–55.
27. Griffith, "Sing-Ins, Brams, and the Odd-Pedal," 198–99.
28. Ibid., 199.
29. I use Carol Myers-Scotton's definition of code-switching: "alterations of linguistic varieties within the same conversation" (*Social Motivations for Codeswitching*, 1).
30. The dilemma is reminiscent of the one faced by LuMing Mao in *Reading Chinese Fortune Cookie*. "Is it rhetorically appropriate," asks Mao, "to try to define and articulate an object of study with a narrative that is inextricably infused with and deliberately constituted by the same object?" (12).
31. In *Solibo Magnificent*, Patrick Chamoiseau describes the experience of such interplay as being "rooted in interlectal space" (22).
32. "A whole set of": many; "digging real horrors": to be deeply bothered by a situation, person, or practice.
33. "Jumbieing": to bother, to interfere with inordinately, or to derail or prevent. The term is derived from the noun *jumbie*, which denotes a ghost, especially a bad one.
34. "Taking basket": to accept unreliable advice or to be fooled, as in the proverbial "taking a basket to hold water."
35. In her examination of cognitive and social mechanisms that facilitate sociolinguistic negotiation, particularly code-switching, Myers-Scotton has claimed that speakers' interactions are conducted against a common social backdrop of shared values and salient factors; these factors include the activation and reliance on identical cognitive faculties, which abstract socio-psychological intent from interactions and facilitate common experiences against which to test those abstractions (*Social Motivations for Codeswitching*, 61).
36. Ashcroft, Griffiths, and Tiffin, *The Empire Writes Back*, 37.
37. Collins, "Shadowboxing," 60, emphasis added.
38. Walcott, "Pocomania," 31, emphasis added.
39. Smith, "Mi Cyaan Believe it," 37–38.
40. Ibid.
41. For example, in many Caribbean parties, the song "Hey Pocky A-way," by the New Orleans funk group the Meters, is often translated as a call, "Hey Fuck Away," to which the response is usually an emphatic "Haul your mothercunt!"
42. Carter, "Dr. Cassandra."
43. The song appears on more than a dozen albums between 1965 and 1988.
44. Manwarren et al., "Mud Madness."
45. Overheard, San Fernando, Trinidad, ca. 2007.
46. Breeze, "Sunday Cricket," 346–47.
47. Lovelace, *The Dragon Can't Dance*, 63–66.
48. There is an obvious correlation here with the practice of "signifyin," which Smitherman highlights as one of the definitive modes of African American discourse.

49. Lovelace, *The Dragon Can't Dance*, 21, emphasis added.
50. Smitherman, *Talkin and Testifyin*, 104.
51. Ibid.
52. This and the previous interactions are traditional.
53. Lee, *Give Me Some More Sense*, viii–ix.
54. Ibid. The closing exchange in patois appears to be a francophone pronunciation of "Crick? Crack."
55. De Freitas, "Rollo the Ganja."
56. Chamoiseau, *Solibo Magnificent*, 56–58.
57. Lamming, *In the Castle of My Skin*, 180.
58. Ibid., 181.
59. These three aphorisms may be rendered as follows. "T'ief f'om t'ief make God smile": an evocation of karma, cosmic irony, or divine justice, this suggests that God need expend little energy to punish, for the actions of the wicked are eventually visited upon them; "Good sense beat obeah": sometimes logic is more effective than magic; "When you come a church, bring you own hymn book": handle your own affairs, or what's mine is mine, so get your own.
60. Roberts, *West Indians and Their Language*, 157.
61. Abrahams, *Everyday Life*, 30, 31.
62. St. John, "Bajan Litany," 39.
63. Bennett, "Independance," 35–36.
64. Lovelace, *The Wine of Astonishment*, 59–61, emphasis added.
65. Lamming, *In the Castle of My Skin*, 179.
66. Ibid., 180.
67. Lovelace, *The Wine of Astonishment*, 61.
68. Dowe and McNaughton, "Rivers of Babylon," borrowing lines from Psalm 137:1.
69. Psalm 137:7–9 (NKJV).
70. Rickford, *African American Vernacular English*, 170.
71. Goodison, "Turn Thanks to Miss Mirry," 12.
72. Rickford, *African American Vernacular English*, 159–60.
73. The interaction in this case is not invented per se because the means by which that unity can be achieved is represented in a greeting that already exists. So, while *invention* is a central tenet of Caribbean rhetorical tradition, this particular performance expresses a deep reliance on aspects that are extant—such as a greeting—for its effectiveness in delivery.
74. Shotter, "Creating Real Presences," 274.
75. Ibid.
76. Sloat, ed., *Caribbean Dance*, viii.
77. Cogil and Barrett, "Dem Belly Full," 64. The poem served as the lyrics for a song by Bob Marley on the album *Natty Dread*.
78. Ibid.

79. Marshall, *Praisesong for the Widow*, 249.

80. Mirzoeff, *Introduction to Visual Culture*, 13.

81. This is despite Shotter's well-reasoned critique of what one is likely to do with a text rather than what ought to be done. See Shotter, "Creating Real Presences," 274.

82. Foss, "Framing the Study," 303.

83. I limit the discussion here to photographs only so they can serve as a representative example of the vast array of images the vernacular rhetor is able to create.

84. Szarkowski, *The Photographer's Eye*, 70.

85. Ibid.

86. I do not include the outboard motors, which are hoisted out of the water and laid in the pirogues, oriented toward the starboard. This is incidental, a matter of the way the engines themselves are designed and their placement is determined by the position of the rudder handle.

87. An overarching irony, of course, is that the photograph is equally capable of undermining the photographer's (my) intended vernacular sensibilities in favor of what appears to be a more "sophisticated" assertion that opts for the esoteric. A similar thing occurs with *Middle Class*, wherein the particular composition—the house, the car, the yard—almost strives to transcend its vernacular limitations.

88. The dish belonged to the Guide family and overlooked a workshop where caskets were made. The Belgrove family owned the funeral home directly across from Guide's on Coffee Street. And Clark and Battoo is a relatively short distance away, on Royal Road.

89. Foss, "Framing the Study," 303.

90. De Certeau, *Practice of Everyday Life*, 38.

91. Of course, others may operate with different goals or strategies when producing vernacular images in photographs, drawings, and so on.

92. Houses further inland exhibit the same form, though to address flooding, not tidal surges.

93. Froude, *The English in the West Indies*, 347.

94. Walcott, *What the Twilight Says*, 16.

95. In *Imaging the Caribbean*, Patricia Mohammed makes the crucial point that "Caribbean peoples have . . . come to resist and resent the camera lens, partly because they feel that the photographer benefits from their image, [and] others because they want to protect their privacy from a prurient outsider gaze" (335). I do not disagree with this point, for I have encountered similar reticence among those I have had the privilege to photograph. However, I have chosen not to include human subjects (with the exception of 3canal) among the images I discuss because I thought ones without them would more effectively illustrate the interplay of symbol, material, and space. That these images depict scenes wherein people exist is obvious. Where I have included biographical detail, it has been to circumvent the conundrum Mohammed faced in photographing a human subject and how they both contribute to the stereotype of what

Notes to Pages 82–85

she calls "the Caribbean picturesque." I have avoided that term in this section because the images have a rhetorical purpose that, I believe, supersedes their arguably picturesque qualities. Whatever the case in our differing ideas, both Mohammed and I share the conflicts that come with explaining our selves.

CHAPTER 3. From the Darker Side of a Schism: Performance and the Prophetic Masque

1. Manuel, *Caribbean Currents*, 1.

2. Alternatively, the original French spelling, *chantuelle*, is used.

3. See Rohlehr, *Calypso and Society*, 43. In addition, these songs also functioned as epilogues or chronicles of failed stickfighting encounters, as "Bagai Sala que Pocheray Moin" illustrates, or as supplication for having lost, as "La Reine Maribones" exemplifies.

4. In *Carnival, Canboulay and Calypso*, Cowley notes that, even after the French "capitulated" the island of Trinidad to the British in 1797, "black culture also reflected [an] African-French-Caribbean bias, including the establishment of 'patois' (Caribbean French Creole) as a lingua franca" (10).

5. It is also important to note that, by this time in the late nineteenth century, *calenda* had become a general term for the range of ritual music (and dance) retained from early celebrations among the underclass. It therefore illustrates the synthetic evolution of indigenous strategies that provided the urban underclass with reliable means of responding to specific formations of circumstances that were hewn from the rock of imperialist ideology.

6. Traditional calenda; a similar version is sung by Neville "Growling Tiger" Marcano. Both versions can be put in contrast to the bilingual calendas, such as "Fire Brigade," which employ the same (or similar) melody and syllabic structure but use both English and French creole. In the liner notes to *Trinidad Loves to Play Carnival: Carnival, Calenda and Calypso from Trinidad 1914–1939*, John Cowley notes that bilingualism was a strategy of defiance that allowed singers to mask their lyrics.

7. Regis, *Political Calypso*, 230.

8. Brereton, *History of Modern Trinidad*, 48, 51.

9. Cowley, *Carnival, Canboulay, and Calypso*, 72, 84. The Canboulay Riot followed the banning of Canboulay processions, where celebrants marched through the streets with torches (the festival's name is a creolized form of Cannes Brulées, or "burning canes"). Traditional stickfighting bands organized in protest to the restriction.

10. Ibid., 100. Additionally, Rohlehr notes that the abandonment of the traditionally symbolic kaiso songs—the first of which were sung by women (whence the term *chantuelles*)—for even more confrontational songs of protest was exacerbated by the very attempt to silence them (*Calypso and Society*, 54).

11. Noblett, "Golden Age of Calypso."

12. Along with Atilla, other calypsonians, including Roaring Lion, Neville "Growling Tiger" Marcano, and Philip "Lord Executor" Garcia, who had all secured notori-

ety at home, would see their musical rivalries span oceans and cultures in the 1930s, their "wars" against opponents like Wilmoth "Houdini" Hendricks being played out in the Decca recording studios. Their performances were revolutionary in that these artists managed to record and distribute songs of protest in an international market. They seemed aware of the historical and rhetorical significance of the moment and took opportunities to comment on this new dimension of experience. Nonetheless, many more were engaged in bitter censorship and licensing battles with the local colonial government. Notable examples were the concurrent banning of Lion's songs "Netty Netty" and "Sally Water" in 1936 and 1937, a development that, despite ongoing censorship, was followed by performances in New York, including one where Lion performed for Roosevelt himself at the Waldorf-Astoria Hotel.

13. Quevedo, *Attila's Kaiso*, 60.
14. Quevedo, "Roosevelt in Trinidad."
15. Quevedo, *Atilla's Kaiso*, 63.
16. U.S. Congress, *U.S. Statutes at Large*, 2406–8. See also Fullberg-Stolberg, "The Caribbean in the Second World War," 82–140.
17. Glissant, *Caribbean Discourse*, 125. Glissant characterizes "verbal delirium" as "improvisations, drumbeats, acceleration, dense repetition, slurred syllables, meaning the opposite of what is said, allegory and hidden meanings" (128).
18. Patton, "Calypso as Rhetorical Performance," 56.
19. West, *Restoring Hope*, 4–5 (interview with Harry Belafonte).
20. Glissant, *Caribbean Discourse*, 123.
21. Rohlehr, *Calypso and Society*, 17. See also Liverpool, *From the Horse's Mouth*, 3.
22. Ordinance no. 11 (1883), for instance, made "every Owner or Occupier, or their Agents, responsible for the Rogues, Vagabonds, and such like, assembling in the yards premises, and singing or dancing to the drum, chac chac, or any other instrument" (qtd. in Rohlehr, *Calypso and Society*, 35, citing *The Trinidad Review*, August 9, 1883).
23. This construction of the heroic in Caribbean music directly challenged the trope of the "grateful slave" that was dominant in the emergence of race as a category in British and American literature of the previous centuries.
24. As calypso grew in legitimacy as an art form at the dawn of the twentieth century, efforts continued to silence the calenda, enticing performers to discard the sentiments of the traditional calenda. The anthropolgist J. D. Elder notes that this was a period of flux, managed by attempts to "improve the calypso in literary style, introducing more complex musical form while using the litany forms of the kalinda-songs as the basic melodic framework" ("Evolution of the Traditional Calypso," 7).
25. It was also obvious that the growing trend of corporate preference, under the pretense of shying away from the disconcerting songs of the calenda and moving toward a more dignified aesthetic, was seen by some as more pointedly a rejection of the already ill-treated vernacular masses and thus a further crippling of the possibilities for economic strides that so few performers had been able to make.

26. Established by the British Caribbean Federation Act of 1956, the federation included Antigua and Barbuda, Barbados, Dominica, Grenada, Jamaica, Montserrat, (what was then) St. Kitts-Nevis-Anguilla, St. Lucia, St. Vincent, and Trinidad and Tobago.

27. That is, a pejorative twist on "personal monarch," a local representation of imperial rule.

28. According to Burke, "implicit in the idea of protection there is the idea that something needs to be *protected against*" (*Philosophy of Literary Form*, 61).

29. Regis, *Political Calypso*, 231, emphasis added.

30. Calliste, "Burn Them."

31. Patton, "Calypso as Rhetorical Performance," 57.

32. Turner, *Anthropology of Performance*, 22.

33. Devines, "Progress."

34. Rohlehr, introduction to *Voiceprint*, 21.

35. Regis, *The Political Calypso*, 211.

36. Phillip, "Dis Place Nice."

37. Ibid.

38. There is no direct reference to "death" in the song.

39. See Cowley, *Carnival, Canboulay, and Calypso*.

40. Rohlehr, "We Getting the Kaiso," 82–95.

41. This sense of urgency would be further underscored with the death of another music legend, the rapso trailblazer Andre Tanker, in 2003. Rudder offers tribute in a similarly transformative fashion, with a search that doubles as a commentary on the state of the Caribbean soul in need of what Tanker, the ancestor, offered. The musicoreligious link also occurs on an intertextual level in "One More Hosannah." Rudder refers to Tanker's "chain of cultures," described in detail in "Sayamanda." Incidentally, the song's title invokes another Tanker song, "Hosanna." Rudder signifies directly on Tanker's musical vision, specifically in his most recognizable chant, "Sayamanda." In Tanker's version, the singer describes the "chain of culture" that represented the mutuality in diasporic expression: "From pole to pole and corner to corner . . . / Behind the bridge and across the border." Rudder appropriates these lyrics to describe the scope and desperation of his own search for Tanker: "I looking from pole to pole. Behind the bridge, across the border. To find you I had to talk to one or two orisha."

42. This is by no means to elide songs such as Black Stalin's "Caribbean Unity" (1979).

43. Rudder interview, *No Restriction: The Concert*.

44. Nora, "Between Memory and History," 12.

45. Epstein, *Sinful Tunes and Spirituals*, 3–17.

46. The confluence of these religious traditions goes beyond the categorizations of the traditionally Christian and so beyond simply folding under the pressures of religious impositions (though the tendency for dogma lingers). Even the practice of syncre-

tism, then, served a dual purpose: to incorporate European practices both as religious veneers and as a means of strategically resisting the hegemonic imposition of European religion.

47. There is no firm consensus on the origin of calypso in Trinidad or when exactly it transformed from the calenda to a more recognizable form. Its roots, both the etymological ones of the name itself and the stylistic ones of the genre, are variously located in African, Amerindian, and European traditions (as I think they should be). The first calypso to be recorded was by Lovey's Band, led by Gerald Clark, in the studios of the Victor Talking Machine Company. The band played a melody entitled "Mango Vert." The first calypso to include vocals was Julian "Iron Duke" Whiterose's "Iron Duke in the Land," in 1914. Note, however, that the performer who would later dub himself the "Duke of Iron," Cecil Anderson, was only a child at the time of Whiterose's recording.

48. The Roaring Lion performs a version of this traditional chant in "African War Call."

49. Ironically, in *Calypso from France to Trinidad*, Roaring Lion argued that calypso originated not in Africa or the songs of indigenous tribes, as others posited, but in France.

50. The calypsonian's role is an undertaking that aligns with Burke's idea of an aesthetic text, which provides its audience with *"equipment for living,* as a ritualistic way of arming us to confront perplexities and risks" (*Philosophy of Literary Form*, 61).

51. The transcription of these vocalizations is original and interpretive; they do not appear among the formal lyrics of De Leon's "African War Call" or in any of the liner notes to albums where the song has appeared.

52. Glissant, *Caribbean Discourse*, 124.

53. Nora, "Between Memory and History," 12.

54. Rudder, "Calypso Music."

55. Based on Rudder, "Bahia Girl." These particular vocalizations are original transcriptions and do not appear among lyrics or in any of the liner notes to albums where the song has appeared.

56. Based on Rudder, "Bahia Girl." These particular vocalizations are original transcriptions and do not appear among lyrics or in any of the liner notes to albums where the song has appeared.

57. The prophetic calypsonian is a purveyor of inconvenient truths, a chronicler of society's shortcomings. So while Rudder's performance here can appear aloof, one should not confuse his message for solipsism, particularly when the imperative and its related practice are directed to the public, demanding its participation through reciprocity, sacrifice, and enactment of a shared agenda.

58. Rudder, "Bahia Girl." These vocalizations are original transcriptions and do not appear among lyrics or in any of the liner notes to albums where the song has appeared.

59. Rudder, "Tales from a Strange Land II: Crossing the Bridge."

60. See Manuel's introduction to *Caribbean Currents* (2) on this. Manuel posits these as opposing concepts, but I regard this as another example of the Caribbean ethos, which is constantly negotiating apparent contradictions with respect to its identity formation.

61. Cooper, *Noises in the Blood*, 5.

Chapter 4. "We Is People": Earl Lovelace, Ethos, and a Rhetoric of Vernacular Fiction

1. Rahim, "Nation/A World/A Place."
2. Burke, *Philosophy of Literary Form*, 20.
3. Ramchand, *West Indian Novel*, 179.
4. Daniel, *Dancing Wisdom*, 57–63.
5. I want to align my course in this chapter with that of Wayne Booth, who writes, "in a time when too much criticism, pursuing 'autonomy,' floats off into the Great Inane, with never a reference to anything but its own concept-spinning, there is surely room for a criticism that is openly embedded in and respectful of the stuff that it criticizes" (*Rhetoric of Fiction*, xii).
6. The name of this activity is spelled variously as *kalinda*, *kalenda*, and *calenda*. I use the variant shown here to highlight the stickfighting dance practiced in Trinidad, where the novel is based, as well as Haiti and Martinique.
7. Lovelace, *The Wine of Astonishment*, 19.
8. Ibid., 22.
9. Rohlehr, *Calypso and Society*, 53.
10. Lovelace, *The Wine of Astonishment*, 94.
11. Lovelace, "Meeting Place of Creole Culture," 10–22.
12. This ordinance lasted from 1917 to 1951, when it was finally repealed.
13. Lovelace, *The Wine of Astonishment*, 22.
14. Ibid., 37.
15. Ibid., 129.
16. Ibid., 118.
17. Lovelace, *The Dragon Can't Dance*, 162.
18. Lovelace, *The Wine of Astonishment*, 19.
19. Thorpe, introduction to ibid., ix.
20. Lovelace, *The Wine of Astonishment*, 129.
21. Ibid., 25.
22. Lovelace, "Meeting Place of Creole Culture," 14.
23. Lovelace, *Salt*, 167–68.
24. Ahye, "In Search of Limbo," 247–61.
25. Ahye has noted, importantly, that the limboing rhetor "is not really alone in the true sense ... as his friends and family are there to cheer him on as well, with much singing, drumming, bamboo stamping, and hand clapping" (ibid., 255).

26. Stanley-Niaah, "Mapping of Black Atlantic Performance," 193–217, emphasis added.
27. Ibid., emphasis added.
28. Ahye, "In Search of Limbo," 255.
29. Lovelace, *Salt*, 8, emphasis added.
30. Ibid., 10.
31. Ibid., 44.
32. Ibid., emphasis added.
33. It is interesting that such frustration stems not from competition or ambition but from an apparent lack of it.
34. Lovelace, *Salt*, 173, emphasis added.
35. Ibid., 171–72.
36. Ibid., 122, 129, 130, 258, emphasis added.
37. Ibid., 35.
38. Harris, *Selected Essays*, 157.
39. Ibid., 158.
40. Lovelace, "Meeting Place of Creole Culture," 13.
41. Lovelace, *Salt*, 22. Ironically, this statement also helps feed Lovelace's humanist agenda while not explicitly turning the notion of parochialism on its head. The demons to which I refer, however, are certainly recognizable and thus generalizable.
42. Lovelace, *The Dragon Can't Dance*, 3.
43. Ibid., 27–28.
44. Ibid., 31, 28–33.
45. Ibid., 115.
46. Aching, *Masking and Power*, 61.
47. Lovelace, *The Dragon Can't Dance*, 115.
48. Harris, *Carnival Trilogy*, xix.
49. Ramchand, *West Indian Novel*, 179.
50. Lovelace, *The Dragon Can't Dance*, 102.
51. Ibid.
52. Ibid., 178.
53. Ibid., 115.
54. In *Masking and Power*, Gerard Aching explains this further as the tripartite interplay of "dispossession, nonpossession, and self-possession . . . [which] constitute a discourse that is the inverse of the utopian cry 'all o' we is one' that is enunciated during the carnival celebrations in the novel but increasingly rings false as degrees of alienation in Aldrick's community become manifest" (52).
55. Lovelace, *The Dragon Can't Dance*, 103, emphasis added.
56. Harris, *Carnival Trilogy*, xiii.
57. Lovelace, *The Dragon Can't Dance*, 6, emphasis added.

58. Dixon, "Black Writer's Use of Memory," 21.

59. For an exposition of these sensibilities, see Hodge, "Language of Earl Lovelace."

60. Lovelace, *Growing in the Dark*, 226; Roffey, "A Certain Presence"; Burke, *Philosophy of Literary Form*, 9.

61. Dance, "Earl Lovelace," 277, emphasis added.

62. Kavalski, "'All o' We Is One,'" 29, emphasis added.

63. Ibid., 30, 32.

64. Ibid., 30.

65. Sylvia Wynter, for instance, notes that "the cultural tradition out of which the West Indian, who is fed by the Caliban culture of the West Indies[,] writes is an inherently revolutionary one. That was always its intention" ("We Must Learn," 341).

66. Hewson, "Interview with Earl Lovelace."

67. Lamming, *Pleasures of Exile*, 38–39.

68. Lovelace, *Salt*, 6.

69. Rahim, "Nation/A World/A Place."

70. Ibid., emphasis added.

71. Lovelace, "Meeting Place of Creole Culture," 10–22. For notion on which Lovelace draws, see Farrell, "Practicing the Arts of Rhetoric," 79–100.

72. According to Ramchand, "the effect of an all-embracing omniscient method as an instrument in characterisation and as a source of the novel's lyrical tone has been carried out as a necessary preliminary. The procedure permits, and helps to justify the generalisation that the world of *The Dragon Can't Dance* is a web in which each character is in turn the main character visibly bound to the other characters" (*West Indian Novel*, 179).

CHAPTER 5. Inhabiting the Digital Vernacular: The Old Talkers, the Caribloggers, and the Jamettes

1. Howard Rheingold defines virtual communities as "social aggregations that emerge from the Net when enough people carry on those public discussions long enough, with sufficient human feeling, to form webs of personal relationships in cyberspace" (*Virtual Community*, 5).

2. Chela Sandoval, for example, has argued that "colonized peoples of the Americas have already developed the cyborg skills required for survival under techno-human conditions as a requisite for survival under domination over the last three hundred years" ("New Sciences," 375). Sandoval suggests that a "methodology of the oppressed ... [relies, in part, on] the technology of 'semiotics,' 'deconstruction,' 'meta-ideologizing,' 'democratics,' and 'differential movement'" (382).

3. In her book *The Digital Divide*, Norris analyses the titular concept into the components listed here: "The concept of the digital divide is understood as a multidimensional phenomenon encompassing three distinct aspects. The *global divide* refers

to the divergence of Internet access between industrialized and developing societies. The *social divide* concerns the gap between information rich and poor in each nation. And finally within the online community, the *democratic divide* signifies the difference between those who do, and do not, use the panoply of digital resources to engage, mobilize, and participate in public life" (4).

4. Lévy, in *Cyberculture*, writes, "To say that technology conditions is to imply that it provides access to certain possibilities, that certain cultural or social options couldn't seriously be contemplated without its presence" (7).

5. Aycock, "Technologies of the Self."

6. Bailey, "Gossiping."

7. That is, one "macos" or is being "fast."

8. Senior, "The Story as *Su-Su*," 50 (old talk); McIntosh, "Social Media Swirls," 32–35.

9. For a discussion of supplementary discourse strands, see Jäger and Maier, "Theoretical and Methodological Aspects," 47.

10. Anonymous correspondence, Mar. 22, 2009. All further quotations from "Brian" and "Peter" are drawn from this exchange.

11. Premiering on December 21, 1973, Cowboy X is a character from a *Sesame Street* cartoon insert. The character, voiced by the satirist Jean Shepherd, was an outlaw who terrorized the town of Sniveler's Gulch by branding everything with the letter X. When the townspeople had had enough, they approached Cowboy X, humbly requesting that he no longer brand things with an X. He readily agreed, vowed never again to be known as Cowboy X, and chose to be known from then on as Cowboy O. The people accepted the compromise of having everything branded with an O instead of an X "because they really weren't very smart."

12. They communicate freely and personally, the confessional reference reinforcing the familiarity (and necessity) of display. That is, it also allows them to engage in a form of syncretically charged skepticism—while they admit belief in the abstractions of a "higher power," they resist subscribing to traditional forms of worship and ritual, choosing instead to reaffirm their personal identification.

13. Hyde, *Ethos of Rhetoric*, xvi.

14. See Meraz, "International Perspective on Citizen Media." See also McIntosh, "Blogging in the English-Speaking Caribbean."

15. Wells, "Portrait of Early Internet Adopters."

16. I use the term *cariblogger* generically; it should not be confused with the website cariblogger.com.

17. Rampersad, "KnowProSE.com Blog," emphasis added. All further quotations of Rampersad come from this source, unless noted.

18. Rampersad, "Blogging/Writing."

19. Springer, "Dear Rihanna," emphasis added. All further quotations of Springer come from this source.

20. Bajegirl, "Six Reasons."

21. See Carolle Charles's "Popular Imaginaries," a study of poor and working-class Haitian women's discourse, particularly their self-identification of the bodies as "my piece of land" (169–70).

22. In Bajegirl, "Six Reasons."

23. For a discussion of such "starting points, see Blair, "Contemporary U.S. Memorial Sites," 18. According to Glissant, "A forced poetics [as opposed to a natural poetics] is created from the awareness of the opposition between a language that one uses and a form of expression that one needs. . . . [It] is instituted by a community whose self-expression does not emerge spontaneously, or result from the autonomous activity of the social body" (*Caribbean Discourse*, 121).

24. The strategic localization of the issue of domestic violence among "we Bajans" thus implies a critical recognition of mutual forms of dehumanization involved in the violence done to women's bodies, occurring both locally *and* globally.

25. Bajegirl, "How Many More?"

26. Ibid., emphasis added.

27. Ibid.

28. Cooper, *Sound Clash*, 106, 127.

29. Ibid., 125–26.

30. Helfand, *Screen*, 35.

31. Hauser, *Vernacular Voices*, 8.

32. 5Management155, "NO INTRO NEEDED," posted November 25, 2006, comments by niniloco, AbsoluteLust, zeesims, breezz00, and BKZMA718, http://www.YouTube.com/watch?v=AIZ3T8-4Z8E.

33. Ibid., comments by bigrayray11, babyboi3000, and LordBlacknWild.

34. Ibid.

35. Flexio7, YouTube channel, posted May, 2008, http://www.youtube.com/user/flexio7.

36. Butler, *Excitable Speech*, 17, emphasis added.

37. Lovelace, *The Dragon Can't Dance*, 127.

38. Nayar, *Introduction to New Media*, 79.

39. According to Lévy, "the digital encoding [of an image] . . . is not, strictly speaking, 'immaterial' but simply occupies less space and weighs less than [the material that makes up the original image]. . . . Fluid and volatile, the digital recording occupies a unique position in the succession of images: implicit in their visible manifestation, it is neither unreal nor immaterial, but *virtual*" (*Cyberculture*, 35–36). In Lévy's example, the photograph of an object is used as the original text, its "material" representation being the paper on which the image is reproduced before being digitally encoded (that is, scanned for electronic display). The same principle applies to the digital encoding of the body.

40. Sheller, "Work That Body," 357; emphasis in original, with additional emphasis.

41. Best, *Politics of Caribbean Cyberculture*, 7, 11.

42. Ibid., 11.

43. Springer, "Dear Rihanna"; Bajegirl, "How Many More?"

44. For information about this organization, see its website, about.me/redforgender.

45. In *Multiliteracies for a Digital Age*, Selber describes these subject positions in order to "help students learn to exploit the different subjectivities that have become associated with computer technologies ... [and that signify our profession's] obligation to formulate better alternatives, to offer approaches and practices that are more responsible, broad-based, and productive" (24–26). My examination serves, in some way, as an extension of Selber's categories beyond the classroom, wherein one considers an even broader applicability of these multiliteracies for achieving effective employment, informed critique, and reflective praxis.

46. In fact, Nayar notes that the "paradigm [of reembodiment] does not split the body and identity between a real-material self and the virtual one. Instead, the virtual is experienced through the real, just as the material-real is mediated by the virtual" (*Introduction to New Media*, 79).

47. "Chris Brown Concert Cancelled after Guyana Protests," Caribbean360.com, November 26, 2012, http://www.caribbean360.com/index.php/news/guyana_news/638510.html#axzz2QueFUO07.

48. Following the incident, Rihanna and Brown have been seen repeatedly in each other's company, even collaborating on a recording, "Nobody's Business" (2012). Tellingly, the cover art for the album features Rihanna nude from the waist up. The image was released on Instagram.com (in contravention to the second item listed on their "Terms of Use," Instagram.com http://instagram.com/about/legal/terms/). Overlaid on her body are a number of words—adjectives, salutes, the album title. "Love" is scrawled across her face. Ironically, the only actual inscriptions visible on her body are two tattoos: on her torso, the Egyptian goddess Isis; and on her right shoulder, the words "Never a failure, always a lesson," written in reverse (http://instagram.com/p/QpTuWYBMym/). According to Rihanna's official website, *Rihanna Daily: The Official Rihanna Fansite for Your Daily Dose of Rihanna* (rihannadaily.com), the Isis tattoo commemorates her grandmother, while the second tattoo was inscribed in reverse so Rihanna could read it in the mirror, reaffirming the personal philosophy (see http://rihannadaily.com/rihanna/tattoos/#).

49. Sheller, "Work That Body," 362.

50. Nayar, *Introduction to New Media*, 76.

51. Lévy, *Cyberculture*, 30.

52. I use the term in the sense outlined by Jenkins in *Convergence Culture*, 2.

53. Rampersad, "Blogging/Writing."

54. Lévy, *Cyberculture*, 57.

Conclusion; or, Reprise for the Carnivalesque

1. For a list showing numbers of murders and other violent crimes in Trinidad and Tobago, see "Crime in Trinidad and Tobago," ttcrime.com, http://www.ttcrime.com/stats.php.

2. Lovelace, *The Dragon Can't Dance*, 127.

3. I cannot help but recall Matthew Lewis's observations in 1816. In "A West India Journal" he wrote, "Besides their (the Negroes') occasional amusements of poisoning, stabbing, thieving, etc., a plan has just been discovered in the parish of St. Elizabeth for giving themselves a grand fête by murdering all the whites in the island" (14).

4. Plato has Socrates speak of recognizing the limits of his knowledge in the *Apology* 21d.

5. Nettleford, "Ideology, Identity, Culture," 557.

6. James, "Lincoln, Carnival, George Padmore," 288.

7. Rudder, "Trini 2 de Bone."

8. For a video of such an incident, see "UTECH Guards Brutally Beating Gay Man in Jamaica," UrbanIslandz.com, November 2, 2012, http://urbanislandz.com/2012/11/02/gay-man-brutally-beaten-in-jamaica-video. According to reports, the man had run into the guard station to escape the wrath of a mob. Voices from the mob can be heard calling for his death. The additional irony brings to mind King Austin's song "Who Will Guard the Guards?"

9. Prelli, *Rhetorics of Display*, 5.

10. Mohammed, *Imaging the Caribbean*, 289.

BIBLIOGRAPHY

Abrahams, Roger. *Everyday Life: A Poetics of Vernacular Practices*. Philadelphia: University of Pennsylvania Press, 2005.

———. "Introductory Remarks to a Rhetorical Theory of Folklore." *Journal of American Folklore* 81, no. 320 (1968): 143–58.

———. *The Man-of-Words in the West Indies: Performance and the Emergence of Creole Culture*. Baltimore, MD: Johns Hopkins University Press, 1983.

Aching, Gerard. *Masking and Power: Carnival and Popular Culture in the Caribbean*. Minneapolis: University of Minnesota Press, 2002.

Ahye, Molly. "In Search of the Limbo." In *Caribbean Dance from Abakua to Zouk: How Movement Shapes Identity*, edited by Susanna Sloat, 247–61. Gainesville: University Press of Florida, 2002.

Alleyne, Mervyn. "Caribbean Linguistic Perspectives and Situation." In *Caribbean Contours*, edited by Sidney Mintz and Sally Price, 155–80. Baltimore, MD: Johns Hopkins University Press, 1985.

Aristotle. *On Rhetoric: A Theory of Civic Discourse*. Translated with introduction, notes, and appendices by George Kennedy. New York: Oxford University Press, 1991.

Ashcroft, Bill, Gareth Griffiths, and Helen Tiffin. *The Empire Writes Back: Theory and Practice in Post-Colonial Literatures*. 2nd ed. New York: Routledge, 2003.

Aycock, Alan. "Technologies of the Self: Foucault and Internet Discourse." *Journal of Computer-Mediated Communication* 1, no. 2 (1995). http://jcmc.indiana.edu/vol1/issue2/aycock.html.

Bajegirl. "How Many More?" *Cheese-on-Bread* (blog), April 1, 2009. http://cheese-on-bread.blogspot.com.

———. "Six Reasons Why Rihanna Would Marry Chris Brown." *Cheese-on-Bread* (blog), March 9, 2009. http://cheese-on-bread.blogspot.com.

Barthes, Roland. *Mythologies*. Translated by Annette Lavers. New York: Farrar, Straus and Giroux, 1991.

Benítez-Rojo, Antonio. *The Repeating Island: The Caribbean and the Postmodern Perspective*. Translated by James E. Maraniss. 2nd ed. Durham, NC: Duke University Press, 2001.

Bennett, Louise. "Dry-Foot Bwoy." In *Out for Stars 1: An Anthology of Poetry for Carib-*

bean Secondary Schools, edited by Neville Giuseppi and Undine Giuseppi, 65–66. London: Macmillan Caribbean, 1975.

———. "Independance." In *The Penguin Book of Caribbean Verse in English*, edited by Paula Burnett, 35–36. New York: Penguin, 1986.

Best, Curwen. *The Politics of Caribbean Cyberculture*. New York: Palgrave Macmillan, 2008.

Bitzer, Lloyd. "The Rhetorical Situation." *Philosophy and Rhetoric* 1, no. 1 (1968): 1–14.

Blair, Carole. "Contemporary U.S. Memorial Sites as Exemplars of Rhetoric's Materiality." In *Rhetorical Bodies*, edited by Jack Selzer and Sharon Crowley, 16–57. Madison: University of Wisconsin Press, 1999.

Booth, Wayne. *The Rhetoric of Fiction*. 2nd ed. Chicago: University of Chicago Press, 1983.

Brathwaite, Kamau. *History of the Voice: The Development of Nation Language in Anglophone Caribbean Poetry*. New York: Beacon, 1984.

Breeze, Jean Binta. "Sunday Cricket." In *The Oxford Book of Caribbean Short Stories*, edited by Stewart Brown and John Wickham, 344–47. New York: Oxford University Press, 1999.

Brereton, Bridget, *A History of Modern Trinidad 1783–1962*. London: Heinemann, 1981.

Bryan, Patrick. "Proletarian Movements (1940–90)." In *General History of the Caribbean*, vol. 5, *The Caribbean in the Twentieth Century*, edited by Bridget Brereton, 141–73. London: UNESCO/Macmillan, 2004.

Bryce-LaPorte, Roy Simon. "Introduction: New York City and the New Caribbean Immigration, a Contextual Statement." *International Migration Review* 13, no. 2 (1979): 214–34.

Burke, Kenneth. *The Philosophy of Literary Form*. 3rd ed. Berkeley: University of California Press, 1973.

Burnett, Paula, ed. *The Penguin Book of Caribbean Verse in English*. New York: Penguin, 1986.

Butler, Judith. *Excitable Speech: A Politics of the Performative*. New York: Routledge, 1997.

Carew, Jan. *Black Midas*. London: Secker and Warburg, 1958.

Cassá, Roberto. "The Economic Development of the Caribbean from 1880–1930." In *General History of the Caribbean*, vol. 5, *The Caribbean in the Twentieth Century*, edited by Bridget Brereton, 7–41. London: UNESCO/Macmillan, 2004.

Césaire, Aimé. *Notebook of a Return to My Native Land*. 1947. Reprint, Middletown, CN: Wesleyan University Press, 2001.

———. *A Tempest*. Translated by Richard Miller. 1969. Reprint, New York: Theatre Communications Group, 1999.

Chamoiseau, Patrick. *Solibo Magnificent*. New York: Anchor, 1999.

Charles, Carolle. "Popular Imaginaries of Gender and Sexuality: Poor and Working-Class Haitian Women's Discourses on the Use of Their Bodies." In *The Culture of*

Gender and Sexuality in the Caribbean, edited by Linden Lewis, 169–70. Gainesville: University Press of Florida, 2003.

"Circular Despatch from the Secretary of State for the Colonies," January 25, 1847. *British Parliamentary Papers*, vol. 37, 28. London, 1847.

Cogil, Legon, and Carlton Barrett. "Dem Belly Full." In *The Penguin Book of Caribbean Verse in English*, edited by Paula Burnett, 64. New York: Penguin, 1986.

Collins, Merle. "Shadowboxing." In *Blue Latitudes: Caribbean Women Writers at Home and Abroad*, edited by Elizabeth Nunez and Jennifer Sparrow, 58–69. New York: Seal, 2006.

Connor, Geraldine, and Max Farrar. "Carnival in Leeds and London: Making New Black British Subjectivities." In *Carnival: Culture in Action—the Trinidad Experience*, edited by Milla Cozart Riggio, 259–69. New York: Routledge, 2004.

Conquergood, Dwight. "Performance as a Moral Act: Ethical Dimensions of the Ethnography of Performance." *Text and Performance Quarterly* 5, no. 2 (1985): 1–13.

Cooper, Carolyn. *Noises in the Blood: Orality, Gender, and the "Vulgar" Body of Jamaican Popular Culture*. Durham, NC: Duke University Press, 1995.

———. *Sound Clash: Jamaican Dancehall Culture at Large*. New York: Palgrave Macmillan, 2004.

Cowley, John. *Carnival, Canboulay and Calypso*. London: Cambridge University Press, 1996.

Cozart Riggio, Milla, ed. *Carnival: Culture in Action-the Trinidad Experience*. New York: Routledge, 2004.

Crichlow, Michaeline A. *Globalization and the Post-Creole Imagination: Notes on Fleeing the Plantation*. Durham, NC: Duke University Press, 2009.

Crowley, Daniel J. "The Traditional Masques of Carnival." *Caribbean Quarterly* 4, nos. 3–4 (1956): 194–223.

Cudjoe, Selwyn. *Beyond Boundaries*. Amherst: University of Massachusetts Press, 2003.

Dance, Daryl Cumber. "Earl Lovelace." In *Fifty Caribbean Writers*, edited by Daryl Cumber Dance, 276–83. Westport, CN: Greenwood, 1986.

Daniel, Yvonne. *Dancing Wisdom: Embodied Knowledge in Haitian Vodou, Cuban Yoruba, and Bahian Candomblé*. Urbana: University of Illinois Press, 2005.

De Certeau, Michel. *The Practice of Everyday Life*. Berkeley: University of California Press, 1988.

Dixon, Melvin. "The Black Writer's Use of Memory." In *History and Memory in African-American Culture*, edited and with an introduction by Geneviève Fabre and Robert O'Meally, 18-27. New York: Oxford University Press, 1994.

Elder, Jacob Delworth. "Evolution of the Traditional Calypso of Trinidad and Tobago: A Socio-Historical Analysis of Song-Change." PhD dissertation, University of Pennsylvania, January 1966. http://repostiory.upenn.edu/dissertations/AAI6703066.

Epstein, Dena. *Sinful Tunes and Spirituals: Black Folk Music to the Civil War*. Urbana: University of Illinois Press, 2003.

Fabre, Geneviève, and Robert O'Meally, eds. *History and Memory in African-American Culture*. New York: Oxford University Press, 1994.

Fanon, Frantz. *Black Skin, White Masks*. 1952. Reprint, New York: Grove, 1967.

Farrell, Thomas. "Practicing the Arts of Rhetoric: Tradition and Invention." In *Contemporary Rhetorical Theory*, edited by John Louis Lucaites, Celeste Michelle Condit, and Sally Caudill, 140–52. New York: Guilford, 1999.

Foss, Sonja K. "Framing the Study of Visual Rhetoric: Toward a Transformation of Rhetorical Theory." In *Defining Visual Rhetorics*, edited by Charles A. Hill and Marguerite Helmers, 303–13. Mahwah, NJ: Lawrence Erlbaum, 2004.

Froude, James Anthony. *The English in the West Indies; or, The Bow of Ulysses*. 1888. Reprint, Cambridge: Cambridge University Press, 2010.

Fullberg-Stolberg, Claus. "The Caribbean in the Second World War." In *General History of the Caribbean*, vol. 5, *The Caribbean in the Twentieth Century*, edited by Bridget Brereton, 82–140. London: UNESCO/Macmillan, 2004.

Garvey, Marcus. "African Fundamentalism." *Negro World*, June 6, 1925.

Glissant, Edouard. *Caribbean Discourse: Selected Essays*. Translated by J. Michael Dash. Charlottesville: University Press of Virginia, 1989.

Goodison, Lorna. "Turn Thanks to Miss Mirry." In *Turn Thanks: Poems*, 12–13. Urbana: University of Illinois Press, 1999.

Griffith, Ezra. "Sing-Ins, Brams, and the Odd-Pedal." In *Under the Perfume Tree: Stories Weaving Patterns of Past Lives*, edited by Willi Chen et al., 184–234. Oxford: Macmillan, 2006.

Hall, Stuart. "Negotiating Caribbean Identities." In *Postcolonial Discourses: An Anthology*, edited by Gregory Castle, 281–92. Oxford: Blackwell, 2001.

Harris, Wilson. *The Carnival Trilogy*. London: Faber and Faber, 1993.

———. "The Limbo Gateway." In *The Post-Colonial Studies Reader*, edited by Bill Ashcroft, Gareth Griffiths, and Helen Tiffin, 378–82. New York: Routledge, 1995.

———. *Selected Essays of Wilson Harris*. Edited and with an introduction by Andrew Bundy. New York: Routledge, 1999.

Hauser, Gerard. *Vernacular Voices: The Rhetoric of Publics and Public Spheres*. Columbia: University of South Carolina Press, 1999.

Helfand, Jessica. *Screen: Essays on Graphic Design, New Media, and Visual Culture*. New York: Princeton Architectural Press, 2001.

Hewson, Kelly. "An Interview with Earl Lovelace." *Postcolonial Text* 1, no. 1 (2004). http://postcolonial.org/index.php/pct/article/view/344/802.

———. *Trinidad Carnival: Mandate for a National Theatre*. Austin: University of Texas Press, 1972.

Hodge, Merle. "The Language of Earl Lovelace." *Anthurium* 4, no. 2 (Fall 2006). http://anthurium.miami.edu/volume_4/issue_2/hodge-thelanguage.html.

Hopkinson, Nalo. *Midnight Robber*. New York: Aspect, 2000.

Howard, Robert Glenn. "The Vernacular Web of Participatory Media." *Critical Studies in Media Communication* 25, no. 5 (Dec. 2008): 490–513.

Hyde, Michael, J., ed. *The Ethos of Rhetoric*. Foreword by Calvin O. Schrag. Columbia: University of South Carolina Press, 2004.

Jäger, Siegfried, and Florentine Maier. "Theoretical and Methodological Aspects of Foucauldian Critical Discourse Analysis and Dispositive Analysis." In *Methods for Critical Discourse Analysis*, edited by Ruth Wodak and Michael Meyer, 34–61. London: Sage, 2009.

Jakobson, Roman. *Fundamentals of Language*. Janua Linguarum. Series Minor. 2nd edition. 1980. Reprint, The Hague: Mouton de Gruyer, 2002.

James, C. L. R. "Lincoln, Carnival, George Padmore: Writings from *The Nation*." In *The C. L. R. James Reader*, edited by Anna Grimshaw, 281–95. Oxford: Blackwell, 1993.

James, Louis. *Caribbean Literature in English*. Longman Literature in English Series. London: Longman, 1999.

Jenkins, Henry. *Convergence Culture: Where Old and New Media Collide*. 2nd ed. New York: New York University Press, 2008.

John, Catherine A. *Clear Word and Third Sight: Folk Groundings and Diasporic Consciousness in African Caribbean Writing*. Durham, NC: Duke University Press, 2003.

Kavalski, Emilian. "'All o' We Is One': Imaginary Federation or the Federation of the Imagination of the West Indies." *Journal of West Indian Literature* 13, nos. 1–2 (Apr. 2005): 28–56.

Kennedy, George. Introduction to *On Rhetoric: A Theory of Civic Discourse*, by Aristotle, 3–22. New York: Oxford University Press, 1991.

Lacan, Jacques. *Freud's Papers on Techniques*. Book 1 of *The Seminar of Jacques Lacan*. New York: Norton, 1991.

Lamming, George. *In the Castle of My Skin*. 1970. Reprint, Ann Arbor: University of Michigan Press, 1991.

———. *The Pleasures of Exile*. 1960. Reprint, Ann Arbor: University of Michigan Press, 1992.

Lawton, David. "Grammar of the English-Based Jamaican Proverb." *American Speech* 59, no. 2 (1984): 123–30.

Lee, Jacintha. *Give Me Some More Sense: A Collection of Caribbean Island Folk Tales*. London: Macmillan, 1988.

Lévy, Pierre. *Cyberculture*. Translated by Robert Bononno. Minneapolis: University of Minnesota Press, 2001.

Lewis, Matthew. "A West India Journal." 1815–17. In *West Indian Narrative: An Introductory Anthology*, edited by Kenneth Ramchand, 12–16. London: Thomas Nelson, 1966.

Liverpool, Hollis. *From the Horse's Mouth: An Analysis of Certain Significant Aspects* in the Development of the Calypso and Society as Gleaned from Personal Communication with Some Outstanding Calypsonians. Diego Martin, Trinidad: Juba, 2003.

Lovelace, Earl. *The Dragon Can't Dance*. London: Faber, 1979.

———. "The Emancipation-Jouvay Tradition and the Almost Loss of Pan." *TDR* 42, no. 3 (1998): 54–60.

———. *Growing in the Dark: Selected Essays*. Edited by Funso Aiyejina. San Juan, Trinidad: Lexicon Trinidad, 2003.

———. "The Meeting Place of Creole Culture: A Conversation with Earl Lovelace." Interview with Patricia Saunders. *Calabash* 1, no. 2 (1999): 10–22.

———. *Salt*. New York: Persea, 1997.

———. *The Wine of Astonishment*. London: Heinemann, 1982.

Manuel, Peter. *Caribbean Currents: From Rumba to Reggae*. Philadelphia: Temple University Press, 1995.

Mao, LuMing. *Reading Chinese Fortune Cookie: The Making of Chinese American Rhetoric*. Logan: Utah State University Press, 2006.

Marshall, Paule. *Praisesong for the Widow*. New York: Plume, 1983.

McIntosh, Karel. "Blogging in the English-Speaking Caribbean." October 31, 2006. http://www.caribbeanprblog.com/archives/2006/10/31/blogging-in-the-english-speaking-caribbean/.

———. "Social Media Swirls in the Caribbean." *Communication World*, May–June 2008, 32–35.

McKerrow, Raymie. "Critical Rhetoric: Theory and Praxis." In *Contemporary Rhetorical Theory*, edited by John Louis Lucaites, Celeste Michelle Condit, and Sally Caudill, 441–63. New York: Guilford, 1999.

Meraz, Sharon. "An International Perspective on Citizen Media: Using Social Network Analysis to Examine Hybridity in the Caribbean Blogosphere." Paper presented at the annual meeting of the International Communication Association, San Francisco, May 23, 2007. http://www.allacademic.com/meta/p169560_index.html.

Mirzoeff, Nicholas. *An Introduction to Visual Culture*. New York: Routledge, 2003.

Mohammed, Patricia. *Imaging the Caribbean: Culture and Visual Translation*. London: Macmillan, 2009.

Myers-Scotton, Carol. *Social Motivations for Codeswitching: Evidence from Africa*. New York: Oxford University Press, 1993.

Nayar, Pramod. *An Introduction to New Media and Cybercultures*. West Sussex, U.K.: Wiley-Blackwell, 2010.

Nettleford, Rex. "Ideology, Identity, Culture." In *General History of the Caribbean*, vol. 5, *The Caribbean in the Twentieth Century*, edited by Bridget Brereton, 537–58. London: UNESCO/Macmillan, 2004.

Noblett, Richard. "The Golden Age of Calypso." *Musical Traditions* 4 (1985). Article MT099, http://www.mustrad.org.uk/articles/calypso.htm.

Nora, Pierre. "Between Memory and History: *Lieux de Mémoires.*" Translated by Marc Roudebush. *Representations* 26 (1989): 7–25.

Norris, Pippa. *Digital Divide: Civic Engagement, Information Poverty, and the Internet Worldwide.* New York: Cambridge University Press, 2001.

Oravec, Christine. "'Observation' in Aristotle's Theory of Epideictic." *Philosophy and Rhetoric* 9 (1976): 162–74.

Parsons, Elsie Clews. "Proverbs from Barbados and the Bahamas." *Journal of American Folklore* 43, no. 169 (1930): 324–25.

Patton, John H. "Calypso as Rhetorical Performance: Trinidad Carnival 1993." *Latin American Music Review/Revista de Música Latinoamericana* 15, no. 1 (1994): 55–74.

Perelman, Chaïm, and Lucie Olbrechts-Tyteca. *The New Rhetoric.* Translated by John Wilkinson and Purcell Weaver. South Bend, IN: University of Notre Dame Press, 1971.

Plato. *Apology.* Translated by John M. Cooper. Indianapolis: Hackett, 2002.

———. *Phaedrus.* Translated by Robin Waterfield. New York: Oxford University Press, 2002.

Prelli, Lawrence J., ed. *Rhetorics of Display.* Columbia: University of South Carolina Press, 2006.

Quevedo, Raymond. *Atilla's Kaiso: A Short History of Trinidad Calypso.* St. Augustine, Trinidad: University of the West Indies (SOCS) Press, 1983.

Rahim, Jennifer. "The Nation/A World/A Place to Be Human: Earl Lovelace and the Task of 'Rescuing the Future.'" *Anthurium* 4, no. 2 (2006). http://anthurium.miami.edu/volume_4/issue_2/rahim-thenation.html.

Ramchand, Kenneth. *The West Indian Novel and Its Background.* London: Heinemann, 1983.

Rampersad, Taran. "Blogging/Writing." *Open Depth* (blog), February 24, 2008. http://www.opendepth.com.

———. "KnowProSE.com Blog." *KnowProSE* (blog). Accessed November 9, 2008. http://www.knowprose.com/blog.

Regis, Louis. *The Political Calypso: True Opposition in Trinidad and Tobago, 1962–1987.* Gainesville: University Press of Florida, 1999.

Rheingold, Howard. *The Virtual Community: Homesteading on the Electronic Frontier.* Reading, MA: Addison-Wesley, 1993.

Rhetorica ad Herennium. In *The Rhetorical Tradition*, edited by Patricia Bizzell and Bruce Herzberg, 2nd ed., 243–82. New York: Bedford/St. Martins, 2001.

Rickford, John R., *African American Vernacular English: Features, Evolution, Ethical Implications.* Malden, MA: Blackwell, 1999.

———. *Dimensions of a Creole Continuum.* Stanford, CA: Stanford University Press, 1987.

Roaring Lion [Raphael De Leon]. *Calypso from France to Trinidad: 800 Years of History.* San Juan, Trinidad: General Printers of San Juan, 1986.

Roberts, Peter A. *West Indians and Their Language*. London: Cambridge University Press, 1988.

Roffey, Monique. "A Certain Presence: An Interview with Earl Lovelace." *Writer's Hub*. http://www.writershub.co.uk/features-piece.php?pc=832.

Rohlehr, Gordon. *Calypso and Society in Pre-Independence Trinidad*. Port of Spain, Trinidad: The author, 1990.

———. Introduction to *Voiceprint: An Anthology of Oral and Related Poetry from the Caribbean*, edited by Stewart Brown, Mervyn Morris, and Gordon Rohlehr, 1–23. Longman Caribbean Writers Series. Essex, U.K.: Longman, 1989.

———. "We Getting the Kaiso That We Deserve: Calypso and the World Market." *Drama Review* 42, no. 3 (1998): 82–95.

Sandoval, Chela. "New Sciences: Cyborg Feminisms and the Methodology of the Oppressed." In *The Cyborg Handbook*, edited by Chris Gray, 374–87. London: Routledge, 1995.

Scott, James. *Domination and the Arts of Resistance: Hidden Transcripts*. New Haven, CT: Yale University Press, 1990.

Selber, Stuart. *Multiliteracies for a Digital Age*. Carbondale: Southern Illinois University Press, 2004.

Senior, Olive. "The Story as *Su-Su*, the Writer as Gossip." In *Writers on Writing: The Art of the Short Story*, edited by Maurice Lee, 41–50. Westport, CN: Praeger, 2005.

Sforza, John. *Swing It: The Andrews Sisters Story*. Lexington: University Press of Kentucky, 2004.

Shakespeare, William. *The Tempest*. Edited by Jonathan Bate and Eric Rasmussen. Modern Library Classics. New York: Norton, 2003.

Sheard, Cynthia Mieczinikowski. "The Public Value of Epideictic Rhetoric." *College English* 58 (1996): 765–94.

Sheller, Mimi. "Work That Body: Sexual Citizenship and Embodied Freedom." In *Constructing Vernacular Culture in the Trans-Caribbean*, edited by Holger Henke and Karl-Heinz Magister, 345–76. Lanham, MD: Lexington, 2008.

Shotter, John. "Creating Real Presences: Displays in Liminal Worlds." In *Rhetorics of Display*, edited by Lawrence J. Prelli, 273–89. Columbia: University of South Carolina Press, 2006.

Sloat, Susanna, ed. *Caribbean Dance from Abakua to Zouk: How Movement Shapes Identity*. Gainesville: University Press of Florida, 2002.

Smith, Michael. "Mi Cyaan Believe It." In *Voiceprint: An Anthology of Oral and Related Poetry from the Caribbean*, edited by Stewart Brown, Mervyn Morris, and Gordon Rohlehr, 37–38. Longman Caribbean Writers Series. Essex, U.K.: Longman, 1989.

Smitherman, Geneva. *Talkin and Testifyin: The Language of Black America*. Detroit, MI: Wayne State University Press, 1977.

Springer, Attillah. "Dear Rihanna." *Four Fingers and a Thumb* (blog), March 7, 2009. http://tillahwillah.wordpress.com/2009/03/07/dearrihanna/.

Stanley-Niaah, Sonjah. "Mapping of Black Atlantic Performance Geographies: From Slave Ship to Ghetto." In *Black Geographies and the Politics of Place*, edited by Katherine McKittrick and Clyde Woods, 193–217. Cambridge, MA: South End, 2007.

St. John, Bruce. "Bajan Litany." In *The Penguin Book of Caribbean Verse in English*, edited by Paula Burnett, 39. New York: Penguin, 1986.

Sutton, Jane. "The Taming of the Polos/Polis: Rhetoric as an Achievement without Woman." In *Contemporary Rhetorical Theory*, edited by John Louis Lucaites, Celeste Michelle Condit, and Sally Caudill, 101–26. New York: Guilford, 1999.

Szarkowski, John. *The Photographer's Eye*. New York: Museum of Modern Art, 2007.

Thomas, John Jacob. *The Theory and Practice of Creole Grammar*. Port of Spain, Trinidad: Chronicle Publishing Office, 1869.

Thorpe, Marjorie. Introduction to *The Wine of Astonishment*, by Earl Lovelace, vii–xiv. London: Heinemann, 1982.

Turner, Victor. *The Anthropology of Performance*. Baltimore, MD: Johns Hopkins University Press, 1988.

U. S. Congress. *U.S. Statutes at Large*. Vol. 54. Washington, DC: Government Printing Office, 1941.

Vatz, Richard. "The Myth of the Rhetorical Situation." *Philosophy and Rhetoric* 6 (1973): 154–61.

Walcott, Derek. "The Antilles: Fragments of Epic Memory." Nobel Lecture. 1992. In *What the Twilight Says: Essays*, 65–84. New York: Farrar, Straus and Giroux, 1998.

———. "Pocomania." In *Collected Poems: 1948–1984*. New York: Farrar, Straus and Giroux, 1987.

———. *What the Twilight Says: Essays*. New York: Farrar, Straus and Giroux, 1998.

Wells, Amy Tracy. "A Portrait of Early Internet Adopters: Why People First Went Online—and Why They Stayed." Pew Internet and American Life Project, February 6, 2008. http://www.pewinternet.org/~/media/Files/Reports/2008/PIP_Early_Adopters.pdf.pdf.

West, Cornel. *Restoring Hope: Conversations on the Future of Black America*. Edited by Kelvin Shawn Sealey. New York: Beacon, 1997.

Wilbur, Shawn. "An Archaeology of Cyberspaces." In *The Cybercultures Reader*, edited by Barbara M. Kennedy and David Bell, 45–55. New York: Routledge, 2001.

Wynter, Sylvia. "We Must Learn to Sit Down Together and Talk about a Little Culture: Reflections on West Indian Writing and Criticism." In *Caribbean Women: An Anthology of Non-Fiction Writing, 1890–1980*, edited by Veronica Marie Gregg, 329–54. Notre Dame, IN: University of Notre Dame Press, 2005.

DISCOGRAPHY

Bailey, Winston. "Gossiping." *Dingolay!* Kiskidee Records, 1994.
Batson, Nadia. "Caribbean Girl." *Caribbean Girl*. Dynamic Entertainment, 2007.
Calliste, Leroy. "Burn Them." *I-Time*. B's Records, 1987.
Caribbean Voyage: Trinidad Carnival Roots. The Alan Lomax Collection. Rounder 1166117252, 2000.
Carter, Anthony. "Dr. Cassandra." *Fire in de Wave*. Ice 941502, 1994.
De Freitas, Vasco. "Rollo the Ganja." *Caribbean Voyage: Trinidad Carnival Roots*. The Alan Lomax Collection. Rounder 1166117252, 2000.
De Leon, Rafael, and Cyril Monrose Orchestra. "African War Call." *Calypso Callaloo: Early Carnival Music in Trinidad*. Rounder B000002TN, 2008.
Devines, Winsford. "Progress." Performed by Austin Lewis ("King Austin"). *Progress/Billy Jean*. Play Me PM-014, 1980.
Francisco, Slinger. "Congo Man." *Congo Man/Patsy*. National NSP-052.
Grant, Rupert. "Rum and Coca-Cola." *Calypso in New York*. Smithsonian Folkways 40454, 2000.
Henry, Winston. "In Parliament They Kicksing." *Positive Vibrations*. Semp SWH 01, 1979.
Isaacs, Gregory. "Night Nurse." *Night Nurse*. Island Records, 1982.
Manwarren, Wendell, et al. "Mud Madness." *Heroes of Wha?* Rituals Records, 2001.
Marley, Bob. "Talkin' (no. 3)." *Talkin' Blues*. Island Records, 1991.
Phillip, Emrold. "Dis Place Nice." Label unknown, 1975.
Quevedo, Raymond. "History of Carnival." Brunswick, 1935.
———. "Roosevelt in Trinidad." *Roosevelt in Trinidad: Calypsos of Events, Places, and Personalities, 1933-1939*. Rounder 1142, 1999.
Rudder, David. "Bahia Girl." *The Hammer*. Charlies, 1986.
———. "Calypso Music." *This Is Soca with David Rudder and Charlies Roots*. London, 1987.
———. "Crossroads." *Tales from a Strange Land*. Lypsoland, 1996.
———. "The Hammer." *The Hammer*. Charlies, 1986.
———. "High Mas I." *Beloved*. Lypsoland, 1998.
———. Interview. *No Restriction: The Concert*. Lypsoland, 1998.

———. "Madness." *This Is Soca with David Rudder and Charlies Roots.* London, 1987.
———. "The Ministry of Rhythm." *Ministry of Rhythm*, Lypsoland, 1992.
———. "No Restriction (on the Friction)." *Tales from a Strange Land.* Lypsoland, 1996.
———. "One More Hosannah." *Eclectica.* Lypsoland, 2005.
———. "Pull Together." *No Restriction: the Concert.* Lypsoland, 1998.
———. *Tales from a Strange Land.* Lypsoland, 1996.
———. "Visions of Paradise." *Farewell to the Flesh.* Lypsoland, 2002.
Rudder, David, and Carl Jacobs. "Tini 2 de Bone." *Blessed.* Lypsoland, 2003.
Span, Norman, et al. "Don't Break It, I Say." 1934. *Trinidad Loves to Play Carnival: Carnival, Calenda and Calypso, 1914-1939.* Matchbox Calypso Series 302-2. Flyright Records, 1993.
Tanker, Andre. "Sayamanda." *Andre Tanker Greatest Hits, Vol. 1.* Andre Tanker Music, 2003.
Tosh, Peter. "Stepping Razor." *Equal Rights.* Columbia, 1977.

INDEX

Note: Page numbers in italic type indicate illustrations.

Abrahams, Roger, 30, 31, 32, 53
accountability, 101, 132, 163
Aching, Gerard, 15–16, 180n54
action, interaction and, 59
activism, 109, 130, 162
activities, 7, 11; enthymematic, 53, 142, 151; rhetorical, 4, 18, 20, 22, 92, 139, 141, 151, 152, 153, 156, 158, 161; vernacular, 142
aesthetics, 69, 70, 79
"African Fundamentalism" (Garvey), 10
"African War Call" (Rudder), 99, 100, 178n48, 178n51
agenda, 22, 104, 180n41; Caribbean, 27; rhetorical, 64, 65
Ahye, Molly, 111, 179n25
Aldrick, 46, 47, 117, 118–19, 122; community and, 180n54; dance and, 120, 121; mas making and, 118, 120
Alleyne, Mervyn, 34
American International Group (AIG), 133
Anderson, Cecil "Duke of Iron," 178n47
Andrews Sisters, 80, 81
aphorisms, 55, 102, 173n59
"Apocalypse" (Lambkin), 94
appeal, 55; dialogic, 56, 57, 58; dogmatic, 56, 57, 58; pathetic, 56, 57, 58, 60
Arab Spring, 163

Aristotle, 24, 103
assimilation, 10, 35
audiences, 28, 89, 160; accountability of, 101; bloggers and, 137; Caribbean, 18, 101, 146; dancers and, 123; identification with, 142; literacy of, 152; nonvernacular, 19; participatory role of, 48; speakers and, 8; vernacular, 12, 137
awareness, 90, 93, 126, 130, 138; psychic, 63

babyboi3000, 148
bacchanalist, 1
badjohns, 105
"Bahia Girl" (Rudder), 92, 98, 99, 100, 159, 178nn55–56, 178n58
Bailey, Winston "the Mighty Shadow," 130
"Bajan Litany" (St. John), 53
Bajans, 6, 49, 140, 142, 144, 183n24
Bajegirl, 143–44, 145; enthymematic/metaphoric approaches and, 151; material realities and, 142; proverb and, 149
Bakhtin, Mikhail, 14, 15
"Banana Boat Song" (Belafonte), 87
banga season, 36, 158
Barthes, Roland, 21
batonniers, 84, 106
Batson, Nadia, 49
Beg Pardon, 64, 95
behavior, 45, 55, 160
Belafonte, Harry, 87

"Bendwood Dick" (Francisco), 43
Benítez-Rojo, Antonio, 12, 14, 15
Bennett, Louise, 35, 53
Best, Curwen, 151
Bible Society of the West Indies, 34
Big Drum, 64, 95
bigrayray11, 148
binarisms, 15, 68
Bishop, Maurice, 88
Bitzer, Lloyd, 167n10
black bodies, colonized, 11
Black Midas (Carew), 36
Black Power Revolution, 88
Blair, Carole, 16, 168n15
bloggers, 50, 136, 137, 138, 140, 141, 145
Blue Devils (band), 1
boasting, 38; shaming and, 50–52
Bolo, 105, 115, 159; character of, 107; death of, 108, 109; on ethos, 109; kalinda and, 106, 108, 110
Booth, Wayne, 103, 179n5
Botha, P. W., 89
Bradman, Don, 39
Brathwaite, Kamau, 34
Breeze, Jean Binta, 45
"Brian," 131–32, 134, 135, 147, 153; discursive model of, 136
British Caribbean Federation Act (1956), 177n26
British West Indies Federation, 88
Brother Austin, 71, 73
Brother Austin's House, San Fernando, 70, 71, 71; *Pink House, Palo Seco* and, 69
Brown, Chris: Rihanna and, 139–40, 142, 144, 152, 184n48
Browne, Layla, 128
Bryan, Patrick, 36
Burke, Kenneth, 4, 30, 103, 178n50
"Burn Them" (Calliste), 89, 94
Burnett, Paula, 32

bwa, 107
bwoy, 35, 36

Calenda, 83, 84, 175n5, 176n24, 179n6; bilingual, 175n6; songs of, 176n25
Caliban, 36, 171n25, 181n65
call and response, 38, 47–50, 99
Calliste, Leroy "Black Stalin," 89, 93, 94
calypso, 43, 81, 84, 88–92, 96, 122; ballad, 95; features of, 82–83; first, 178n47; formative years of, 95; literary style and, 176n24; oratorical, 85; origin of, 178n47, 178n49; prophetic, 86; social influence in, 90
Calypso from France to Trinidad (Lion), 178n49
"Calypso Music" (Rudder), 95, 101
Calypso Rose, 93
calypsonians, 84, 85, 87, 89, 90, 97, 102, 130, 189, 178n50; audience of, 88; composing by, 101; prophetic, 92, 178n57
Canboulay, 87, 98, 159, 160
Canboulay Riot (1881), 84, 175n9
Cannes Brulées, 159, 175n9
Capolino, Lesley Ann, 155
Carew, Jan, 36
Carib Street House, Western Side, San Fernando, 73, 73
Caribbean, 1, 3, 5, 116; abstractions of, 78; becoming, 6, 113, 141
Caribbean Diaspora, 95
Caribbean discourse, 6, 15, 20, 39, 135; rhetorical modes of, 38 (table)
Caribbean Discourses (Glissant), 10, 30
Caribbean exceptionalism, 163
Caribbean gaze, 18
"Caribbean Girl" (Batson), 49
Caribbean orality, negative views of, 38
Caribbean reality, 38
Caribbean texts, 16, 28, 135

Index

Caribbean360, 152
Caribbeanness, 13, 14, 15, 20, 24, 27, 35, 39, 49, 80, 86, 93, 104, 115, 124, 126, 128, 135, 141, 154, 158; conceptions of, 129; enactment of, 8–9; expressions of, 136; metaphor for, 25; productive understandings of, 123
Caribbeans, 80, 93, 128, 129, 160, 161, 162; of African descent, 167n8; authentic, 47; conditions for, 8; conversation about, 9; depictions of, 16; images/representations by, 167n8; issues relevant to, 137; online, 134; participation of, 5; rhetoric of, 9, 27; roots of, 4; technology and, 151
Caribloggers, 129, 136, 142, 143, 145, 153, 182n16; individuality of, 137; mainstream bloggers and, 138; role of, 139
Cariblogosphere, 135–41
Carnival, 2–3, 7, 14, 24, 25, 28, 45, 51, 91, 103, 117, 121, 122, 125, 145, 150, 155, 159; Bakhtinian reading of, 16; celebrations, 160; corporatization of, 93; European sensibilities and, 11; formalized, 13; glorious, 85; liberatory potential of, 163; masque and, 23; narrative, 151; naturalization-neutralization of, 22; participation in, 10; as privilege, 12; Trinidadian, 20
"Carnival in Leeds and London" (Connor and Farrar), 10
carnivalesque, 15, 16, 17, 24, 28, 29, 59, 80, 86, 101, 105, 107, 112, 117, 129, 136, 146, 151, 155, 162; Bakhtinian, 14; Caribbean, 7, 11, 12, 15, 17 (table), 20, 156, 163; characteristics of, 17 (table); discourse, 13; effectiveness of, 149; enactments of, 8; European, 21; manifestations of, 12, 159; manipulation of, 127; notions of, 18; social action and, 13; vernacular, 22

Carriacou, 64
Carter, Anthony "Gabby," 42, 43
cascadoo, 4
Cassá, Roberto, 10
celebrations, 23, 127, 160
censorship, 42, 84, 176n12
chantwell, 83, 84, 106
chantuelle, 85, 175n2, 175n10
characteristics, 126; carnivalesque, 17 (table); subnational, 81; vernacular, 78
Charles, Rudolph, 92, 93
Charlie's Roots (band), 92
Cheese-on-Bread: From Barbados to the World (Bajegirl), 142
chiasmus, 53, 54
Cicero, 30, 270n32
circumlocution, 38, 46–47, 52
citizenship, 18, 27; belonging and, 24; Caribbean, 19, 26, 152; global, 129, 161; Clark and Battoo, 174n88
Clark, Gerald, 85, 178n47
Cocoa House, Roxborough, 65, 65
Code Red for Gender Justice, 151
code-switching, 38, 40–42, 172n29, 172n35
collaboration, 84, 105, 134, 135, 139
collective practice, 11, 153
collective resolve, 59, 60, 125
Collins, Merle, 41
colonialism, 4, 19, 21, 25, 27, 33, 70, 87, 124; legacy of, 91; metropolitanism and, 18
communication, 6, 127, 136; attitudes toward, 33–38; polydialectal, 41; rhetoric and, 8
community, 5, 120, 121, 164, 180n54; activism, 109; discourse, 86, 145; interdependency of, 71; resilience of, 52–53; transnational, 126; virtual, 128, 129, 181n1; West Indian, 31
composition process, 62, 138
concealment, 23, 42

concept, dancing, 122–27
confession, 55, 56
"Congo Man" (Francisco), 43
Connor, Geraldine, 10
consciousness, 22, 82; critical, 81; cultural, 112; liberation through, 63; moral, 26; public, 143; rhetoric of, 21; vernacular, 59, 60, 130
construction, 17, 70
consumption, 21, 44, 146
convergence, 17, 49, 153
Cooper, Carolyn, 145, 146
Corbeaux, Erin I, 69, 69
corruption, 90, 115, 146
Cowboy O, 182n11
Cowboy X, 132, 182n11
Cowley, John, 13–14, 175n6
creole, 14, 35, 38, 63, 97, 134, 147; continuum, 33–34; perspectives, 101; standardizing, 41; vernacular, 39
Creole Bible Translation Project, 34, 171n18
creolization, 14, 32, 35, 36
critical response, 27, 155, 156
critique, 24, 144, 148, 174n81
Crowley, Daniel, 23, 119
Cudjoe, Selwyn, 14, 15
cultural amnesia, 50
cultural commentary, 135
cultural heritage, 100
cultural memory, 21, 37, 89
cultural production, 13, 81, 87, 164
cultural unity, 7, 15
culture, 18, 27, 116, 156, 160, 162; black, 175n4; Caribbean, 28–29, 95, 100, 129, 161; expressive, 4, 42; oral display of, 38; underground, 14
cyberculture, 129, 145, 150, 153; Caribbean, 151, 154
cyberspace, 129, 136, 137, 138, 151, 152

Daisley, Liesl, 144
Dame Lorraine, 169n24
dance, 119, 120, 122–27, 160; bodies, 149; dragon, 121, 138; inclusiveness of, 122–23; language, 63; prison, 121; as rhetoric, 64, 122; ritualistic, 111; sacred, 64
Dance, Daryl Cumber, 123
dancing of attitude, spiritual/physical, 101
De Certeau, Michel, 74
De Freitas, Vasco, 50, 51
De Oratore (Cicero), 30, 170n32
"Dear Rihanna" (Springer), 130–40
DeCamp, David, 33
"Dem Belly Full" (Cogill and Barrett), 63
democracy, 120, 167n7, 181n2, 182n3
desires, 26, 113, 154
Destroyers for Bases Agreement, 86
Diab-Anba-Feuilles, 51
Diable-Diable, 117
dialectic, 11, 19–20, 146
dialogism, 15
dialogue, 87, 138, 164; monologue and, 137
diametre, 13, 17, 84, 170n24
diaspora, 64, 95, 115
Digital Divide, The (Norris), 181n3
"Dis Place Nice" (Phillip), 91, 92
discourse, 13, 16, 137, 141, 161, 168n10; African American, 172n48; audience, 146; Caribbean, 6, 15, 20, 38 (table), 39, 135; civil/civic, 154; community, 86, 145; conflicting, 29; creolized, 132; dominant, 157; epideictic, 26; familiar, 128; feminist, 160; public, 153; supplementary strands of, 131; women's, 183n21
disenfranchisement, 87, 106, 123, 160
disorder, order and, 68
display, 17, 120; oral, 35, 38; parrhesiastic, 86; public, 22, 80, 141; rhetorical, 100, 106, 124, 127; self-conscious, 122; vernacular, 19, 103

"Dr. Cassandra" (Carter), 42
Dowe, Brent, 59
dragon, 119, 120
Dragon Can't Dance, The (Lovelace), 46, 103, 104, 105, 108, 150, 181n72; Carnival and, 122; daemonic transformation in, 117–22
"Dry-Foot Bwoy" (Bennett), 35
dystopian critique, 17, 94

Eastern Parkway, 157, 163
Elder, J. D.: on calypso, 176n24
emancipation, 60, 123, 161, 170n28
"Emancipation-Jouvay Tradition, The" (Lovelace), 170n28
Emmanuel, Maclean "Short Shirt," 93
empowerment, 111, 160, 169n23
English in the West Indies; or, The Bow of Ulysses, The (Froude), 21, 169n18
English language, as agent of civilization, 33
enthymematic activity, 53, 142, 151
enthymeme, 4
epideictic, 24–25, 63, 83, 157, 170n32; collective, 26; vernacular, 23, 81, 100
escapism, 59, 60
ethics, 7, 20, 101, 162
ethos, 18, 20, 27, 49, 52, 83, 102, 109, 111, 116, 117, 121, 137, 151, 153, 179n60; Caribbean, 8–9, 10, 12, 17, 50, 101, 119, 122, 124, 125, 126, 127, 139, 158, 162; collective, 108; concept of, 26; digital vernacular and, 130–35; display of, 120; emergence of, 10, 105, 127; post-Caribbean, 154; prophetic, 91; rhetors and, 80; self-discovery and, 110; theory of, 105; vernacular, 19, 25, 26, 125, 137
everyday struggle, negotiations of, 87
exhibitionism, 146
exigence, 16, 19, 165
exoticism, 8, 66, 113

expressions, 22, 171n9; Caribbean, 12, 31, 78, 134, 136; cultural, 38, 80, 156, 162; folkloric, 32; nonverbal, 66; rhetorical, 11, 26; vernacular, 39, 41, 87

Facebook, 129, 131
Fanon, Frantz, 35
Farrar, Max, 10
Farrell, Thomas, 4, 126
Farrow, Rene, 155
Fastbook, 130
festivals, 9, 28, 45, 111, 112, 121
Firearms Act, 88
Fisheye, 46, 47, 51, 108, 121
flexi07, 148, 149, 151
"Flying Squad," 88
Foss, Sonja, 66, 72
Four Pirogues, Charlotteville, 68, 68
fragmentation, 82, 100, 125
Francisco, Slinger "the Mighty Sparrow," 43–44
Froude, James Anthony, 21, 75, 169n18, 171n12

Gairy, Eric: coup versus, 88
Garcia, Philip "Lord Executor," 175n12
Garvey, Marcus, 10
Gaye, Marvin, 90
George, Alford, 114, 115, 116, 117, 159; epiphany for, 120
Gerald Clark's Serenaders, 85
Glissant, Edouard, 10, 30, 31–32, 78, 97; forced poetics and, 143; verbal delirium and, 176n17
god-as-voyeur narrative, 132
"God Save the King," 91
"Good Morning Neighbor," performance of, 62
Goodison, Lorna, 60, 61
Google+, 129
gossip, characterization of, 130

"Gossiping" (Bailey), 130
Griffith, Ezra, 39, 41
Gun Court Act, 88

Hall, Stuart: on Caribbeanness, 27
"Hammer, The" (Rudder), 92
Harder They Come, The (Henzell), 77
Harris, Wilson, 8, 115, 119, 122
Hauser, Gerard: on publics, 18
hegemony, 7, 74, 106
Helfand, Jessica, 146
Hendricks, Wilmoth "Houdini," 176n12
Henry, Winston "Explainer," 45
Henzell, Perry, 77
"Hey Pocky A-way" (Meters), 172n41
"High Mas I," 94
Hill, Errol, 12
history, 100, 103, 118, 160
"History of Carnival" (Atilla), 85
Homer, Aristotle and, 103
Hopkinson, Nalo, 1
"Hosanna" (Tanker), 177n41
Howard, Robert Glenn: vernacular and, 19, 169n23
humanism, 68
"Humpty Dumpty" (nursery rhyme), 42

idealism, 66, 115
identification, 7, 130, 142, 163, 182n12; collective, 49; criteria for, 141; cultural, 41; rhetorical, 23
identity, 18, 116, 120, 130, 146, 162, 163, 179n60; African American, 167n8; Caribbean, 6, 17, 27, 28, 79, 103, 108, 125, 136, 140, 160; cultural, 34; eccentricities of, 164; expressions of, 80; postcolonial, 124; rhetors and, 129; sense of, 30, 37; subnational/supranational, 6; vernacular, 78, 141
Illustrated London News, 10

images, 65, 174n91; vernacular, 64, 66, 71, 74
imperialism, 18, 22, 75, 91, 169n17, 175n5
improper, proper and, 35
"In Parliament They Kicksing" (Henry), 45
In the Castle of My Skin (Lamming), 36–37, 58
independence, 92, 103, 104, 110
"Independence" (Bennett), 53
individualism, 4, 101, 111, 125, 139
inquiry, 73; intuition and, 155
Instagram.com, 184n48
Institutio (Quintilian), 170n32
interaction, 63, 153; action and, 59
International Criminal Court, 89
Internet, 129, 136; commercialization of, 130; divergence of, 182n3
Internet chat, orthographic features used in, 133 (table)
invisibility, 3, 19; visibility and, 129
"Iron Duke in the Land" (Whitehorse), 178n47
irony, 53, 54, 174n87; metaphor and, 169n16
Isaacs, Gregory, 43
Isocrates, 170n32

Jakobson, Roman, 168n16
Jamaica Labour Party, 88
James, C. L. R., 163
jamette, 13, 148, 149; de/en/coding, 145–54
"Jamiekan Baibl" project, 41
Jeremiadic thesis, 55, 56, 58
Jiizas: Di Buk Wi Luuk rait bout Im, 34
John, Catherine, 5–6
Johnson, Avey, 64
"Jook for Jook" (Francisco), 43

kaiso songs, 175n10
kalinda, 106, 108, 109, 110, 179n6
Kavalski, Emilian: on postcolonial symbol, 123–24

Kewley, Stanton, 62
Khaidji, poem by, 143
kicksing, 45
knowledge, 23, 116, 141, 142; power and, 11; rhetorical, 5, 24; shared, 143; transmission of, 127
Kongo cosmogony, limbo and, 111
Kumina/Pocomania, 64, 95

Labor Day, memories of, 1–2, 155–56, 156–57
Lambkin, Franz "Delamo," 94
Lamming, George, 36–37, 58, 125
language, 40, 80, 129, 150, 160; Caribbean, 32, 34–35, 39; creolized, 132; dance, 63; English, 33; imposition of, 37; manipulation of, 16; oral displays of, 35; standard, 35, 60; varieties, 41
"Leggo Meh Stick" (Francisco), 43
Lévy, Pierre, 153, 154, 183n39
Lewis, Austin "King Austin," 90, 185n8
Lewis, Matthew, 185n3
liberation, 23, 120
limbo, 110–16, 129
linguistic codes, 143
linguistic dynamics, 33, 34, 37, 52
LinkedIn, 129
Lion, Roaring, 96, 97, 99, 175n12, 178n48; calypso and, 178n49; songs by, 176n12
"Little Boy Blue" (nursery rhyme), 42
Liverpool, Hollis "the Mighty Chalkdust," 93
LordBlacknWild, 148
Louboutin, Christian, 156
Lovelace, Earl, 46, 55, 59, 60, 103, 105–9, 112, 115, 150, 159; agenda of, 104, 180n41; Aldrick and, 118–19; argument of, 110–11; awareness and, 126; Caribbean identity and, 125; carnivalesque, 127; dragon dance and, 121; ethos and, 105, 109, 110, 116, 121, 124; formative/transformative practices and, 123; intellectual maneuvers and, 119; materiality and, 122; memory and, 116; New World challenge and, 123; nostalgia and, 109; personhood and, 123; postcolonial identity and, 124; self-awareness and, 117; self-determination and, 126; self-discovery and, 126; veils and, 120; work of, 108, 111, 127
Lovey's Band, 178n47

Macobook, 130
Macoumba, 95
Man-of-Words in the West Indies, The (Abrahams), 31
Mandela, Karega, 93
"Mango Vert" (Lovey's Band), 178n47
Manuel, Peter, 82, 179n60
Manwarren, Wendell, 62
Mao, LuMing, 172n30
Marcano, Neville "Growling Tiger," 175n6, 175n12
marginalization, 26, 123, 129
Marley, Bob, 63, 80, 173n77
Marshall, Paule, 64
mas, playing, 29, 92–102, 118, 120, 121
Masimba, Lutalo "Brother Resistance," 93
masques, 42, 75, 81, 108, 109, 120, 144, 149, 150, 153, 161, 162, 169n24; carnival and, 23; making, 120; of sexually ambiguous reference, 44; wearing, 20, 23–29
masquing, 64, 85, 86, 87, 95, 117, 129, 135, 149, 157; body proverbial and, 141–45; epideictic role of, 104; rhetorical, 23, 141
material, 16, 68, 100, 142; symbol and, 160
materiality, 4, 96, 97, 122, 137; symbolism and, 143
maxim, exclamations and, 133
McIntosh, Karel: on social media, 131

McKerrow, Raymie, 8, 11
McNaughton, Trevor, 59
meditation, 55, 56, 58
memory, 116, 118
Meraz, Sharon, 136
metaphor, 53, 54, 75, 109, 111, 151, 168n16; dramatistic, 170n2; irony and, 169n16; metonymy and, 16, 17
methodologies, 9, 10, 139
metonymy, 18, 20, 104, 168n16; metaphor and, 16, 17; synecdoche and, 169n16
Metropolitanism, colonialism and, 18
"Mi Cyaan Believe It" (Smith), 42
Middle Class, Roxborough—Parlatuvier Road, 74, 75, 174n87
Midnight Robber, 50, 51, 62, 119
Midnight Robber (Hopkinson), 1
"Ministry of Rhythm, The" (Rudder), 93
(mis)representation, 14, 16–22
Mitchum, Robert, 81
Mohammed, Patricia, 164, 169n17, 174n95, 175n95
moral practice, 98, 141
Morton, Ivan, 107
motives, 41, 118, 141; collective awareness of, 138; common store of, 26
mslikklebit, 148
"Mud Madness" (3canal), 44–45
music, 50, 82; Caribbean, 82, 84, 101, 176n23
Myal, 95
Myers-Scotton, Carol: code-switching and, 172n29, 172n35

National Science Foundation Network (NSFNET), 130
National Union of Freedom Fighters, 88
nationalism, 4, 88
Natty Dread (Marley), 173n77
Nayar, Pramod, 150, 153, 184n46
negotiation, 14, 111, 146; rhetorical, 149, 156

neocolonialism, 4
Nettleford, Rex, 162
Negue Jadin, 169n24
"Netty Netty" (Lion), 176n12
New York City Police Department, protesting, 163
"Night Nurse" (Isaacs), 43
nihilism, 8, 101
"No Restriction" (Rudder), 94
"Nobody's Business" (Rihanna and Brown), 184n48
nonverbal/visual semantics, 38, 60–75, 77–79
nostalgia, 3, 66, 89, 100, 101, 155, 156
obscurities, 65–66
old talk, 50, 131, 135
"One More Hosannah" (Rudder), 177n41
oppression, 16, 110, 128
order, 88; disorder and, 68

Panama Canal, 11
Panegyricus (Isocrates), 170n32
pappyshow, 31, 114
parochialism, 125, 180n41
parody, power of, 114
participation, 8, 20, 28, 129; democratic, 156; mass, 91; vernacular, 152
Patton, John, 90
Peace Preservation Ordinance, 84
peasantry, 10; plantations and, 11
People's National Movement (PNM), 44
People's National Party, 88
perception, 22, 31
performances, 7, 15, 20, 42, 48, 49, 50, 59, 63, 64, 84, 90, 102, 109, 122, 123, 141, 148, 149, 151, 157, 158, 160, 161, 162, 164; antisocial, 31; authenticating, 132; carnivalesque, 11; common wisdom/divine knowledge and, 83; conception of, 119; consequences of, 100; dancehall, 145, 146, 150, 152; dehistoricizing,

21; derivative, 19; dialogic, 12; epideictic, 25, 39; folkloric, 30; masqued, 29; musicoreligious, 93; normative, 31; outcome of, 81; physical, 62; prophetic, 95; public, 19, 21, 80; rhetorical, 3, 28, 86, 117, 120–21; self-consciousness, 118; symbolic, 101; verbal, 60; vernacular, 26
personhood, quest for, 123
"Peter," 131–32, 134, 135, 147, 153; discursive model of, 136
Phaedrus (Plato), 1
Phillip, Emrold "Brother Valentino," 91, 92, 93
Phillips, Karl Hudson, 89
Phillips, Sophia, 144
Philosophy of Literary Form, The (Burke), 103
picturesque, 18, 169n17, 175n95
Pink House Doorway, Palo Seco, 70, 72
Pink House, Palo Seco, 70; *Brother Austin's House, San Fernando* and, 69
pirogues, 68, 69, 174n86
plantations, peasantry and, 11
plantocracy, 13, 20, 21, 103
Plato, 1, 161, 185n4
"Pocomania" (Walcott), 41
poetics, forced, 143, 183n23
politics, 78, 116, 118, 152; partisan, 42; sexual, 142
popular culture, Caribbean, 3, 156
postcolonization, 27, 124
power: asymmetrical, 40; knowledge and, 11; relations, 127; structure, 5, 18; supernatural, 59, 60
practices, 100; formative, 123; rhetorical, 80, 118, 123, 162, 167n7; transformative, 123
practitioners: Caribbean, 11, 19, 32, 40, 48–49, 128; discourse of, 145; vernacular, 21, 130

Praisesong for the Widow (Marshall), 64
primitivism, 68
Primus, Brother, 108
Prince, Corporal, 107
"Progress" (Austin), 90
proper, improper and, 35
proverbs, 38, 52–53, 55, 149; sample forms of, 54 (table)
Psalm 137, 59, 173n68
public consumption, 27, 141
public opinion, 9, 141, 143, 169n18
Public Order Act, 88
"Pull Together" (Rudder), 94
puns, 43, 86

Quevedo, Raymond "Atilla the Hun," 85, 86, 87, 96, 175n12
Quintilian, 270n32

Rabelais, 15
radicalism, 88
Rahim, Jennifer, 104, 126
Ramchand, Kenneth, 104, 120, 181n72
Rampersad, Taran, 137, 138, 139, 145, 153
Rastafarian Nyabinghi rituals, songs of, 60
Rawlins, Weston "Cro-Cro," 93
Reagan, Ronald, 89
Regis, Louis, 84, 89
(re)invention, rhetorical, 104, 130, 152
remasquing, historiographic/revisionist, 17
remembering, legacy of, 116
representation, 66, 135; cultural, 17; material, 283n39; metonymy of, 20; polyrhythmic, 99; symbolic, 118; virtual, 150; visual, 169n17
responsibility, 48, 52, 110, 123; social, 82
Rheingold, Howard, 181n1
rhetoric, 6–7, 23, 26, 39–40, 59, 60, 71, 79, 89, 115, 141, 151, 158; Caribbean, 3, 5, 7,

rhetoric: Caribbean (*cont.*), 8, 9, 12, 15, 16, 17, 19, 24, 27, 28–29, 161, 162; collective/individual, 6; colonial, 14; communication and, 8; critical, 11; from cultural perspective, 2; democratic impulses in, 161; epideictic, 24–25; formation of, 160; performance of, 164; persuasive aspect of, 6; phenomenon of, 161; pictorial turn of, 66; popular, 22; real dimension of, 16; requirements of, 7; understanding of, 5; unexplored dimension of, 18; vernacular, 18, 67, 160
Rhetoric of Fiction, The (Booth), 103
Rhetorica ad Herennium, 169n16
rhetorical activities, 4, 22, 92, 141, 156; Caribbean, 20, 139, 151, 152, 153, 158, 161; vernacular, 18
rhetorical choice, 104, 109, 113, 116
rhetorical effectiveness, 78, 81
rhetorical exchanges, 145, 162
rhetorical features, 32, 145
rhetorical flexibility, 19–20
rhetorical implication, 19, 81
rhetorical invention, 20, 99
rhetorical methods, 28, 157–58
rhetorical modes, 32, 38–53, 38 (table), 55–75, 76–79
rhetorical negotiation, 149, 156
rhetorical significance, 78, 120
rhetorical situations, 8, 167n10
rhetorical tradition, 4, 80, 91, 123, 129; Caribbean, 5, 6, 7, 45, 55, 78, 173n73
rhetors, 4, 9, 37, 68, 111, 117, 135, 157–58; absence of, 66; ethos and, 80; identity and, 129; limboing, 179n25; literacy of, 152; participation among, 5; perspective of, 120; symbolic/material suspension of, 113; vernacular, 32, 72–73, 77, 78, 81, 106, 112, 127, 156, 157, 159, 174n83
Rickford, John, 33–34, 36, 60, 62

Rihanna: Chris Brown and, 139–40, 142, 144, 152, 184n48; ethos of, 140–41
"Rivers of Babylon" (Dowe and McNaughton), 59
Roberts, Peter, 32, 53
Roberts, Roger, 62
Rohlehr, Gordon, 83, 90, 106, 175n10
romanticism, decline of, 168n16
Roosevelt, Franklin D., 86, 176n12
"Roosevelt in Trinidad" (Atilla), 86
Rudder, David Michael, 44, 80, 92, 94, 163, 178n55; chorus and, 98–99; cultural/religious influences and, 93; intimacies and, 100; performance by, 95–96, 97, 98, 100–101, 178n57; polyrhythmic representations and, 99; prophetic intention of, 101; Tanker tribute by, 177n41; titles for, 92; vision of, 93; vocalizations and, 100
"Rum and Coca-Cola" (song), 81

St. John, Bruce, 53
"Sally Water" (Lion), 176n12
Salt (Lovelace), 104, 105, 117, 120; negotiating limbo silence in, 110–16; social pressures in, 113–14
"Saltfish" (Francisco), 43
Sandoval, Chela, 128, 181n2
Santeria, 95
"Sayamanda" (Tanker), 177n41
Scott, James C.: on hidden transcript, 170n38
Second Industrial Revolution, 11
Sedition Act, 88
self-assertion, 84, 109, 126
self-awareness, 90, 110, 112, 113, 117, 122
self-consciousness, 9, 122
self-definition, 7, 14, 104, 124, 126, 136, 146, 157
self-destruction, 119, 122
self-determination, 84, 104, 110, 126, 152

self-discovery, 98, 100, 110, 126
self-identification, 6, 167n8, 183n21
self-interest, 9, 137
self-representation, 136, 146
semantics, nonverbal/visual, 38, 60–75, 77–79
Serenaders, 85
sermonic, 38, 55–60, 89; rhetorical action/social change and, 59; strategic characteristics of, 56 (table)
Sesame Street, 132, 134, 182n11
Sforza, John, 80
"Shadowboxing" (Collins), 41
Shakers, 95
Shakespeare, William, 171n25
shaming, 38, 146; boasting and, 50–52
Shango, 92, 118
Shango Baptists, 64
Sheller, Mimi, 150, 151
Shepherd, Jean, 182n4
shit talk, 39, 50, 131
Shotter, John, 18, 63, 174n81
Shouter Baptists, 64
Shouter Prohibition Ordinance, 106
Shrovetide festivals, 45, 112
"Six Reasons Why Rihanna Would Marry Chris Brown," 142
skills, 114; rhetorical, 113, 119
slavery, 4, 12
Slavery Abolition Act, 168n2
slaves, 82, 95, 168n10, 169n24, 170n28
Sloat, Suzanna, 63
Smith, Michael, 42
Smitherman, Geneva, 47, 48, 172n48
Sniveler's Gulch, 182n11
"So Confused" (Khaidji), 143
social action, 13, 50, 109
social class, vernacular, 20
social forces, vulnerability/susceptibility to, 7
social formation, 5, 6, 7, 27

social groups, 2, 167n7
social injustice, 42, 63, 78
social interaction, 7, 131–32
social media, transparency of, 131
social practices, 8, 11, 129
social pressures, 82, 85, 113–14, 115
social reality, 28, 32, 36
social situations, 39, 96, 120–21
social status, vernacular, 19
social tensions, 23, 35, 127
socioeconomic issues, 83, 87, 158
sociolinguistic evolution, 36
Socrates, 161, 185n4
Solibo Magnificent (Chamoiseau), 51
speakers: audiences and, 8; vernacular, 33
spelling: creolized/phonetic, 132; inflectional, 133
Spiritual Baptists, 95, 116, 118
Springer, Attillah, 148, 182n19; Caribbean identity and, 140; enthymematic/metaphoric approaches and, 142, 151; post by, 139–40; Rihanna's ethos and, 139–41
@staceyannchin, 128
Stanley-Niaah, Sonjah, 111
"State of the Blogosphere" (Technorati.com), 136
"Stepping Razor" (Tosh), 50
steups, 61, 62, 66
stickfighters, 105, 107
"Stop and Frisk" campaign, protesting, 163
strategies, 4; discursive, 146; indigenous, 175n5; mythmaking, 22; rhetorical, 80, 89, 109, 162; vernacular, 84
subject, 49, 133; virtualization/reembodiment of, 153
subjectivity, 18, 27, 74, 138, 152, 161, 169n24, 284n45
subjects, absence of, 66
"Sunday Cricket" (Breeze), 45
Suppression of Crime Act, 88

Sutton, Jane, 128
Swing It (Sforza), 80
symbol, 67, 68, 157, 162; manipulation of, 16; material and, 160
symbolism, 6, 31, 53, 55, 96, 100, 119, 120, 127; Christian, 84; materiality and, 143; rise of, 168n16
symmetry, 53, 54
syncretic, 17, 59, 82
synecdoche, 168n16; metonym and, 169n16
Szarkowski, John, 67, 68

"Tales from a Strange Land II: Crossing the Bridge" (Rudder), 80
"Talkin" (Marley), 80
"Taming of the Polos/Polis, The" (Sutton), 128
Tanker, Andre, 177n41
technology, 129, 130, 151, 152
Technorati.com, 136
Tempest, The (Shakespeare), 36, 171n25
Thatcher, Margaret, 89
Theater and Dance Halls Act, 85
Theory and Practice of Creole Grammar, The (Thomas), 33
Thomas, J. J., 33, 34, 171n12
Thorpe, Marjorie, 108
3canal, 44–45, 61, 64
Torch Ordinance, 84
Tosh, Peter, 50
tourism, industry and, 66
tradition, 113, 146; ethos of, 126; rhetorical, 4, 5, 6, 7, 45, 55, 78, 80, 91, 123, 129, 173n73
transnationalism, 81, 157
trickster, 17
Trinidad Legislative Council, 85
Tumblr, 130
"Turn Thanks to Miss Mirry" (Goodison), 60
twist-mouth, 61
Twitter, 129, 137

Umbanda, 95
Unlocked on Coffee Street, 65, 66

Vallee, Rudy, 85
Vatz, Richard E., 167n10
verbal delirium, 86, 176n17
vernacular, 17, 23, 24, 53, 65, 66, 72, 87, 111, 129, 140, 144, 145, 162, 169n23; Caribbean, 18, 25, 31, 37; colonial, 25, 26; complex, 128; dialectical, 19; digital, 130; ethos and, 130–35; subaltern, 19
vernacular class, 104, 111, 160
vernacular gaze, material realness of, 74
vernacular practice, ethic of, 138
vernacular tradition, 8, 116, 123, 150
Victor Talking Machine Company, 178n47
violence, 88, 141, 143; domestic, 144, 183n24; privatization of, 150
virtual, 153, 154, 184n46
visibility, 18; invisibility and, 129
vision, 64, 93; prophetic, 17, 89; rhetorical, 119
"Visions of Paradise" (Rudder), 98
vocalizations, 96, 100
Vodun, 95

Walcott, Derek, 2, 77
Water Riot, 84
Wells, Amy Tracy, 136
West, Cornel, 87
West African Pidgin Portuguese hypothesis, 33
West Indies Federation, 4, 162
What the Twilight Says (Walcott), 77
"What's Going On?" (Gaye), 90
"When It Bald It Better" (Francisco), 43
Whiterose, Julian "Iron Duke," 178n47

who don't hear will feel, threat of, 81
who vex, loss, 86
"Who Will Guard the Guards?" (Austin), 185n8
Williams, Eric "Pussonal Nonarch," 88
Windward Road House I, Outside, 74, 76
Windward Road House II, Inside-Outside, 74, 76
Windward Road House III, Inside, 74, 77

Wine of Astonishment, The (Lovelace), 55, 59, 104; emergent ethos in, 105–9, 110
wordplay, 38, 42–46, 50, 86
WordPress, 130
Worrell, Frank, 39
Wynter, Sylvia, 181n65

Yard, San Fernando, 66–67, 67, 73, 74
YouTube, 130, 145, 148, 150